JUDICIAL POLICIES

JUDICIAL POLICIES

Implementation and Impact
Second Edition

Bradley C. Canon
UNIVERSITY OF KENTUCKY

Charles A. Johnson
TEXAS A&M UNIVERSITY

A Division of Congressional Quarterly Inc.
Washington, D.C.

Copyright © 1999 Congressional Quarterly Inc.

Printed in the United States of America

Library of Congress Cataloging-in-Publication Data

in process

To three teachers who stimulated my interest in law and politics:
—in high school, the late Catherine Dinnen
—in my undergraduate years, Marian D. Irish
—my graduate professor, David Fellman
B. C. C.

To my sister, Pat Chlebda, her husband, Chris, and their two sons,
Charlie and Michael
C. A. J.

Contents

Tables, Figures, and Boxes

Preface

The first edition of *Judicial Policies: Implementation and Impact* was published in 1984. Political scientists, law professors, and other scholars had been conducting research on the impact of judicial policies over the previous quarter century, and even magazines and newspapers had examined the effectiveness or unintended consequences of judicial decisions. But in the mid-1980s no one had taken a general stock of such research; it had not been synthesized in organized form. We believed that a book giving comprehensive coverage to what was known or not known about the implementation and impact of judicial policies would be highly useful in both research and teaching, so we wrote such a book.

The first edition was well received and continues to be cited by scholars. However, after almost fifteen years, we believe it is time for a new edition. New judicial policy issues, such as affirmative action and equity in school financing, have come to the fore, and courts have modified some older policies, such as school desegregation and abortion. Scholars have done a considerable amount of research since 1984 both on the impact of judicial policies and on other questions surrounding the courts, such as how judges make decisions and whether court decisions affect public opinion and vice-versa.

We have made sure that the second edition retains the basic structure of the first, but with updated decisions and policies and new research, hypotheses, and examples. At the same time, to make it more manageable as a supplemental text, we have shortened this edition considerably.

We have organized our synthesis of relevant research according to a heuristic model of populations and responses. We posit four categories of persons, each of which stands in a particular relationship to any given judicial policy: the interpreting, implementing, consumer, and secondary populations. We also posit two responses that affected persons must make when reacting to a judicial policy: the acceptance decision and the behavioral response decision. This model has the advantage of comprehensiveness: no research is added or left out awkwardly. This organizational scheme links together in the same chapter the literature on people whose functions in the process are similar regardless of which judicial policy is involved and which theory, if any, is used.

Chapter 1 introduces the heuristic model—the populations and response sequences. Chapters 2 through 5 discuss the interpreting, implementing, consumer, and secondary populations in turn. In Chapter 6, we turn to theory development, focusing on nine theories—some formal, some more intuitive—that scholars have offered to explain implementation and impact patterns. We look at the extent to which these theories have been verified by research and discuss the applicability of each theory to each population.

In Chapter 7, our final chapter, we offer an overall assessment of the impact of judicial policies on American society. We take two approaches here. First, we look at courts as entities in the larger political system and examine research that assesses the abilities of courts at all levels to initiate or maintain major policies, especially in the face of opposition or indifference from other political institutions. Second, we discuss Gerald N. Rosenberg's 1991 book *The Hollow Hope: Can Courts Bring About Social Change?* In this widely read work, Rosenberg argues that the U.S. Supreme Court simply does not have much of an impact on major policy change in America. We disagree with this blanket assessment and address the impact question in seven areas where the Supreme Court has initiated major policy changes over the past half century.

In writing *Judicial Policies* we have goals other than making our own and our colleagues' teaching and research easier. One is to stimulate more research about the implementation and impact of judicial policies. To this end, our book points to what we do not know about implementation and impact as well as to what we do know. We also borrow theories from the political science subfield of public policy that is focused in part on the implementation and impact of policies made by legislative bodies and executive agencies. Judicial policy is as much public policy as is that made by the other branches. We hope our overview will encourage public policy researchers to include court decisions in the ambit of their work.

A second goal is to inform a larger set of readers about what happens after judicial decisions are made. Many citizens unfamiliar with how the legal system works may assume that court decisions are automatically carried out by lower court judges, prosecutors, police, and other agencies, or that if they are not it is the result of some nefarious plot. Reality, of course, is more complex, and we try to explain it. While *Judicial Policies* is not primarily aimed at the popular market, we have written it so that intelligent lay people can understand what we write.

Observant readers of this edition who are familiar with the first one will note that the Johnson and Canon order of authorship in the first edition has changed to Canon and Johnson here. The publication of a second edition allows us to alternate names as a way of acknowledging the truly shared nature of our coauthorship.

Many people have contributed their time and energy to helping us turn a mass of research and ideas into what we hope is a complete and coherent book. We remain grateful to Lawrence A. Baum of Ohio State University, Sheldon Goldman of the University of Massachusetts, and Robert L. Peabody of Johns Hopkins University for their review of the penultimate draft of the first edition. Our thanks also go to Jennifer A. Segal of the University of Kentucky, who read drafts of four chapters of the second edition. Tom White, a graduate student at Texas A&M University, assisted with research, especially for Chapters 1 and 5. Charles Johnson thanks Diane Adams for typing parts of the manuscript. Both authors are grateful to their respective departments for logistical support. At CQ Press, we thank Brenda Carter for encouraging us to undertake the second edition and for her advice and support while we were writing it. Nola Healy Lynch was a thoroughly professional copy editor; her suggestions have done much to enhance the quality of this book. Finally, once again we thank our wives, Rose Canon and Barbara Johnson, for their understanding.

Bradley C. Canon
Charles A. Johnson
August 1998

JUDICIAL POLICIES

CHAPTER ONE

Responses to Judicial Policies

President Andrew Jackson, unhappy with a Supreme Court decision, is said to have retorted: "John Marshall has made his decision, now let him enforce it." His remark reminds us of a central fact of American democracy: judicial policies do not implement themselves. In virtually all instances, courts that formulate policies must rely on other courts or on nonjudicial actors to translate those policies into action. Inevitably, just as making judicial policies is a political process, so too is the implementation of the policies—the issues are essentially political, and the actors are subject to political pressures.

STUDYING RESPONSES TO JUDICIAL POLICIES

This book examines the implementation and impact of judicial policies. There are important substantive and theoretical reasons for studying what may at first appear to be a very narrow part of the judicial process and for studying it as a political process instead of as a legal process. From the substantive perspective, few areas of the American political system remain untouched by judicial decision making. In our litigious society many disputes that have public policy ramifications are decided by the judiciary.

Although judicial policies differ from legislative actions and executive orders in their origin, they are also public policies: they too must be implemented before disputes or problems are resolved, and they have an impact on the public. Racial segregation, for example, did not end with the announcement of *Brown v. Board of Education* in 1954. Ten years after the Supreme Court decided that "separate but equal" is inherently unequal, a great majority of the South's black students continued to attend overwhelmingly black schools. The Court's policy was given meaning only after considerable efforts by lower courts; the Department of Justice; the Department of Health, Education and Welfare; Congress; and civil rights groups. Our knowledge about desegregation and the judiciary would be quite incomplete if we limited our analysis to the *Brown* decision. Knowing how events lead to a judicial decision and what the decision itself means gives us an incomplete picture of the judicial process.

Studying the reaction to judicial policies is also important from a theoretical perspective. To a certain degree, evaluating the implementation of judicial policies is in the mainstream of the field of policy analysis. Important theoretical questions in this field may be answered by studying the aftermath of judicial decisions: Why are some policies implemented while others are not? Why do some organizations change policies while others do not? Why do some policies have the intended impact while others fail to do so or have unintended consequences? The varied outcomes of judicial policies provide ample opportunities to examine the impact of public policies.

Responses to some court decisions have been immediate and implementation almost complete. For example, in the years following the Supreme Court's 1973 abortion decision in *Roe v. Wade,* several million women ended their pregnancies with legal abortions and new pro-choice and pro-life groups emerged as powerful forces in our political system. By contrast, the events following *Brown v. Board of Education* demonstrate that the implementation of other decisions may be prolonged.

Still other decisions meet with varied responses across the country. The Supreme Court's decision in *Gregg v. Georgia* (1976), for example, cleared the way for states to impose the death penalty after serious challenges in the 1970s. Although some states passed no legislation reauthorizing the death penalty, others chose to adopt new legislation on death penalties. Today there are many prisoners on death row.[1]

The aftermath of these decisions and others raises important questions about the ability of the judiciary to make public policy effectively and about how individual citizens and political institutions relate to the judiciary. Moreover, studying the implementation of judicial decisions may shed some light on such longstanding issues as the relationship between law and human behavior and the role of the judiciary in our political system.

If studying the implementation of judicial policies is important, then we must study it as a political process. In a general sense, the implementation of *any* public policy is a political process. The notion that the administration of policy is apolitical has long since been discarded (if it was ever in vogue). Political scientist Michael Lipsky remarks on how postdecision factors may enter the implementation process: "There are many contexts in which the latitude of those charged with carrying out a policy is so substantial that studies of policy implementation should be turned on their heads. In these cases, policy is effectively 'made' by the people who implement it."[2]

As we will see in later chapters, many judicial decisions afford a great deal of latitude for interpretation and implementation. Political actors and institutions who follow through on the decisions make the judicial policy. Certainly, the judges who enforced civil rights decisions were subject to political pressures from a variety of sources. Similar pressures affected public and private institutions after court decisions on affirmative action. Even presidential politics may become intertwined with judicial policies, as did Richard Nixon's 1968 "law and order" presidential campaign criticizing the Supreme Court's criminal justice decisions or the explosive issue of abortion in virtually every presidential election since 1980.

Like Congress and the president, the Supreme Court and other courts must rely on others to translate policy into action. And like the processes of formulating legislative, executive, and judicial policies, the process of translating those decisions into action is often a political one subject to a variety of pressures from a variety of political actors in the system.

ROE V. WADE: A CASE STUDY OF JUDICIAL IMPACT

The best way to illustrate the political nature of the events that follow a judicial decision is to review the implementation and impact of a decision that remains controversial decades after its announcement by the U.S. Supreme Court. We will use the Supreme Court's 1973 abortion decision in *Roe v. Wade* to show what may happen after a judicial policy is announced. Later in this chapter we will suggest a conceptual scheme by which the events following any judicial decision may be effectively organized and compared with the events following other judicial decisions.

The Decision

On Monday, January 22, 1973, Associate Justice Harry Blackmun announced the decision of the Court in two cases concerning the rights of women to end unwanted pregnancies with legal abortions, *Roe v. Wade* and *Doe v. Bolton*. According to Bob Woodward and Scott Armstrong's revealing inside account of the Supreme Court during the 1970s, *The Brethren,* this decision was the result of considerable conflict and compromise within the Court.[3] The justices fully expected a public outcry after the decision was announced. They were not disappointed.

The cases before the Court challenged the laws prohibiting abortion in Texas and Georgia. In both cases the Court decided in favor of the plaintiffs—women who were identified only as Jane Roe and Mary Doe. The direct effect of the decision was to void the antiabortion laws in these two states. Indirectly, of course, the Court also voided laws in forty-four other states that prohibited or limited abortion. The results and policy options for the states were summarized in the concluding parts of the majority opinion in *Roe:*

1. A state criminal abortion statute of the current Texas type, that excepts from criminality only a (lifesaving) procedure on behalf of the mother, without regard to pregnancy stage and without recognition of the other interests involved, is violative of the Due Process Clause of the Fourteenth Amendment.

(a) For the stage prior to approximately the end of the first trimester, the abortion decision and its effectuation must be left to the medical judgment of the pregnant woman's attending physician.

(b) For the stage subsequent to approximately the end of the first trimester, the state, in promoting its interest in the health of the mother, may, if it chooses, regulate the abortion procedure in ways that are reasonably related to maternal health.

(c) For the stage subsequent to viability, the state in promoting its interest in the potentiality of human life may, if it chooses, regulate, and even proscribe, abortion except where it is necessary, in appropriate medical judgment, for the preservation of the life or health of the mother.[4]

In effect, the Supreme Court had given women the right to abortion on demand during the first two trimesters of pregnancy and had allowed the state to regulate abortions only to protect the mother's health during these two trimesters. The Court held that during the third trimester the state could regulate or even prohibit abortions, except where the life or the health of the mother was endangered.

Immediate Responses

The reactions from several corners of the political system were immediate, and they were mostly negative. A few reactions were aimed directly at the justices. In *The Brethren,* Woodward and Armstrong recount one type of reaction by noting that

> thousands of letters poured into the Court. The guards had to set up a special sorting area in the basement with a huge box for each Justice. The most mail came to Blackmun, the decision's author, and to Justice William Brennan, the Court's only Catholic. Some letters compared the Justices to the Butchers of Dachau, child killers, immoral beasts, and Communists. A special ring of hell would be reserved for the Justices. Whole classes from Catholic schools wrote to denounce the Justices as murderers. "I really don't want to write this letter but my teacher made me," one child said. Minnesota Lutherans zeroed in on Blackmun. New Jersey Catholics called for Brennan's excommunication. Southern Baptists and other groups sent more than a thousand bitter letters to Justice Hugo Black, who had died sixteen months earlier. Some letters and calls were death threats.[5]

But not all reactions were negative. The president of Planned Parenthood, Alan F. Guttmacher, called the decision a "courageous stroke for right to privacy and for the protection of a woman's physical and emotional health." A similar reaction came from women attorneys at the Center for Constitutional Rights, who cited the decision as a "victory for [the] women's liberation movement."[6] A more direct and personal reaction to the decision is reported in *The Brethren.* Several months after the abortion decision Justice Blackmun gave a speech at Emory University Law School, in Atlanta, Georgia, where a woman embraced him after his speech, saying, "I'll never be able to thank you for what you have done. I'll say no more. Thank you." Unknown to Blackmun at the time, this rare positive response came from "Mary Doe," the woman from Texas who had challenged the Texas abortion law.[7]

Reactions also came from members of Congress. A week after the Supreme Court's decision, Rep. Lawrence J. Hogan, R–Md., introduced the first of several "right to life" amendments to the U.S. Constitution. By November 1973, more than two dozen resolutions to overturn some aspect of the Court's decision were introduced in Congress. Two of the proposals eventually enacted into law were added to the Health Programs Extension Act of 1973, which was amended to permit institutions receiving federal funds to refuse to perform abortions, and the 1973 Foreign Assistance Act, which was amended to prohibit the use of U.S. funds to pay for abortions overseas.[8]

Response was also immediate from women who sought abortions. In the first three months of 1973, over 180,000 abortions were performed in the United States; during the first year following the Supreme Court's decision a total of 742,460 abortions were performed nationwide. The variation in the number of abortions from state to state was considerable; the greatest number of abortions was performed in New York, a state that had previously liberalized its abortion law, while two states—Louisiana and North Dakota—reported no abortions during 1973.[9] Data from the first year of nationwide legal abortions suggest that almost one of every five pregnancies was terminated with an abortion.[10]

Whether a woman secured an abortion depended heavily on whether there was a physician or medical facility willing to provide abortion services. A study by Jon R. Bond and Charles A. Johnson found that fewer than half of the hospitals in their national sample changed abortion policies after *Roe*.[11] Indeed, for many hospitals in the sample (85.6 percent), the abortion issue was not a subject of heated staff or board discussions. Whether hospitals provided abortion services depended strongly on whether the hospital staff was in favor of abortions; factors such as community need or demand for abortion services were largely unrelated to the hospitals' decisions.

A national survey by the research division of Planned Parenthood, the Alan Guttmacher Institute, in 1973 revealed that less than one-third (30.1 percent) of the non-Catholic short-term general hospitals in the United States provided abortion services. Another survey revealed that 75 percent of the hospitals providing abortion services were privately controlled, rather than publicly controlled or government operated. In the year following the abortion decision, a relatively small number of nonhospital clinics provided abortion services (178 nationwide), and only a few physicians (168 nationwide) reported performing abortions in their offices. Nonetheless, in the first year after the decision, the largest percentage of abortions occurred in clinics (44.5 percent), and most of the remaining abortions (41.1 percent) were performed in private hospitals.[12]

The Alan Guttmacher Institute concluded that in the twelve months following the Supreme Court's abortion decision, "the response of health institutions in many areas to the legalization of abortion in 1973 was so limited as to be tantamount to no response at all."[13] This widespread non-response had a considerable effect on *Roe v. Wade*'s impact—after being granted the *constitutional* right to an abortion, many women could not exercise that right, at least locally, because medical facilities in their communities refused to provide such services.

Later Responses

Despite the limited availability of abortion providers noted in reports by the Alan Guttmacher Institute, the number of abortions nationwide continued to increase for several years after the Supreme Court's abortion rights decision. Data reported in Figure 1-1 show these increases over time, regardless of whether they are measured in terms of absolute numbers or as a ratio of the number of abortions per 1,000 live births in the United States.

The data reported in Figure 1-1 can be interpreted in different ways and thus can lead to varying conclusions about the actual impact of *Roe v. Wade*. Gerald N. Rosenberg notes that the "largest numerical increases in legal abortions occurred in the years prior to initial Supreme Court action."[14] He concludes that the Court's decision could be viewed as one element in a national trend of already increasing abortion rates. Rosenberg also acknowledges, however, that without granting abortion rights constitutional protection, it is possible that "no more states would have liberalized or repealed their restrictive laws"[15] Thus, we do not know whether the trend line would have been different if *Roe* had been decided differently or if the matter had not been addressed by the Court at all.

Although the abortion rate data are subject to interpretation, there has been a clear and continuing shift in the kinds of facilities providing abortion services after *Roe*. An increasing number of abortions are provided by clinics rather than hospitals. Indeed, the number of clinics providing abortions doubled in the three years following *Roe*. In 1992, two-thirds of the nation's abortions were provided by these non-hospital clinics.[16] Regardless of the type of providers, however, national data also reveal that the number of abortion providers has declined after an initial growth following *Roe*.[17]

Figure 1-1 Abortions in the United States, Number and Rate, 1970–1994

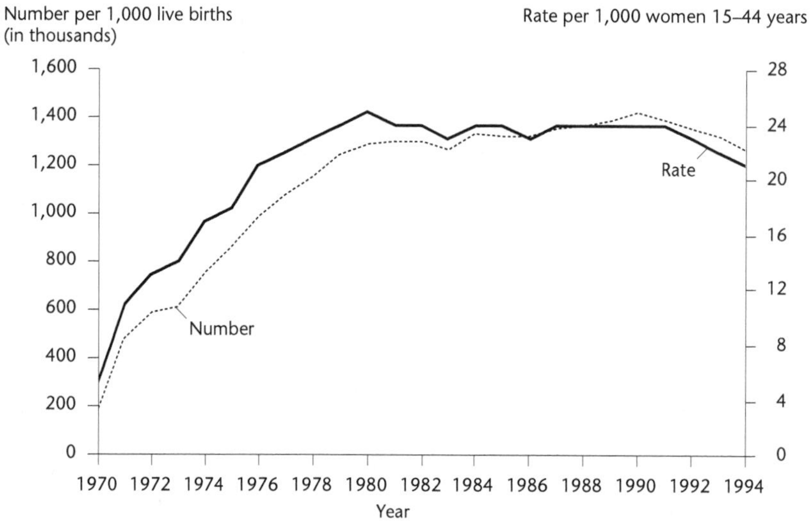

Number per 1,000 live births
(in thousands)

Rate per 1,000 women 15–44 years

Source: "Abortion Surveillance—United States, 1993–1994," *MMWR* 46 (1997): 49.

The decision in *Roe* and changes in the way abortion services are provided have led some social scientists to consider more subtle changes in the aftermath of the Supreme Court's decision. Matthew Wetstein, for example, reports that *Roe* has "substantially influenced where women obtained abortions." Relying on data from the U.S. Centers for Disease Control, Wetstein finds that among women who obtained abortions, the percentage of women who went to out-of-state providers dropped from 44 to 25 percent one year after the *Roe* decision. Within two years of the decision, the percentage had dropped below 10 percent, and it hovered around 7 percent through 1990—the latest year data were available.[18]

Another way to consider abortion rates (number of abortions per 1,000 women aged fifteen through forty-four) after *Roe v. Wade* is to examine the same data at state and local levels. In 1994, for example, the abortion rate varied from a low of 2 per 1,000 women in Wyoming to a high of 42 per 1,000 women in California.[19] The trends within states over time also vary considerably. Abortion rates in Colorado and Pennsylvania, for example, increased substantially after *Roe v. Wade*. In Pennsylvania, where state law had limited abortions, the increase is not surprising. In Colorado, however, a relatively liberal abortion law was in place before the *Roe* decision. However, in contrast to the national trends, Colorado and Pennsylvania's abortion rates after 1978–1980 declined to roughly 1973 rates. These trends differ dramatically from the experience in California, which prior to *Roe* had a permissive law allowing abortions under many circumstances. Abortion rates in California were largely unaffected by *Roe* through 1983.[20] Abortion rates jumped dramatically after 1983 for reasons we will discuss later. The important point here is to appreciate that there are variations in abortion rates across time, in different kinds of facilities, in different kinds of communities, and in different parts of the country.

Politics and Abortion Rights

The Supreme Court's decision in *Roe v. Wade* brought the issue of abortion rights to center stage in American politics. In national institutions, in state and local governments, in political parties, in some interest groups, in some religious denominations, and among the general public, battles were fought between the decision's supporters and its detractors. In many instances, these battles and resulting government actions substantially affected the implementation and impact of the Court's decision.

CONGRESSIONAL ACTIONS.   Within a year of *Roe*'s announcement, fifty constitutional amendments were introduced pursuing a variety of strategies for revising the Court's decision.[21] A subcommittee of the Senate Judiciary Committee held sixteen days of hearings on the proposed amendments in 1974 and 1975, after which the Judiciary Committee voted not to report any of the proposed amendments to the floor for a vote because of legal questions about the proposals. Subsequent attempts to amend the Constitution also failed at various stages of the legislative process, including a vote in 1983 on an amendment that read: "A right to abortion is not secured by this Constitution. The Congress and the several States shall have concurrent power to restrict and prohibit abortion."[22] An attempt to pass ordinary legislation in 1981 called the Human Life Bill (which defined "persons" protected by the Fourteenth Amendment to included fetuses from the point of conception and would have removed federal court jurisdiction in abortion cases) also failed to garner enough congressional support to pass.[23]

Opponents of abortions and the Supreme Court's decisions achieved greater success in Congress with legislative initiatives aimed at curtailing federal involvement in providing or paying for abortions and protecting physicians and hospitals who refused to provide them.[24] Poor women's access to abortion services was significantly diminished by a series of legislative riders to appropriations bills that effectively ended payments through the federal Medicaid program. Passage of this legislation, generally referred to as the Hyde Amendment (for its chief sponsor, Rep. Henry Hyde, R., Ill.), resulted in an almost complete cessation of federally funded abortions—from approximately 250,000 in 1976 to fewer than 2,500 in 1978.[25] While there is evidence that many poor women found alternative funding for abortions, Eva Rubin notes that poor women often "postponed abortions for two or three weeks . . . [which] might mean that the abortion was performed in the second trimester . . . [and with funds] diverted from household money."[26]

A new tactic by pro-life forces in Congress emerged in the mid-1990s with congressional attempts to ban abortions in particular circumstances. The passage in 1996 and 1997 of legislation banning an infrequently used late-term abortion procedure called "partial birth abortion" by abortion opponents and "intact dilation and extraction" by abortion rights proponents marked a new level of proposed federal regulation. This legislation was vetoed twice by President Clinton and became a political issue in the 1996 presidential election. One leader of a pro-life lobby group, Ralph Reed of the Christian Coalition, indicated that this legislation would be followed by other attempts to "outlaw other procedures . . . like a ban on abortion in the last month, and so on . . . ."[27]

ABORTION POLITICS AT THE STATE AND LOCAL LEVELS. Most of the legislation in the United States concerning abortions is state-level legislation. In 1973 *Roe v. Wade* invalidated most laws that flatly prohibited abortions, but states have continued to be prominent players in U.S. abortion policy. Rubin reports that two years after *Roe,* thirty-two states had passed sixty-two laws relating to abortion.[28] Almost all of these laws were aimed at limiting access to abortions, regulating abortion services, or stopping abortions under certain conditions. They are especially frequent in a handful of states that have a strong antiabortion political culture (Pennsylvania, Ohio, Minnesota, Missouri, Louisiana, Utah, and Idaho).

Table 1-1 gives a broad overview of the kinds of laws passed by state legislatures after the *Roe* decision. Interestingly, some of the laws passed in states with strong antiabortion sentiment directly challenged the holding in *Roe.* For example, as Barbara Hinkson Craig and David O'Brien report, "Six states passed laws prohibiting abortion except when necessary to save the life of the woman or in cases of fetal abnormality, rape, or incest."[29]

TABLE 1-1

Laws Passed by State Legislatures Limiting the Implementation of
Roe v. Wade (1973–1996)

Number of States	Nature of Laws Passed by the States
36	Conscience clause that allows medical personnel to decide not to provide abortions when they are opposed to abortion
30	Prohibitions against using tissue from aborted fetuses for experimentation
30	Post-viability standards concerning when viability occurs and regulating abortions after viability
30	Requirements for post-abortion care for the aborted viable fetus
25	Requests made of the U.S. Congress that abortion be banned
22	Laws requiring minors to obtain parental consent or judicial consent before obtaining an abortion
21	Laws requiring a minor's parents to be notified before an abortion is performed
20	Laws requiring that pregnant women be given antiabortion lectures or materials intended to discourage her from having an abortion, that is, "informed consent" laws
20	Requirements that all abortions must be reported to a state agency
12	"Right to Life" laws that make it illegal to kill a fetus in the womb or that require that any fetus born alive during an abortion must be given a chance to live
11	Regulations concerning the disposal of aborted fetuses
11	Private insurance companies permitted to restrict access or to not cover abortion services
10	Feticide laws that outlaw the killing of a fetus after an abortion
8	Laws requiring the husband's or father's consent before a woman obtains an abortion
6	Stipulations that only licensed physicians can perform abortions
6	Specified waiting periods after an abortion is requested
4	Restrictions on the use of public facilities for abortions
2	Restrictions on the use of abortion for gender selection
1	Requirements that physicians inform pregnant women that fetuses feel pain and that anesthetic is available

Source: Kenneth Meier et al., "Assessing the Impact of State Level Restrictions on Abortion," *Demography* 33 (1996): 309–310. Reprinted with permission of the publisher.

Clearly unconstitutional, these laws were not enforced, but their passage registered a protest against the Court's decision and offered opponents the hope of a more restrictive abortion policy should *Roe* be overturned or modified.

Research by social scientists has produced mixed results concerning whether the passage of restrictive laws actually reduced the availability of abortions or affected abortion rates in the states. Kenneth Meier and his associates examined abortion rates in the fifty states over a ten-year period, 1982–1992, and found no evidence that the passage of restrictive state laws resulted in lower abortion rates. This analysis took into account trends in abortion rates and socioeconomic factors that previous analyses had demonstrated were related to state-by-state abortion rates. Even when the analysis focused on laws that were not enjoined by a court decision or held unconstitutional by the state attorney general, no policy "had a significant negative impact on the [state's] abortion rate."[30]

While analysis of restrictive state policies showed little impact on abortion rates, state financing legislation in some states dramatically influenced abortion rates. Data reported by Wetstein for Pennsylvania, Colorado, and California appear to demonstrate this dramatically. The passage of state laws prohibiting the use of Medicaid funds for abortions in Pennsylvania (in 1985) and Colorado (in 1984) resulted in a substantial drop in abortion rates, 12 and 13 percent respectively. The decline in abortion rates continued in these states for several years, eventually stabilizing at rates substantially below the rates of the years immediately following the *Roe* decision. In California, the legislature also eliminated state Medicaid funds for abortions in 1978, but this action did not have the same effect on abortion rates as new laws had in Pennsylvania or Colorado. However, when the state supreme court declared California's restrictions unconstitutional in 1981 (*Committee to Defend Reproductive Rights v. Myers*), forcing the state to fund abortions with Medicaid money, the abortion rate rose dramatically.[31]

INTEREST GROUPS AND ABORTION POLITICS. As has happened with other major issues in American politics, the Supreme Court's establishment of abortion rights in *Roe v. Wade* led to considerable activity by organized interests in the United States. While a few interest groups could be found on either side of the abortion issue before the Court's 1973 decision, their number and the variety of their activities increased dramatically after *Roe*.

Groups opposed to the decision grew rapidly in number, often organizing public demonstrations against the decision and, later, picketing clinics. Opposition groups, more so than supporters, included many people who had the time to picket, orchestrate letter-writing campaigns, call legislators, and participate in other political activities.[32] The orientation and composition of these groups often produced large demonstrations, such as the annual March for Life rallies in Washington, D.C., on the anniversary of the *Roe* decision. These marches attracted nearly 650,000 total participants over a sixteen-year period from 1974 through 1989.[33]

Organized interests opposing abortion were often linked to religious organizations—usually either the Catholic Church or fundamentalist Christian organizations. In November 1975, for example, the National Council of Catholic Bishops adopted a "Pastoral Plan for Pro-Life Activities" that called on all Catholic agencies to support legislation restricting access to abortion. The plan called for individuals and groups to work for the election of pro-life legislators. One direct result of this action occurred in New York, where local groups pressed county governments to stop financing abortions and persuaded three counties to do so in 1978.[34] A 1980 meeting in Dallas, Texas, led to an agreement among several fundamentalist Christian groups to pursue activities in the political system that included

> voter registration drives centered on the churches, church-level laymen's leagues to study candidates and legislation, state and regional training seminars in political tactics, the expansion of an already thriving network of newsletters that "simplify" and "clarify" the issues, a telephone network to bring an avalanche of Christian opinion down on Congress at critical points in the legislative process, and a concerted courting of the media.[35]

These actions are classic interest group initiatives to influence political institutions and government officials.

As many of the interest group initiatives fell short of their primary objective of overturning the *Roe* decision, some organized interests took direct action against abortion providers by attempting to blockade or close clinics. Joseph Scheidler, one advocate of this approach, published a book "listing ninety-nine ways to close abortion clinics."[36] Another national movement led by the Pro-Life Nonviolent Action Project mounted "rescue" attempts to shut down clinics in several cities. Their attempts met with some success in several cities and received a great deal of national attention. Litigation on behalf of abortion providers, however, ended with the conviction of group leaders for violations of federal racketeering laws.[37]

Organized groups that supported the Court's abortion decision were initially happy about *Roe* and did not mobilize a political campaign to support the decision's implementation. As Congress, state legislatures, and other government bodies passed new restrictive legislation, these groups sought to influence abortion policy primarily through litigation. Although the supportive groups organized some public demonstrations and contacted legislators, their most obvious efforts focused upon the courts. A study by Barbara Yarnold illustrates this. In 145 federal district court cases involving challenges to state and local laws that limited access to abortion services, pro-choice interest groups participated in 94 while pro-life groups were, by contrast, involved in only 14. Yarnold attributes the high number of victories for pro-choice forces in these cases (111 out of 145) to the extensive participation of pro-choice groups in organized efforts that included joint litigation strategies.[38]

The differences in strategies among organized interests was demonstrated clearly when the Supreme Court heard a challenge to a Missouri law that limited abortions in several ways. This case, *Webster v. Reproductive Services* (1989), attracted national attention because the Department of Justice explicitly asked the Court to overrule *Roe v. Wade*. Many hoped (or feared) that the Court would do this. (When the decision was announced, only four justices said they would overrule *Roe*.) A record number of seventy-eight amicus curiae briefs (those filed by interest groups who are not parties to the case; see Chapter 5) supported by over 300 organizations were filed in this case in support or opposition to the *Roe* decision. Pro-choice groups' filings or signings outnumbered those from pro-life groups by a 5 to 1 ratio.[39]

ABORTION POLICY QUESTIONS RETURN TO THE COURTS. The actions taken by Congress, state legislatures, and various administrative agencies at all levels of government, as well as the activities of private organizations, often led to the consideration of new policy questions by the courts. The Supreme Court's decision in *Roe v. Wade* had invalidated state laws prohibiting abortion, but it had left unanswered questions about restrictive legislation, especially with regard to the latter stages of pregnancy. Similarly, the Court was silent on policy questions regarding the state's obligation to provide abortion services in public hospitals or to pay for abortions for women who could not afford them. Courts often and necessarily leave important questions open when deciding a core issue; addressing them in subsequent cases gives the judiciary a continuing role in the implementation of its policies.

Appendix Table A-1 gives a summary of major abortion decisions by the U.S. Supreme Court after *Roe v. Wade*. These decisions address such questions as whether states could require various forms of spousal consent or parental consent before minors received an abortion, whether the First Amendment protected advertisements for legal abortions, whether federal and state governments could prohibit payments from public funds for abortion services, and whether states could regulate the time and place of abortions.

Notable among these Supreme Court cases have been several efforts to reverse the decision. As we have noted, in *Webster* the Court was asked to overrule its decision in *Roe*. A highly fragmented Court upheld the essential holding in *Roe*—namely, that women have the right to terminate pregnancies. The Court did, however, allow state regulations limiting access to abortions and imposing conditions on those services. Such legislation had the effect of making abortion more complicated for both pregnant women and providers. Most significantly, *Webster* abandoned the trimester formulation articulated in *Roe;* states could now impose regulations on abortion services tied to the "viability" of a fetus. These changes led Justice Blackmun, the author of the majority opinion in *Roe,* to complain in his *Webster* dissent, "Today, *Roe v. Wade,* and the fundamental constitutional right of women to decide whether to terminate a pregnancy, survive but are not secure."

Three years later the Court was again pressed to reverse *Roe* in *Planned Parenthood of Southeastern Pennsylvania v. Casey* (1992). And again the Court upheld the right to abortion in a fragmented decision, but with six justices signaling that state legislatures could enact laws regulating the circumstances under which women could have abortions, as long as the laws did not place an "undue burden" on the right to obtain an abortion. Sarah Weddington, the attorney for "Jane Roe" who argued before the Court in 1973, commented:

> Up to now, the court has said, "It's a woman's decision, and you people in the legislature, leave her alone." Now they're saying, "It's still her decision, but you people in the legislature can erect hurdles and roadblocks so that only women who are the most determined, who have the most money, who are the most sophisticated make it through."[40]

Nonetheless, the impact of *Webster* and *Casey* is uncertain. The number of abortions has declined slightly, from a high of 1.43 million to 1.27 million, in the mid-1990s, but how much of the change is attributable to the Court cases as opposed to greater sex education, more frequent use of contraceptives, or a rise in abstinence is not known. Fluctuations aside, the number of abortions in the United States each year remains large.

Even more cases concerning abortion services were addressed in lower courts. A few even involved criminal prosecutions of physicians, as did the case of Dr. Kenneth C. Edelin of Massachusetts. Edelin was convicted of manslaughter after he performed an abortion in the sixth or seventh month of pregnancy. His conviction was later overturned on appeal, but reports in the popular press after the conviction suggested that hospitals in several cities began limiting abortions in later stages of pregnancy so as to avoid similar charges.[41]

Appendix Table A-2 gives a sampling of other cases resolved in lower courts where states or local governments attempted to limit abortion services. Each of these decisions sought to clarify the rights of women as set forth in *Roe v. Wade,* and thereby affected the implementation and impact of that decision.

A MODEL OF THE IMPLEMENTATION AND IMPACT OF JUDICIAL POLICIES

Chronicling the events that followed the Supreme Court's abortion decision gives some idea of the range of reactions and actors that may become involved in the implementation of a judicial decision. Similar case histories could be supplied for other court decisions. But our aim is not to study the aftermath of every judicial decision; instead, we want to make general statements about what has happened or may happen after any judicial decision. That is, we hope to move away from idiosyncratic, case-by-case or policy-by-policy analyses and toward a general theoretical understanding of the events that may follow a judicial decision. The remainder of this book is devoted to explaining the responses one may encounter to any given judicial decision—who may react to the decisions and how; what types of reactions may occur; and what effects those reactions may have on the implementation of the judicial policy.

The first step in understanding any political process is to develop a conceptual foundation upon which explanations may be built. We will organize our presentation of what happens after a court decision around two major elements: *the actors* who may respond to the decision and *the responses* that these actors may make. Focusing on these two elements enables us to define more precisely who is reacting and how. In studying the

Figure 1-2   Populations and Lines of Communication Involved in the Implementation and Impact of Judicial Policies

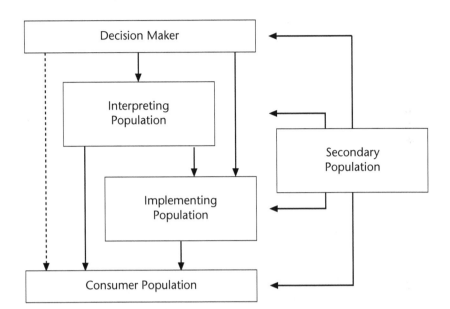

Source: Adapted from Charles A. Johnson, "The Implementation and Impact of Judicial Policies: A Heuristic Model," in *Public Law and Public Policy,* ed. John A. Gardiner (New York: Praeger, 1977), 107–126, with permission of the publisher.

responses to judicial policies, we describe and attempt to explain the behavior following a court decision—specifically, what the behavior is, its antecedents, and its consequences. Hence, when we discuss impact, we are describing the general reactions and changes (or lack thereof) that follow a judicial decision. When we discuss implementation, we are describing the behavior of lower courts, government agencies, or other affected parties as it relates to enforcing a judicial decision. When we discuss what many would call compliance/noncompliance or evasion, we are describing behavior that is in some way consistent or inconsistent with the behavioral requirements of the judicial decision.

Figure 1-2 presents a schematic diagram of the different sets of actors, referred to as populations, that may respond to a judicial policy.[42] The organization of these populations is essentially a functional one, in which their roles in shaping the impact of judicial decisions and their influence on the ultimate impact of judicial policy differ. We now turn to a discussion of these populations and their responses, illustrated with examples drawn from the events after the Supreme Court's abortion decision as well as other recent court decisions.

The Interpreting Population

For any appellate court decision, the actor most often charged with responding to a decision is a particular lower court, often a trial court. Moreover, in our common law system many appellate court decisions become policies used in deciding future cases. In a general sense, therefore, a higher court's policy affects all lower courts within its jurisdiction. This set of courts is known as the interpreting population. (This population may include state attorneys-general or other non-judges who have an official role in interpreting the law.) The interpreting population, as the name implies, responds to the policy decisions of a higher court by refining the policy it has announced. Such refinements can have the effect of enlarging or limiting the original policy. This population, in other words, interprets the meaning of the policy and develops the rules for matters not addressed in the original decision. Of course, all populations must "interpret" the decision in order to react to it. Interpretations by lower courts, however, are distinguished from other interpretations since theirs are viewed as authoritative in a legal sense by others in the political system. Hence, this population provides "official" interpretations of a court policy applicable to the other populations under its jurisdiction.

The Supreme Court's *Roe* decision launched the judiciary into a new area of the law, which required considerable refining before complete implementation. Shortly after the decision was announced, lower state and federal courts began hearing cases presenting issues that had not been directly addressed in *Roe*. In Florida, for example, the issue of a father's rights were raised by a father who brought legal action to restrain the mother of his unborn child from obtaining an abortion. The lower court denied relief and the Florida Supreme Court affirmed that decision, arguing that the U.S. Supreme Court's abortion decision was based on the mother's "right of privacy" (*Jones v. Smith*, 1973). The decision to terminate a pregnancy was, therefore, purely the right of the mother and could not be subject to interference by the state or private individuals.

Meanwhile, in Arizona, another matter was before the courts. Arizona law prohibited the advertisement of any medicine or procedures that facilitated abortions. New Times, Inc., a local publisher, was convicted under this statute and appealed to the state supreme court. The conviction was reversed, since the Arizona abortion statutes were found to be similar to the Texas statute struck down in *Roe v. Wade,* even though the issue before the court was different from that decided in the original abortion cases (*State v. New Times, Inc.,* 1973).

In each of these instances, and in others such as those cases summarized in Appendix Table A-1, the issue before the court had not been addressed directly in the original decision. Consistent with the common law tradition, the lower courts had the responsibility of making authoritative interpretations of policy in light of the original Supreme Court decision. In their interpretations these courts could limit the application of the original policy, as did the Arizona trial court in convicting the publisher, or could facilitate its implementation, as did the Florida courts. Chapter 2 describes and offers explanations for the reactions of lower courts that authoritatively interpret judicial decisions.

The Implementing Population

The lower courts apply a higher court's policy only in cases that come before them. Higher court policies, however, usually affect a wider set of actors than those involved in lawsuits. We refer to this set of actors as the implementing population. In most instances, this population is made up of authorities whose behavior may be reinforced or sanctioned by the interpreting population. The implementing population usually performs a policing or servicing function in the political system—that is, implementors apply the system's rules to persons subject to their authority. Prominent examples of this population are police officers, prosecutors, university and public school officials, and welfare and social security workers. In many instances, the original policy and subsequent interpretations by lower courts are intended to impose requirements or set limits on the behavior of the implementing population. A clear example of this activity involves decisions concerning police behavior with regard to the rights of criminal suspects.

When the services or practices of private concerns are subject to a judicial policy, the implementing population is composed of private individuals or institutions. For example, court decisions may require or strongly suggest that corporations implement policies against racial or gender discrimination or harassment. As we will explain in Chapter 4, however, when a private organization has a choice (is not obligated to follow a policy), it is part of the consumer population.

The implementing population will vary from decision to decision. For criminal justice decisions, prosecutors, police officers, and defense attorneys are the primary implementors. For environmental protection decisions, the implementors are most often federal and state environmental protection agencies. Reapportionment decisions usually involve legislators as the implementing population. When judicial decisions require no action by government agencies, nongovernmental service agencies may be the implementors. Sometimes there is no implementing population at all. For example, no one is charged with implementing a case such as *New York Times Co. v. Sullivan* (1964), which significantly decreased the applicability of libel law to public officials. The decision held that when public officials initiated libel suits against the media, they had to show a much greater degree of fault than did private persons who filed libel suits. *Sullivan* is implemented solely through court rulings made in the course of litigation.

The degree to which a court decision actually benefits those it was intended to benefit depends on the implementing actors and institutions whose activities are affected by the decision. Implementors' reactions may range from full compliance to doing nothing. These reactions have been extensively studied by social scientists and legal scholars; the results provide a basis for our discussion of the implementing population in Chapter 3.

The Consumer Population

Those for whom the policies are set forth by the court are identified as the consumer population. This population is the set of individuals (usually not affiliated with the government) who would or should receive benefits or suffer disabilities as a result of a judicial decision; that is, they gain or lose desired rights or resources. Criminal suspects, for example, benefit from judicial policies announced by the Supreme Court in a series of decisions in the 1960s. African American students presumably benefited from school desegregation decisions following *Brown v. Board of Education* (1954). But they were disadvantaged by more recent judicial decisions limiting affirmative action programs in many public universities. Thus, some consumer populations do not benefit from a judicial policy. For example, juvenile court defendants suffer because they do not have the right of trial by jury; stockholders can suffer when their corporation is split up as a result of an antitrust ruling. And there are decisions under which members of the consumer population may either benefit or suffer, depending on their attitudes toward the policy. When led prayer was banned in the public schools (*Abington School District v. Schempp*, 1963), children who wanted to pray became disadvantaged and those who did not want to pray became advantaged.

The consumer population, depending on the policy involved, may include the entire population of the political system, as with judicial decisions concerning general tax legislation. For some decisions, however, a very limited population may be directly involved, such as criminal suspects under arrest. When the policy affects a specific sector but supposedly is for the public good (for example, antitrust decisions), a distinction between direct and indirect consumption must sometimes be made. Also, for some decisions there are two levels of consumer population, those who have to decide whether to offer some previously prohibited service and those who decide whether to use the service. For example, after *Roe* women could still not obtain legal abortions unless hospitals, clinics, and physicians were willing to perform them. As we noted, most medical facilities and doctors choose not to offer abortion services.

Specifying the consumer population exactly may be troublesome in some cases. For example, while few would dispute that women with unwanted pregnancies are the consumers for the Supreme Court's abortion decision, opponents would likely argue that unborn children are also consumers and receive catastrophic negative benefits from the abortion decision. Others might argue that fathers of unborn children or parents of underage, pregnant girls are part of *Roe*'s consumer population.

In studying the reactions of consumers to judicial policies, several questions need to be addressed. Do the potential consumers of a judicial policy know of the policy? If they know of the policy, why and how do they modify their attitudes or behavior because of it? What effect, if any, does the policy have on the attitudes and behavior of the consumer with regard to the judiciary or other political institutions? These questions and the issue of who may be identified as a member of the consumer population will be considered in Chapter 4.

The Secondary Population

The populations we have discussed so far are those directly (at least potentially) affected by a judicial policy or its implementation. The secondary population is a residual one. It consists of everyone who is not in the interpreting, implementing, or consumer population for any given decision.

Members of the secondary population are not directly affected by a judicial policy; however, some members may react to a policy or its implementation. This reaction usually takes the form of some type of feedback directed toward the original policy maker, another policy maker, the implementing population, or the consumer population.

The secondary population may be divided into four subpopulations: government officials, interest groups, the media, and the public at large. First, there are government officials. This subpopulation includes legislators and executive officers who are not immediately affected by the decision. Though usually unaffected directly, these individuals are often in a position to support or hinder the implementation of the original policy. This subpopulation is distinguished from other secondary subpopulations in that its members have direct, legitimate authority in the political system, and they are often the recipients of political pressure from the public. Clearly, for example, Congress and state legislatures substantially affected implementation of *Roe v. Wade* with the passage of laws restricting the funding of abortions.

The second subpopulation is interest groups, which are often activated by court policies even when they are not directly affected by them. Subsequent pressures by these groups may help facilitate or block effective implementation of the judicial policy. National, state, and local pro-life organizations have worked diligently to discourage providers from offering abortion services and women from obtaining abortions. These groups have also maintained considerable pressure on public officials and the courts to limit the implementation of pro-choice policies.

The third subpopulation is the media, which communicate the substance of judicial policies to potentially affected populations. Included here are general and specialized media, which may affect implementation or consumption by editorial stance or simply by the way they report (or do not report) judicial policies. Media attention to a policy, descriptions of reactions to it, and support or criticism of it can play a large role in determining the amount and direction of feedback courts and implementors get. Media reports of activities by pro-choice and pro-life groups have helped keep the abortion issue at the forefront of American politics.

The fourth subpopulation consists of members of the public at large, insofar as they do not fall within the consumer population. The most important segment of this subpopulation is attentive citizens—those who are most aware of a judicial policy. This segment includes individuals who may be related to the consumer population (e.g., parents of teenage girls seeking an abortion), politically active people (e.g., political party workers), or just people who follow the news pretty regularly. The reactions of secondary populations and how they may influence the implementation process are considered in Chapter 5.

Fluidity and Linkage Among Populations

The basis for the foregoing classification of populations is primarily functional. We may, therefore, on some occasions find that particular individuals are members of different populations in different circumstances. For example, it is entirely possible for a state attorney general to be an interpreter for one judicial policy and an implementor for another. In the former instance, the attorney general would be issuing an authoritative, legally binding statement interpreting a judicial decision; in the latter instance, the attorney general would be charged with the responsibility of applying a judicial policy to some consumer population or of carrying out some order of the court. School boards or superintendents may be implementors of a schoolhouse religion decision and consumers of a court decision changing the way the state finances the schools. Media outlets are consumers of a libel decision like *Sullivan,* but more often they are in the secondary population. Obviously, private citizens are in both the consumer and secondary populations, depending on the nature of the judicial policy.

Attorneys constitute a special set of participants whose function may vary from one setting to another. They assist the interpreting population when they argue for a particular interpretation of a higher court's decision in briefs or oral arguments before lower court judges. They have a role in implementation when they insist that agencies follow policies promulgated by a higher court. When they advise clients to take advantage (or not to do so) of a judicial policy, attorneys are playing a role as quasi-members of the consumer population.

Perhaps even more often, attorneys are called upon to give their interpretations of judicial policies to potential consumers, implementing groups, and, occasionally, secondary groups such as interested citizens or legislative bodies. Such interpretations are not official like those of the interpreting population. Often, however, their interpretations can be final, since paying clients usually act on lawyers' advice; so it is reasonable to assume that such interpretations play an important role in accounting for the reactions of others to judicial policies. As we have mentioned, attorneys also assist in interpreting higher court policies for lower courts.

In a broad sense, as they perform these functions, attorneys serve as links between various populations. They provide a means for the communication of decisions downward from higher courts to relevant actors, as well as being unofficial interpreters of these decisions. Their linkage activities may also prompt new litigation or feedback to the courts or other agencies, which, in turn, may affect the implementation of a decision.

Acceptance Decisions and Behavioral Responses

In this book, we focus on the responses to judicial policies by all of the populations we have identified. We may observe a large variety of responses to judicial decisions, so precise distinctions are difficult to make. Nonetheless, we believe two general categories of responses are captured in the concepts of acceptance decisions and behavioral responses. The *acceptance decision* involves psychological reactions to a judicial policy, which may be generalized in terms of accepting or rejecting the policy. An individual's acceptance decision is shaped by several psychological dimensions: intensity of attitude, regard for the policy-making court, perceptions of the consequences of the decision, and the person's own role in society.

The *intensity of a person's attitude* toward the policy prior to the court's decision can be important. Most white southerners, for example, were extremely hostile toward policies of racial integration before *Brown;* thus their unwillingness to accept the decision was not surprising. Many people had similarly intense attitudes about abortion and about prayers in the public schools. Many minority groups felt strongly about affirmative action. For most policies, though, feelings are not so intense. Few people feel strongly about such issues as the size and composition of juries, whether a high school newspaper can be published without the principal's approval, or the application of the First Amendment guarantees to commercial advertising. In such instances the acceptance decision is less likely to be governed by prior attitudes.

Another dimension of acceptance reflects people's *regard for the court* making the decision. People who view the U.S. Supreme Court favorably may be more inclined to accept a decision as legitimate and proper. Those who generally view the Court negatively or who believe it has taken on too much authority may transfer their views to particular decisions of the Court.

A third psychological dimension takes into account a person's *perception of the consequences of a decision*. Those who may not quarrel with a decision in the abstract but believe it will have a serious and detrimental effect on society may be reluctant to accept it. In the 1950s, for example, many citizens feared that communism would expand in the United States as a result of the Supreme Court's decisions granting due process to persons suspected of engaging in subversive activities. In the late 1990s many people worry that court decisions voiding affirmative action programs will make it more difficult for minority applicants to obtain jobs.

Finally, acceptance decisions are shaped by a *person's own role in society.* An ambitious judge, school superintendent, or police chief may be reluctant to accept (publicly, at least) an unpopular judicial policy for fear that it will harm his or her career. Corporate officers or citizens may be unwilling to accept a decision if they think it will reduce their profits or cause them great inconvenience. Conversely, people may accept quite willingly decisions that are popular with the public or that bring them financial or other benefits.

Behavioral responses involve reactions that may be seen or recorded and that may determine the extent to which a court policy is actually realized. These responses are often closely linked to acceptance decisions. Persons who do not accept a judicial policy are likely to engage in behavior designed to defeat the policy or minimize its impact. They will interpret it narrowly, try to avoid implementing it, and refuse or evade its consumption. Those who accept a policy are likely to be more faithful or even enthusiastic in interpreting, implementing, and consuming it. Of course, nonacceptors may not always be in a position to ignore a decision or to refuse completely to comply with it. Malapportioned state legislatures, for instance, had little choice but to reapportion themselves after the Supreme Court established a "one person, one vote" criterion for legislative representation in the 1960s. People may adjust some of their behavioral responses to meet the decision's requirements while they have other, less visible, behavioral responses that may more truly reflect their unwillingness to accept the decision. Conversely, acceptors may for reasons of inertia never fully adjust their behavioral responses to a new judicial policy.

Changes in policy often entail *changes in rules or formal directives* within an organization. But at the day-to-day level, norms, informal understandings, or even behavioral habits within an organization may set the tone. Public and private employers may, for example, adopt formal policies prohibiting sexual harassment, but many informally tolerate violations of those policies. Policy changes may also lead to changes in organizational structure or function. As we have indicated, the delivery of abortion services changed after *Roe v. Wade* to the extent that currently most abortions are performed in clinics, not hospitals.

Another type of behavioral response is the *actions or inaction* of those who consume the policy. Consumption decisions can be affected by the way the interpreting and implementing populations act. Consumers may respond to a court decision by using, ignoring, or avoiding it. For example, many lawyers do not advertise, even through the Supreme Court has ruled that they can do so (*Bates v. Arizona Bar,* 1978). We must examine actual behavior, in addition to policy changes of corporations and agencies, if we are to better understand the consumption of judicial policies.

Feedback is another behavioral response to judicial policies. It is directed toward the originator of the policy or to some other policy-making agency. The purpose of feedback behavior is usually to provide support for or make demands upon political actors (including judges) regarding the judicial policy. Feedback is often communicated through interest groups or the media. Almost immediately after the Supreme Court announced its abortion decision, feedback in the form of letters to the justices began. Also, some members of Congress let the Court know of their displeasure with the abortion decision by introducing statutory restrictions or constitutional amendments to overturn *Roe.* Manifestations of displeasure or support by various interest groups have been directed at the Court and other political institutions, such as Congress and state legislatures. In varying degrees, these types of feedback have led to modifications of the policy—as we can see in the Court's *Webster* and *Casey* decisions abandoning the trimester system and allowing the states greater leeway in regulating abortion.

SUMMARY

In this chapter we have introduced the notion that judicial decisions are not self-implementing; courts must frequently rely on lower courts or on nonjudicial actors in the political system to turn law into action. Moreover, the implementation of judicial decisions is a political process; the actors upon whom courts must rely are usually political actors and are subject to political pressures as they allocate resources to implement a judicial decision. The events and actors following the Supreme Court's 1973 abortion decisions illustrate the initial premises underlying the remainder of this book.

NOTES

1. Fox Butterfield, "Behind Death Row Bottleneck," *New York Times,* January 25, 1998 (http://www.nytimes.com/library/review/012598death-penalty-review.html).

2. Michael Lipsky, "Implementation on Its Head," in *American Politics and Public Policy,* ed. Walter Burnham and Martha Weinberg (Cambridge, Mass.: MIT Press, 1978), 390–402, as cited in Robert T. Nakamura and Frank Smallwood, *The Politics of Policy Implementation* (New York: St. Martin's Press, 1980), 19.

3. Bob Woodward and Scott Armstrong, *The Brethren: Inside the Supreme Court* (New York: Simon and Schuster, 1979).

4. *Roe v. Wade,* 410 U.S. 113 (1973) at 164–165.

5. Woodward and Armstrong, *The Brethren,* 238–239.

6. "Cardinals Shocked—Reaction Mixed," *New York Times,* January 23, 1973, 1, 20.

7. Woodward and Armstrong, *The Brethren,* 240. The authors may have been in error reporting this incident, since "Mary Doe" challenged the Georgia abortion statute, not the Texas statute.

8. David Loomis, "Abortion: Should Constitution Be Amended?" *Congressional Quarterly Weekly Report,* May 3, 1975, 919.

9. Alan Guttmacher Institute, *Abortion 1974–1975: Need and Services in the United States* (New York: Planned Parenthood Federation of America, 1976).

10. Alan Guttmacher Institute, *Abortion 1975* (New York: Planned Parenthood Federation of America, 1975), 62.

11. Jon R. Bond and Charles A. Johnson, "Implementing a Permissive Policy: Hospital Abortion Services after *Roe v. Wade,*" *American Journal of Political Science* 26 (1982): 1–24.

12. Alan Guttmacher Institute, *Abortion 1975,* 62.

13. Ibid., 11.

14. Gerald N. Rosenberg, *The Hollow Hope: Can Courts Bring About Social Change?* (Chicago: University of Chicago Press, 1991), 179.

15. Ibid.

16. Stanley K. Henshaw and Jennifer Van Vort, "Abortion Services in the United States, 1991 and 1992" *Family Planning Perspectives* 26 (May/June 1994): 100–112, 106.

17. Ibid., Table 6.

18. Matthew Wetstein, *Abortion Rates in the United States: The Influence of Opinion and Policy* (Albany, N.Y.: SUNY Press, 1996), 48–50.

19. "Abortion Surveillance—United States, 1993–1994," MMWR 46 (August 8, 1997), Table 4.

20. For a full discussion of these state-by-state differences, see Wetstein, *Abortion Rates,* 52–58.

21. See Eva Rubin, *Abortion, Politics, and the Courts:* Roe v. Wade *and Its Aftermath* (New York: Greenwood Press, 1987), 152–161, for a full discussion of these amendments and subsequent deliberations.

22. Ibid., 157.

23. Ibid., 159–161.

24. See Ibid., 162–163, and Barbara H. Craig and David O'Brien, *Abortion and American Politics* (Chatham, N.J.: Chatham House, 1988), 103–155, esp. Table 4.1 on pp. 112–113.

25. Rich Spencer, "New Curbs Cut Medical-Funded Abortions 99%, HEW Reports," *Washington Post,* March 8, 1979, 1, as reported in Rosenberg, *The Hollow Hope,* 187.

26. Rubin, *Abortion, Politics, and the Courts,* 176.

27. Melinda Henneberger, "House Approves Bill to Overturn Veto on Abortion," *New York Times,* September 20, 1996, 1, 11 (national edition).

28. Rubin, *Abortion, Politics, and the Courts,* 127.

29. Craig and O'Brien, *Abortion and American Politics,* 79–80.

30. Kenneth Meier et al., "Assessing the Impact of State Level Restrictions on Abortion," *Demography* 33 (1996): 310.

31. Wetstein, *Abortion Rates in the United States: The Influence of Opinion and Policy,* 52–57.

32. Craig and O'Brien, *Abortion and American Politics,* 46.

33. Ibid., 51.

34. Ibid., 47; also see Timothy A. Byrnes and Mary Segers, eds., *Abortion Politics in American States* (Armonk, N.Y.: M. E. Sharp, 1995), for a series of case studies on the political actions of the Catholic Church in several states to influence abortion policy.

35. Craig and O'Brien, *Abortion and American Politics,* 52.

36. Ibid., 57.

37. Ibid., and "Abortion Foes Are Held Liable for Harrassment," *New York Times,* April 22, 1998, 1.

38. Barbara Yarnold, *Abortion Politics in the Federal Courts: Right Versus Right* (Westport, Conn.: Praeger, 1995), 16–23.

39. See Craig and O'Brien, *Abortion and American Politics,* 204 and 214–218, for lists of these groups.

40. Quoted in Craig and O'Brien, *Abortion and American Politics,* 326.

41. "Abortion and the Law," *Newsweek,* March 3, 1975, 18–30.

42. This model is drawn from Charles A. Johnson, "The Implementation and Impact of Judicial Policies: A Heuristic Model," in *Public Law and Public Policy,* ed. John A. Gardiner (New York: Praeger, 1977), 107–126.

CHAPTER TWO

The Interpreting Population

Important policy announcements almost always require interpretation by someone other than the policy maker. Even a simple "Keep off the grass" sign may require some interpretation. Does the sign apply when there is a foot of snow on the ground? Does it apply when workers have torn up the sidewalk so that the only access to a building is across the grass? Most policies, moreover, have considerably greater scope and sophistication. Policies are made to govern society or large institutions within it, and they often focus on complex and perhaps interrelated circumstances. Sometimes such policies cannot easily be applied to local situations or unanticipated events, and the policy-making person or organization is rarely available for an immediate interpretation. Other persons, then, must interpret the policy in question, at least temporarily.

This chapter focuses on the population that interprets judicial policy. The actions of this population are the first link in the chain of events that gives a judicial decision its impact. Members of other populations, particularly the implementing population, look to the interpreting population for guidance and are often subject to authoritative commands by the interpreting population. Quite often it is only after this population has interpreted a particular policy that the other populations feel that they can or should implement or consume a judicial decision.

Unlike the other populations, the interpreting population is readily iden-
tifiable and remains quite stable from one judicial policy to another. Broadly
speaking, the interpreting population is composed of those persons whose
regular function in society is telling others what court decisions mean.
Judges are interpreters, of course. Lawyers who interpret a decision for their
clients are in this category—especially if the clients act upon the advice and
do not go to court. Attorneys general, city attorneys, and other officials who
regularly interpret court decisions are also included.[1]

Judges are the heart of the interpreting population. Judges' interpretations—unlike those of lawyers, attorneys general, and others—are authoritative. They must be obeyed under threat of penalty; they are not merely
a form of advice. Because judges have special interpretive status and
because there has been little study of how interpretations by nonjudges
affect the impact of decisions, we will focus on judges in this chapter. As
judicial scholar Jack Peltason put it: "Supreme Court decisions mean what
district courts say they mean."[2]

It will be useful to review briefly the structure of courts in the United
States (see Figure 2-1). Bear in mind that our description is simplified: the
particular titles of courts are not as important as their functions relative to
each other; in fact, courts with similar names in different states may have
generally different jurisdictions. The judicial hierarchy is divided between
federal and state courts and between appellate and trial courts; there are two
levels of appellate courts for the federal level and in about forty of the states.
It is possible for a case originating in a state trial court of general jurisdiction to go through as many as three appeals. State supreme court decisions
regarding state statutes or common law are final, except where a federal
question is involved; then a case can go from a state supreme court to the
U.S. Supreme Court—the ultimate judicial policy maker. Any court to
which a case is appealed is a higher court for that case; thus an appellate
court may be sometimes designated a higher court (in relation to a trial
court, for example) and sometimes a lower court (in relation to a supreme
court).

Once a case is decided by the state supreme court or the U.S. Supreme
Court, a policy has been made. All courts lower in the hierarchy must
attempt to apply the policy to relevant cases, interpreting the policy as necessary to fit the circumstances at hand. The process starts in the trial court;
here the judge must make an initial interpretation and explain it to those
outside the judicial hierarchy, particularly lawyers and litigants. Each appel-

Figure 2-1   The American Court System, Simplified

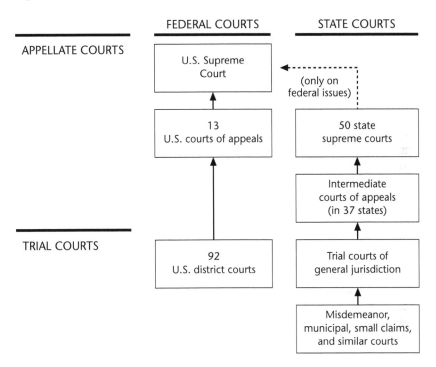

late court in turn interprets U.S. or state supreme court cases and explains them to lower courts and other interested persons.

In this chapter we first discuss some of the reasons lower court judges must interpret higher court policy. Next, we turn to an analysis of the freedoms of and limitations on lower court judges who must interpret higher court policies. Finally, we consider research concerning the responses of judges and look at some explanations of why judges respond as they do when they must interpret higher court policies.

WHY AND WHEN JUDICIAL POLICIES MUST BE INTERPRETED

Judicial policies require interpretation under a variety of circumstances and for a variety of reasons. Some policies (for example, antitrust and labor relations laws) are by nature complex. Opinions in such cases can involve very sophisticated reasoning. Moreover, because policy is usually made by a collegial court (one with several judges), vague phrases may be used to cover differences between the judges. At times, higher court policies are so ambiguous or poorly articulated that a judge *must* exercise some discretion in determining what the higher court intends. Such situations are opportunities for the judge's own biases to enter the decision-making process. Judges are, after all, political actors, and they often have strong views on public policy.

Sometimes lower courts must decide how higher court policies apply to new technology, financial arrangements, or social trends (for example, the First Amendment and the Internet). An opinion may require interpretation or elaboration because it fails to address one or more of its controversial implications. Indeed, since judicial opinions usually come about as a result of a dispute between two parties over a specific situation, most court opinions make little effort to announce a comprehensive policy. But even if the opinion does more than settle a dispute, the decision and opinion do not stand alone. Rather, the decision is usually part of a broader policy shaped by earlier decisions and the new opinion must be enmeshed with them.

Further interpretation is needed when a higher court announces a policy that either opens a new area of the law or changes previous policies. *Roe v. Wade* is an example of the former situation. *Batson v. Kentucky* (1986) illustrates the latter. Here the Court said that it was unconstitutional for prosecutors to strike people from jury pools because of their race, a change from the centuries old policy that no reason need be offered for peremptory (non-cause) challenges to jurors. Did *Batson* apply to Jews, Italian Americans and men or women? To Hispanics and the obese? Using various interpretations, lower courts have applied *Batson* to the former groups, but not the latter.[3] Similarly, in *Meritor Savings Bank v. Vinson* (1986), the Supreme Court held that the 1964 Civil Rights Act's prohibition against discrimination by employers because of sex also prohibited sexual harassment on the job, but the decision gave little guidance about what constituted sexual harassment. Must a threat to fire or not promote a victim accompany a request for sexual favors? Did derogatory sexual remarks suffice? If so, how much of a pattern was required? For twelve years lower federal courts answered these questions in a variety of ways. Even the Court's 1998 decision on sexual harassment (*Ellerth v. Burlington Industries*) leaves some questions unanswered.

DISCRETION AND CONSTRAINTS IN INTERPRETING JUDICIAL DECISIONS

As members of the judicial hierarchy, lower court judges are constrained in interpreting higher court policies, although they also have considerable discretion in their interpretation. In this section we will discuss the factors that permit discretion and impose constraints. Before proceeding, however, we should note that only perhaps one-fifth of trial court decisions each year are appealed and only 15 percent of these are reversed.[4] Very few—only about 100—are decided by the Supreme Court annually. In most cases, lower court decisions, some of which have interpreted Supreme Court policy, are not steps on the way to a final policy decision, but are final decisions themselves. Put otherwise, lower courts have considerable practical freedom from review by the Supreme Court.

Discretion

REMOVAL. In most bureaucracies, incompetent or defiant subordinates are demoted or fired. In the judiciary, however, such mechanisms are not available. Policy-making courts seldom have the legal authority to dismiss lower court judges. The latter are elected or appointed for set terms. Federal judges hold lifetime appointments, and their removal requires the ponderous process of impeachment (trial by the U.S. Senate). In over 200 years only seven federal judges have been so removed. Over the last few decades some states have created judicial disciplinary commissions that can remove judges or impose other sanctions (such as suspension without pay or reprimand) on judges, often subject to the state supreme court's approval. For example, a New York judge was removed from office after he said that spousal protection orders were "foolish and unnecessary" and added that "every woman needs a good pounding every now and then" during a spouse abuse case.[5] Even so, sanctioning lower court judges is rather difficult. Moreover, impeachment or other sanctions usually result from a judge's corruption or untoward behavior rather than his or her misinterpretation of higher court decisions.

In many states judges can be removed by defeat at the polls, or in some states by a majority vote in a recall election. But it would be unseemly and violate judicial ethics for a state supreme court to advocate defeat of a trial judge because the judge refused to apply the higher court's policies. Moreover, a local judge's deviant interpretations may well be quite popular with the voters.

Thus, unlike a bureaucracy, a supreme court cannot easily sanction a lower court judge who is stubborn about adhering to an unwarranted interpretation of its policy. Lower court judges have considerable leeway in applying higher court policies without fear of punishment.

REVERSAL. Reversal by a higher court is also a sanction of sorts for a lower court judge. While all judges suffer reversal on occasion, frequent reversals can harm a judge's professional reputation and chances for elevation to a higher court. One of the most telling criticisms of G. Harrold Carswell, nominated by President Richard M. Nixon to a vacant Supreme Court seat in 1971, was the extremely high reversal rate Carswell had as a U.S. district judge in Florida. In part, the high rate stemmed from his narrow interpretations of the Supreme Court's desegregation decisions. The Senate rejected Carswell's nomination. In addition, frequent reversal is a sign of professional failure. As we note in the next subsection, judges, like most people, value their reputation for professional competence. As one Connecticut trial judge put it, "Do I wince when a decision of mine is reversed by an appeals court? You bet I do." [6] On rare occasions, a reversing opinion can criticize the lower court judge scathingly.[7]

However, in some circumstances judges with strongly held beliefs will risk reversal. This was the case for some southern judges following *Brown v. Board of Education* (1954) and other Supreme Court desegregation cases. Religious convictions may compel a judge to resist applying a policy. A federal district judge in Oregon said: "We try to rule on the side of God. If the 9th circuit wants to reverse, we'll know whose side it is on." [8] In 1997 an Alabama circuit judge defied a higher court's ruling to stop opening his court with a prayer and became something of a local hero in the process.[9]

As the Supreme Court has become more conservative, some liberal judges have courted reversal. Judges on the Ninth Circuit Court of Appeals (the West Coast states) have skirted several conservative Supreme Court policies in the 1980s and 1990s, and have virtually defied the Supreme Court in some death penalty and abortion cases.[10] The Supreme Court once directly ordered the Ninth Circuit to cease issuing stays of execution.[11] Also, judges in federal specialized courts (those considering patent, customs, or international trade issues) sometimes feel their expertise in these areas warrants greater independence from Supreme Court doctrines than is suitable for "generalist" judges of the federal courts of appeals.[12]

Constraints

Although sanctions have only a limited effect, other factors push lower court judges toward being conscientious in interpreting higher court policies.

OBLIGATION. All judges take an oath to support the Constitution; state judges are also bound to support the constitution of their home state. Although there was some debate in the early years of the Republic, it is now universally understood that the U.S. Supreme Court is the final authoritative interpreter of the meaning of the U.S. Constitution. Likewise, state supreme courts have the final authority in interpreting state constitutions. Thus, judges are obligated by their oaths to abide by the policies of these higher courts insofar as they stem from constitutional interpretation.

This obligation can be a powerful reinforcement to a judge who is formulating a decision that goes against social or political pressures—or even against his or her own better judgment. For example, in 1990 in *Oregon Employment Division v. Smith,* a case involving the ritual use of the drug peyote by members of the Native American Church, the Supreme Court overturned the "compelling state interest" doctrine, which it had been using for more than twenty-five years, and adopted the "valid secular policy" doctrine in its place. The earlier doctrine allowed some religious practices to be exempted from laws of general applicability (such as Amish children not having to abide by compulsory education laws) while the new doctrine said that religiously motivated behavior was not a reason for exempting anyone from the reach of a law that had a valid secular purpose. In a case occurring shortly after *Smith,* a Rhode Island federal judge wrote: "While I feel constrained to apply the [Supreme Court] majority's opinion to the instant case, I cannot do this without expressing my profound regret and my own agreement with Justice Blackmun's forceful dissent"[13]

Frank Sorauf's 1976 study of sixty-seven lower court interpretations of *Abington School District v. Schempp* (1963) and related religious exercise cases found numerous judicial protests, but only one actual incident of "judicial heel dragging in the face of an uncongenial precedent."[14] Abortion can also tempt judges' professional commitment. A Louisiana federal judge asserted that *Roe v. Wade* had been wrongly decided; yet, after noting that judges were obligated to obey the Constitution as interpreted by the U.S. Supreme Court, he struck down Louisiana's reenactment of its laws prohibiting abortion.[15]

Appellate courts can reinforce this sense of obligation through praise, especially if a trial court has thrown out charges against an obviously guilty defendant. The Oklahoma Court of Criminal Appeals did so in commending a trial judge for "courageously following the law as laid down by the Supreme Court of the United States, even though it is not always a popular thing to do."[16]

PROFESSIONALISM. Judges are expected to have an excellent understanding of the law and to act accordingly. An opinion that patently misinterprets a higher court policy belies this expectation. It damages a judge's reputation among other judges and attorneys, just as a physician who ignores new medical findings loses the respect of other physicians. Furthermore, most persons in learned professions are socialized to norms of competence if not excellence. This is particularly strong in the case of judges. Society deliberately isolates them from pressures and constantly reminds them of their judicial status (for example, they wear robes, they are addressed as "Your Honor"). Thus both concern for their reputation and their own professional pride encourage judges to render an impartial interpretation of the law as found in higher court decisions.

SYSTEM INTEGRITY. Another important reason that judges adhere to higher court policies is that widespread failure to apply them would lead to a breakdown of the judicial system. Since judges are part of that system, its breakdown would, of course, adversely affect their own status and authority. Judges who publicly defy or evade their superiors' policies must realize that they are inviting similar treatment from those subject to their own rulings. The risks inherent in defiance were cogently recognized when Louisiana Supreme Court Justice Mack Barham dissented from his colleagues' overt unwillingness to apply a U.S. Supreme Court search and seizure decision. Justice Barham wrote:

> We, sitting as the Supreme Court of Louisiana attack with harsh and condemning language our state appellate courts below us for daring to deviate from, or even to question, our jurisprudence. . . . Yet we, who under our oath must obey the supremacy clause of the United States Constitution and respond to the United States Supreme Court decisions, tell that court of final supremacy that we will act on federal issues as we see fit—its pronouncements to the contrary notwithstanding.[17]

The justice then pointedly concluded his dissent by urging Louisiana's trial judges and district attorneys to abide not by his colleagues' decision but by relevant federal courts' search and seizure policy interpretations.

Thus a sense of duty, judicial professionalism, and a fear of undermining the judicial system hold the judicial system together and enable it to transmit judicial policy from Washington or the state capitals to the implementing populations without too much distortion. These constraints usually work. Research by Donald Songer and others shows that U.S. Courts of Appeals almost always abided by unambiguous Supreme Court doctrines in recent times.[18]

INTERPRETIVE RESPONSES BY JUDGES

As we noted in Chapter 1, when members of the interpreting population have to interpret a court case or policy, they must make acceptance and behavioral decisions about how to do it. Scholars have shown that the Supreme Court justices' votes are often based upon their attitudes about the policy at issue.[19] It is thus reasonable to believe that lower court judges' attitudes also affect their decisions. Of course, lower court judges are more constrained than Supreme Court justices (the latter hear more novel cases and have no higher court to answer to), but their attitudes nonetheless affect whether they decide to accept a higher court policy enthusiastically, treat it indifferently, or oppose it. Then they behave (decide and write their opinion) accordingly. Given the judicial environment, however, the opinion may be structured to be most effective (that is, to minimize the chances of reversal or protect the judge's professional reputation). Or as political scientist Jim Gibson summarized: "Judges' decisions are a function of what they prefer to do, tempered by what they think they ought to do, but constrained by what they think is feasible to do." [20]

Judges' reactions can be placed on a continuum from enthusiasm to acceptance to rejection. Most judges react more or less indifferently—that is, their sense of professionalism and obligation overcomes their personal reaction to the policy.[21] Even at this, a judge may well resolve genuine ambiguities in accord with his or her own attitudes or legal philosophy. But occasionally a judge finds a higher court's policy unacceptable. Such a judge might overtly defy the higher court, but more often he or she will try to evade its mandate or will interpret the policy as narrowly as possible. Following *Brown v. Board of Education* in 1954, many judges throughout the South gave the narrowest possible interpretations to the racial integration mandate.[22] At the continuum's other end, a few judges may become very enthusiastic about a higher court decision. They may interpret it broadly, pushing its logic to the limit or expanding the policy to other areas of law.

Techniques of Non-Acceptance

A judge who does not accept a higher court policy has three basic options: defiance, avoidance, and limited application.

DEFIANCE. By defiance we mean that the judge simply does not apply the policy in cases that come before his or her court. As we have noted, overt defiance is highly unprofessional and threatening to the judicial system; thus it is a relatively rare event, especially in more prestigious courts. But it is not unknown. In fact, some cases the Supreme Court decides and sends back to a lower court for final disposition are decided in favor of the party that lost in the high Court, especially when the Court vacates (that is, sets aside) the decision but does not reverse it.[23] After the U.S. Supreme Court held that Utah's law setting the age of majority for women at eighteen and for men at twenty-one was unconstitutional, the Utah Supreme Court refused to implement the policy, saying: "To judicially hold that males and females attain their maturity at the same age is to be blind to the biological facts of life."[24]

Judges may occasionally refuse to apply an obvious precedent. In 1958 a federal district judge in Texas obstinately refused to follow the Supreme Court's decision in *Wickard v. Filburn* (1942), which upheld the crop production limitations of the Agricultural Adjustment Act.[25] And in 1984 an Alabama federal district judge declared that "the United States Supreme Court has erred"[26] in interpreting the Constitution's prohibition against the establishment of religion and refused to enjoin the use of a prayer for public school students adopted by the legislature. Desegregation brought out considerable defiance in trial courts; in one extreme case, a Birmingham, Alabama, municipal judge not only refused to follow Supreme Court decisions desegregating municipal facilities, but also declared the Fourteenth Amendment unconstitutional.[27]

Defiance need not be overt—in some situations, a lower court judge will simply ignore the higher court's policy or rely on another, less appropriate precedent. This tactic is less unprofessional than outright defiance; in fact, the Supreme Court occasionally ignores its own precedents when it wants to change policy.[28] Trial courts may ignore precedents quite often, especially misdemeanor courts where appeals are rare. Indeed, such judges may not even be aware of the relevant precedents. In the 1940s and 1950s, for example, it was common practice for trial courts to order hitchhikers and vagrants to leave town (one author had a personal experience with this), even though in *Edwards v. California* (1941) the Supreme Court had clearly established the rights of indigent citizens to travel and relocate. Likewise, judicial guarantees are sometimes ignored when dealing with deviant lifestyles. In 1988, for instance, a man wearing a dress, high heels, pantyhose, and earrings (and also sporting a mustache) was arrested while eating at a restaurant in a Kentucky mountain town; he was convicted of disturbing the peace on the basis of his appearance alone. He got a ten-day sentence, suspended on condition that he leave town.[29]

AVOIDANCE. When defiance is inconvenient or unseemly, a lower court can sometimes avoid interpreting an unacceptable higher court policy on procedural grounds. There are many rules and doctrines pertaining to judicial procedure, and their application is not as inflexible as we might think; judges have considerable discretion in their use. A judge might decide, for instance, that the plaintiff lacks standing (sufficient interest) to sue. Or that the plaintiff has sought the wrong remedy—for example, the 1866 Civil Rights Act rather than the 1968 Fair Housing Law. Or that the appellant failed to raise a crucial point of law at the trial (a rule that is often invoked, considering that many criminal defendants have inexperienced or unenthusiastic lawyers).

Avoidance tactics certainly can forestall the impact of a disliked judicial policy for some time. But ultimately they only delay implementation. Eventually, a case will come along that cannot be avoided through procedural maneuvering.

One avoidance device that is sometimes available to state supreme courts faced with having to apply a U.S. Supreme Court decision is to decide the case on state constitutional grounds. In a trend called the new judicial federalism, liberal state high courts apply the state constitution to avoid the impact of the Supreme Court's conservative jurisprudence under the leadership of Chief Justices Warren Burger and William Rehnquist.

THE NEW JUDICIAL FEDERALISM

State constitutions generally have provisions similar to those found in the U.S. Constitution; thus a state court can decide some cases on state constitutional grounds instead of relying on the Supreme Court's interpretation of a similar provision of the federal constitution. However, state courts *cannot* interpret a state civil liberties guarantee more narrowly than the Supreme Court has interpreted a similar federal constitutional provision, since the U.S. Constitution protects most rights against encroachment by the states as well as by the federal government. But state courts can construe their constitutional provisions more liberally.

The new judicial federalism is seen most often with regard to the rights of criminal defendants, especially since the Supreme Court has construed the protections against illegal searches and seizures, compelled self-incrimination, and the like, more narrowly in the 1980s and 1990s. For example, in *Michigan State Police v. Sitz* (1990) the U.S. Supreme Court held that roadside sobriety checkpoints did not violate the Fourth Amendment. When the case was returned to the Michigan Supreme Court, it then considered Sitz's case under the state constitution's protection against illegal searches and ruled that Michigan's constitution outlawed sobriety checkpoints.[30] More generally, Barry Latzer examined 730 criminal appeals between 1960 and 1990 in which state supreme courts interpreted the state rather than the federal constitution. In 232 (31.8 percent) of them, the state court interpreted its defendants' rights provisions more broadly than the U.S. Supreme Court interpreted parallel provisions in the federal document (see Box 2-1).[31]

The new judicial federalism can apply to other rights as well.[32] For instance, after the U.S. Supreme Court ruled that there was no First Amendment right to distribute literature at privately owned shopping malls (*Lloyd Corp. Ltd. v. Tanner,* 1972), the supreme courts of California, Massachusetts, and Washington decided that such a right existed under the freedom of speech guarantees in their state constitutions, but six state high courts found no such right in their constitutions.[33] State high courts in Kentucky, New York, Pennsylvania, and Texas have held that their state constitutions' guarantees of liberty protect consensual homosexual acts despite the U.S. Supreme Court's *Bowers v. Hardwick* (1986) decision holding that such acts were not protected by the federal constitution's liberty clause. In 1996, in *Pyle v. South Hadley School Committee,* Massachusetts's highest court protected vulgar student speech in high schools, contrary to the U.S. Supreme Court's *Bethel School District v. Fraser* (1986) ruling. In the equal protection area, Connecticut's highest court ruled that even unintentional racial imbalances in schools resulting from housing patterns violated the state constitution (*Sheff v. O'Neill,* 1996), although the U.S. Supreme Court rejected an argument that the Fourteenth Amendment's equal protection of the laws clause should be so interpreted.[34] Several other state supreme courts have construed state equal protection clauses more broadly than the Supreme Court has applied the Constitution's clause. [35] In his study of state supreme court decisions in right-to-die cases, Henry R. Glick found that states that already followed more liberal policies than the U.S. Supreme Court announced in *Cruzan v. Missouri Health*

BOX 2-1
Politics and the New Judicial Federalism

Some of the state supreme court justices who have expanded defendants' rights have gotten into political trouble for being soft on crime. In 1986 California voters denied state Chief Justice Rose Bird and two colleagues another term because of their votes on crime issues, particularly the death penalty. For similar reasons justices in Wyoming, Texas, Tennessee, and Mississippi lost bids for reelection in the 1990s. Moreover, in the 1980s voters in California, Florida, Massachusetts, and Pennsylvania amended their state constitutions to require that certain defendants' rights provisions be construed in the same manner as the U.S. Supreme Court interpreted analogous federal constitutional provisions. However, in Florida, Indiana, and Oregon justices who practiced the new judicial federalism survived conservative attempts to get them off the court.

Sources: Michael Esler, "State Supreme Court Commitment to State Law," *Judicature* 78 (1994): 25–32; Barry Latzer, "California's Constitutional Counterrevolution," in *Constitutional Politics in the States,* ed. G. Alan Tarr (Westport, Conn.: Greenwood Press, 1996), 149–177; John T. Wold and John H. Culver, "The Defeat of the California Justices: The Campaign, the Justices and the Issue of Accountability," *Judicature* 70 (1987): 348–355; Stephen Bright, "Political Attacks on the Judiciary," *Judicature* 80 (1997): 165–173; and "Goals of Activists Is Judge's Ouster," *New York Times,* October 4, 1984, 16.

Department (1990) continued using them, but the states that had not yet adopted a policy often used *Cruzan* as a guideline.[36]

LIMITED APPLICATION. A judge who does not accept a higher court's decision, but who cannot or will not defy or avoid it, can limit its application. Limiting a precedent or doctrine is not in itself a manifestation of hostility. In any court case, lawyers for both sides cite a variety of precedents in their arguments; a judge could not normally accept all of the precedents as being applicable and still come to a meaningful decision. The heart of a judicial opinion is an explanation of why the court accepts some precedents and limits others. At times, however, the relevance of a precedent to a case under consideration is fairly obvious. In such situations, a judge's finding that the precedent is not a controlling one most likely reflects his or her unwillingness to accept it.

One method of limiting a precedent is to stress factual differences between the earlier case and the situation the judge is called upon to resolve. In legal terminology this is called *distinguishing* the precedent. At times such distinctions can be unimportant. For example, in 1992 the Supreme Court held that public schools could not invite a member of the clergy to say a prayer at a graduation ceremony (*Lee v. Weisman*). In 1997 a federal court of appeals upheld Indiana University's policy of inviting a member of the clergy to offer a prayer at graduation, reasoning that college students were not as susceptible to religious persuasion as were secondary school students (*Tanford v. Brand*). Usually, however, lower courts do not resort to making minor factual distinctions unless they are unwilling to accept a higher court's precedent and can find no more plausible means of evading its application.

A more likely event comes about when a judge ignores the direction of an emerging Supreme Court policy. A classic example occurred when federal district Judge John Bell Timmerman of South Carolina limited the relevance of *Brown v. Board of Education* to a suit seeking the desegregation of Charleston's city buses. Noting that the opinion in *Brown* had stressed the importance of equal educational opportunities to the development of the skills and personality of African Americans, he disdainfully remarked, "One's personality is not developed on a bus."[37] *Brown* had in fact involved only school desegregation, so Judge Timmerman was not technically defying the Supreme Court. Few observers, however—including, we suspect, the judge himself—had any real doubts that the fundamental thrust of the *Brown* decision was that segregation in general, not just in schools, was unconstitutional.

When it is not feasible to focus on factual distinctions, a judge can interpret the precedent in question very narrowly, observing its letter but not its spirit. Sometimes lower courts will openly admit that they are doing this, especially with regard to interpretations of Supreme Court decisions expanding the rights of criminal suspects. Fearful of the real political consequences of applying precedents that would be likely to enable seemingly guilty persons to escape punishment, several state supreme courts announced that they would interpret such decisions "in the interests of the realistic administration of criminal investigations" or so as to forestall "disastrous social consequences."[38]

Sometimes higher court precedents are limited because experience with a broader interpretation leads lower court judges to believe that limiting a precedent is the most practicable course. In the last decade, many federal judges have come to believe that little more can be accomplished in the realm of school desegregation, even though many school districts remain largely segregated (Box 2-2).

Expansion of Higher Court Policies

At the other end of the continuum, lower court judges can sometimes be quite enthusiastic in their acceptance of a higher court policy and behave accordingly. Expanding a precedent's scope is not necessarily a sign of undue enthusiasm. As we noted in Chapter 1's discussion of *Roe v. Wade,* Court opinions traditionally refrain from addressing questions of application not raised in the case, so lower court judges have to decide for themselves when such a question comes to their court. Some expansion will certainly occur if a higher court policy decision is at all important. It is only when the lower court application moves well beyond expectations that the judge's enthusiasm for the policy is apparent.

One well-known example is based upon the Supreme Court's decision in *County of Washington v. Gunther* (1980), which held that women who worked at essentially the same jobs as men (in this case, jail guards) should be paid the same salaries. In 1983 a federal district judge in Washington State ruled that *Gunther* required the state to develop a "comparable worth" classification system that substantially equalized the pay for dissimilar male-dominated job types (such as road repair crews) and largely female job types (such as office workers). The Court of Appeals later overturned the district court decision.[39]

Somewhat similarly, lower court judges can expand a precedent to cover a different type of situation. Judicial decisions often seem to rest on premises or to advance principles that transcend the immediate subject matter. But lower courts are usually rather cautious about transferring the applicability of precedents to considerably different jurisprudential situations. A good example of expansion occurred following *Daubert v. Dow Merrill Pharmaceuticals* (1993), in which the Supreme Court loosened the restrictions on what constitutes scientific evidence in product liability cases. Previously, courts required evidence based upon "well-recognized" scientific principles. *Daubert* relaxed this standard, allowing newer or more experimental scientific research as a source of evidence. Within a few years, several lower courts were citing *Daubert* to allow the admission of polygraph (lie detector) evidence in criminal cases.[40] *Daubert* has also been applied to the use of psychological testimony in child sexual abuse cases.[41]

Box 2-2
Dismantling Desegregation?

In their book *Dismantling Desegregation,* political scientist Gary Orfield and journalist Susan Eaton argue that many federal district judges made decisions in the 1980s and 1990s that effectively recreated largely segregated school systems in metropolitan areas. This resegregation was usually accomplished through rulings declaring that the school system was now "unitary" (that is, that the effects of segregation by law or by school board pupil assignment policies had been cured) and returning full control to local school officials. At that point pupils were assigned to nearby schools and busing was diminished or ended. In returning control, the judges accepted school officials' pledges to maintain high quality schools (supplemented by extra funding) or magnet schools in African American or Hispanic areas. Often these pledges were ignored or diluted, sometimes with the judges openly countenancing the school districts' derelictions. In *Missouri v. Jenkins II* (1995) the Supreme Court seemed to give a green light to less aggressive actions by lower court judges. Orfield and Eaton conclude that *Brown* "has been stripped of much of its power," that judges sometimes "will not even support enforcement of the 'separate but equal' doctrine that *Brown* overturned," and that the nation is "sleepwalking back to *Plessy* [*v. Ferguson,* the 1896 decision establishing the separate but equal doctrine]." [a]

The termination of federal judicial supervision over once-segregated school districts reflects many federal judges' disillusionment with busing and other desegregation plans. Despite twenty or thirty years of effort, minority scores on educational achievement tests still fall below those of whites. Moreover, taxpayers are unwilling to spend much additional money on improving the schools. Funds spent on cross-district busing seem diverted from the classroom. Nonetheless, in northern urban areas more blacks attended majority-black schools in 1992 than in 1967. [b] Thus many observers (including some judges) have come to believe that the disease of segregation has been cured

---

Thus, by broadly interpreting the meaning of a policy, judges may expand it in order to resolve new questions in the same issue area or to decide cases in other issue areas. Lower court policy expansion probably does not occur too often, but a study by Traciel Reid showed that almost half the reported lower court decisions interpreting *Richmond Newspapers Inc. v. Virginia* (1980), which held that criminal trials must be open to the public, expanded the requirement, while only about 5 percent seemed to narrow its holding unduly. [42]

about as well as it can be, given widespread segregated residential patterns, and that it is time for the courts to get out of the business of supervising schools.[c] By 1997 even the NAACP was having second thoughts about busing.[d]

The change in judicial attitudes toward school integration illustrates the dynamic nature of the interpretive process. Lower court judges make interpretive adjustments as the impact of higher court decisions is limited for reasons beyond judicial control. Policies are scaled back. Eventually, as occurred in Jenkins, higher courts accept the lower courts' feedback and ratify the adjustments. The dynamic process also reflects changes in public opinion and political commitments. The Reagan and Bush administrations did not share the Carter administration's willingness to use busing, and even the Clinton administration has paid little attention to school desegregation. New federal judges (including Supreme Court justices) often share the views of their appointing president. Declining enthusiasm and energy for solving difficult problems whose worst features have been curtailed is a common historical phenomenon. This is witnessed by the federal courts' unwillingness to apply Reconstruction-era civil rights laws or the Fourteenth Amendment's equal protection clause after Reconstruction ended.

[a] Gary Orfield, Susan Eaton, and the Harvard Project on School Desegregation, *Dismantling Desegregation: The Quiet Reversal of* Brown v. Board of Education (New York: New Press, 1996), xiv–xv, 33.

[b] Tom Wicker, *Tragic Failure* (New York: William Morrow, 1996), 94–96; see also "Schools See Reemergence of 'Separate But Equal,'" *New York Times,* April 8, 1997, A-10.

[c] Orfield, Eaton, et al., *Dismantling Desegregation,* 19–22, 48, 349–350.

[d] "At NAACP Talk of Shift on Integration," *New York Times,* June 23, 1997, A-1.

FACTORS AFFECTING LOWER COURT INTERPRETATIONS

So far we have discussed why judicial policies must be interpreted, who interprets them, and the range of possible interpretations. Now we will look at the scholarly explanations of what factors affect lower court interpretations. We will focus on three sets of factors: those associated with the judges, those inherent in the policy, and those related to the environment within which the interpretation takes place.

Judges' Attitudes and Roles

ATTITUDES. As we have noted, professional and conscientious judges try to mute the influence of their attitudes. But no judge can totally escape the implicit and explicit ideas about justice and good social order that he or she acquires over a lifetime. Like other people, judges develop liberal, moderate, or conservative political and social attitudes. These, along with their experiences relating to specific issues, undoubtedly shape their interpretations of higher court policies. We cannot overemphasize the importance of attitudes here, although because it is such a general phenomenon, we will not dwell on it.

Judges can also have prejudices—stereotypical or hostile attitudes toward specific groups. Because these run contrary to basic American norms and challenge the concept of equal justice under law, judges seldom acknowledge them. But occasionally they come out. For example, a New York appellate judge, upholding women's exemption from jury duty, stereotyped women as preferring "television soap operas, bridge and canasta, the beauty parlor and shopping [to serving on juries]."[43] Federal district judge Harold Cox of Mississippi referred to African Americans trying to register to vote as "a bunch of niggers" who were "acting like a bunch of chimpanzees"[44] In a custody case, a South Dakota Supreme Court justice spoke harshly of "a lesbian living a life of *abomination* (see Leviticus 18:22)[emphasis in original]."[45] Obviously such biases, even when not articulated and less explicitly held, strongly influence interpretations.

ROLE PERCEPTIONS. Judges' interpretations of higher court policies are also affected by their perception of their role as judge, that is, by their beliefs about how a lower court judge should behave. This is partly a matter of professionalism, but more than that is involved. When higher court decisions allow some interpretive leeway, some judges see their role as "doing justice" by making arguable leaps of logic. Their leaps may later be reversed, as happened in the Washington State comparable worth case we discussed in the previous section, but these judges believe one of their functions is to bring an issue of "doing justice" to the attention of the public and a higher court. Other judges see themselves as strict constructionists of higher court decisions, relying on the earlier cases' clear premises but rejecting undue expansion. Most judges function somewhere between these two ends of the continuum of role perceptions.[46] Thus some judges with similar attitudes but different role perceptions (and vice versa) may arrive at dissimilar interpretations.

Policy Characteristics

CLARITY. Higher court opinions that are ambiguous, vague, or poorly articulated are more likely to produce dissimilar lower court interpretations. In other words, the clarity of a judicial decision or policy may affect the scope of interpretations substantially. Identifying unclear decisions, even by the U.S. Supreme Court, is not a difficult task.

Decisions may lack clarity for several reasons. Occasionally the Court will deliberately write an opinion with few specifics because it wants to await public reaction before becoming more detailed. After *Brown v. Board,* the Court said that desegregation should proceed with "all deliberate speed" (*Brown v. Board II,* 1955, 301). This is an inherently vague phrase, and the Court meant it to be. Most southern judges emphasized the "deliberate" rather than the "speed." Only thirteen years later did the Court adopt a more specific policy requiring school boards to take "positive steps" to end segregation (*Green v. School Board of New Kent County,* 1968). Likewise, the opinion in the Court's breakthrough reapportionment decision (*Baker v. Carr,* 1962) deliberately failed to give lower courts any guidelines about permissible new legislative district lines.

Some judicial policies are ambiguous because the issue is complex or the subject matter is difficult to resolve with consistency. In obscenity cases, for example, it is impossible to fashion a precise judicial policy defining obscene material. Phrases such as "patently offensive" or "without serious redeeming value" necessarily leave room for subjective interpretation among judges, even those who are more or less indifferent to the substance of the Supreme Court's policy. Justice Potter Stewart once expressed his frustration in this regard by writing, "I shall not attempt further to define [obscenity], but I know it when I see it" (*Jacobellis v. Ohio,* 1964, 197).

A Supreme Court opinion can be unclear when the court majority does not agree on the reasons for or the implications of its decision. The Court's initial busing decision in *Swann v. Charlotte-Mecklenburg County Board of Education* (1971), although unanimous, was rather confusing. For example, it held that single-race schools were not necessarily unconstitutional, but it authorized cross-district busing to help districts balance schools racially. One lower court judge characterized *Swann* as having "a lot of conflicting language. It's almost as if there were two sets of view laid side by side."[47]

Moreover, during the last thirty years, Supreme Court justices have written longer and more frequent concurring opinions, dissenting opinions, and opinions that concur in part and dissent in part. This proliferation of opinions has led Justice Rehnquist to call Court policy in some areas "a virtual Tower of Babel from which no definitive principles can clearly be drawn."[48] Such behavior on the part of the Supreme Court obviously makes it difficult for a lower court to render faithful and consistent interpretations.

Clarity is also a problem when the higher court fails to provide consistent, continuing cues to lower courts about the interpretations of important policies. The Supreme Court's affirmative action jurisprudence illustrate this point. The first case resulted in a partly yes, partly no decision on special admissions to medical school for minorities in *University of California v. Bakke* (1978); then the Court then approved policies enhancing minority promotions in 1979 (*Kaiser Aluminum Co. v. Weber*) and job set asides in 1980 (*Fullilove v. Klutznick*); the justices spiritedly disapproved of a set-aside policy in 1986 (*J. A. Crosen Co. v. City of Richmond*), then embraced special minority opportunities in 1990 (*Metro Broadcasting Co. v. Federal Communications Commission*). In 1995 the Court forcefully rejected any special considerations enhancing minority employment (*Adarand Constructors v. Pena*), and in 1996 the justices denied certiorari to *Texas v. Hopwood,* in which the Fifth Circuit had rejected race as a "plus" for admission to law school despite *Bakke*'s explicit allowance of this practice. Yet in 1998 the Court declined to hear a case challenging a practice of minority preferences in academic hiring.[49] This see-sawing reflects both turnover in justices and a couple of changes of attitude. It is quite understandable that lower court judges could be uncertain or confused in many cases about what the Court's policy was.

By contrast, consider John Gruhl's research on lower court follow-up of the *New York Times v. Sullivan* (1964) case, which gave considerable protection to publications against libel suits from public persons. He notes that while the Supreme Court's subsequent decisions in this area "were not exceptionally clear, . . . lower courts did not seem troubled by this lack of clarity." He explains that nonetheless "the Court had continually emphasized its commitment to the *[Sullivan]* doctrine," and he found 100 percent compliance with *[Sullivan]* in federal courts of appeals libel cases through 1974.[50]

Even when a higher court's decision is clearly written, it will probably not answer all questions about its applicability. For example, the Supreme Court's decision establishing the exclusionary rule in search and seizure (*Mapp v. Ohio,* 1961) did not tell lower courts whether a defendant who did not reside at the premises from which the illegal evidence was seized had standing to object to its admission in court, or whether evidence seized by the police acting in good faith on a faulty warrant was admissible. Lower courts split in answering these and other questions.[51] The Supreme Court did not decide the question of standing for nineteen years (answering no) and did not decide the good faith question for twenty-three years (yes).[52]

Thus, whether a higher court decision or policy goal is clearly and consistently articulated will have a substantial effect on lower court interpretations. Conscientious judges frequently have to make their own best guesses about how to interpret a judicial policy and apply it to a particular set of circumstances not considered by a higher court. The greater the ambiguity of the case or the policy, the wider the range of possible interpretations.

COMMUNICATION. If a higher court policy is to be accurately interpreted, lower court judges must read and consider it. In the American judicial system, however, the deciding court makes no direct effort to inform lower courts (other than the one from which the specific case was appealed) of its decisions. Appellate courts are usually aware of Supreme Court decisions; yet California Supreme Court justices have complained that they do not have U.S. Supreme Court decisions easily available.[53] Trial courts often rely on the parties' lawyers to bring relevant cases to their attention. Overworked, lazy, or incompetent attorneys may not always do this. Indeed, the late Chief Justice Warren Burger believed that one-third to one-half the nation's attorneys are not competent to conduct a trial.[54]

Almost no research has been done about the familiarity of lower court judges, professional or lay, with higher court decisions (see Box 2-3). We suspect most are conscientious in this regard. And as the ranks of lawyers have swelled in recent years, there are fewer lay judges. Nonetheless, we should remember that the communication of information about judicial decisions is not an automatic process and that it may work poorly at the lowest echelons of the judicial hierarchy.

PERCEPTIONS OF HIGHER COURT SUPPORT. Lower court judges may be cautious about applying policies that no longer seem to have majority support on a higher court. Over the last two decades especially, Supreme Court justices are often unwilling to apply a precedent they do not like, and normal turnover of the justices may have eroded the original majority.[55] So, despite the doctrine of stare decisis (that a court should abide by its own prior decisions), the Supreme Court sometimes explicitly or

BOX 2-3
Lay Judges and Supreme Court Decisions

Some judges—particularly rural justices of the peace or juvenile court judges—are not lawyers and serve part time. Lay judges often have little interest or skill in reading appellate court opinions. As an extreme (we hope) illustration of the lack of legal knowledge in some local courts, we offer the following questioning of a justice of the peace (JP) in the mountains of eastern Kentucky by a lawyer whose client the JP had found guilty:

Q: Are you familiar with the Fourteenth Amendment to the Constitution of the United States, as to what it provides?

JP: Yes, sir.

Q: What does it provide?

JP: Right off hand I don't . . . something about judicial. I think one of them is judicial procedure or something or another. I'm not for sure.

Q: Do you think the Fourteenth Amendment . . . deals with judicial procedure?

JP: Right off hand, I couldn't tell you.

Q: Are you familiar with the term "due process of law" or "equal protection of the law?"

JP: Yes, sir.

Q: In legal meaning?

JP: No, that's beyond me.

Q: Are you familiar with the rights accorded to a defendant as accused in a criminal case under the Fourteenth Amendment?

JP: As I previously said, I don't know . . . exactly understand this Fourteenth Amendment. I know part of it.

Q: Are you familiar with the *Supreme Court Reports* of the United States Supreme Court?

JP: I am familiar with some of them, but I don't agree with all of them.

Q: What is your understanding with respect to the effect that a judge should give between conflicting rulings made by the Kentucky Court of Appeals and the Supreme Court of the United States? Do you understand the question?

JP: No, I really don't. I don't think I know.

Source: Quoted in Walter Murphy and C. Herman Pritchett, *Courts, Judges and Politics,* 3d ed. (New York: Random House, 1979), 159–160.

implicitly abandons its earlier policies. Recently, for example, the Fifth Circuit Court of Appeals (Louisiana, Mississippi, and Texas) said that the Supreme Court's *Bakke* case, which acknowledged the need for diversity in higher education, was no longer good law and ordered the University of Texas Law School to cease its policy of lower admission standards for African Americans than for whites (*Texas v. Hopwood,* 1996). It acted in the belief that the Court's earlier overturning of a federal preference program for minority road contractors (*Adarand Constructors v. Pena,* 1995), as well as the Court's earlier denial of certiorari to a Fourth Circuit decision striking down a University of Maryland scholarship program available only to African Americans,[56] indicated that the justices were abandoning *Bakke* as a precedent. This supposition was buttressed when the Supreme Court refused to consider the Fifth Circuit's ruling. This placed judges and admissions officers in the remaining forty-seven states in a situation of uncertainty about continuing minority admissions policies. *Hopwood* had a dramatic impact at the University of Texas Law School: black admissions fell from sixty-five students to eleven between 1996 and 1997.[57]

To forestall lower court doubts about support on the Supreme Court, Chief Justice Earl Warren strived to obtain unanimity of both vote and opinion in the 1954 *Brown* decision desegregating southern schools.[58] Southern judges were not going to like the decision regardless of the vote, but Warren hoped that they might accord it minimal acceptance if they knew that the justices were united behind a policy of desegregation. Indeed, the Supreme Court apparently attached such importance to unity on the matter that every major desegregation decision through 1971 was unanimous.

But lower court counting of justices' votes is the exception rather than the rule. Charles A. Johnson analyzed lower federal court citations to 347 Supreme Court decisions from 1961 to 1963. He found that "the degree of Supreme Court support or non-support for a particular case has little or no bearing on eventual treatment of that case by lower courts."[59] His analysis used several indicators of support: size of the deciding majority, number of justices supporting the majority opinion, and size of the dissenting minority. Johnson also considered the presence of dissenting opinions and whether the chief justice wrote the majority opinion. Citations reported in *Shepard's Citations* classifying lower court interpretations as either "compliant" or "evasive" were uncorrelated with these indicators of support for the policy on the Supreme Court.

Environmental Pressures on Interpreting Populations

Formally, judges are supposed to make decisions independent of their environment. Only the parties to a case can communicate with judges, and then only through specific channels. Even though society erects barriers against direct pressure, judges cannot be perfectly isolated. Like all human beings, they are subject to social and political pressures from their environment—their friends, community leaders, voters, the bar, the media, and the like. The pressure may be fairly strong when they must render decisions with social or political overtones. But strong or weak, these are seldom direct pressures. Politicians, newspapers, and neighbors do not tell judges, "You must decide this case for the pro-life side," or whatever. Rather, the pressures are anticipatory. Like the rest of us, judges want to maintain respect and avoid undue criticism, especially among peers. Thus we can expect judges to be sensitive to social and political considerations in their environment as they interpret higher court policies. They must also be sensitive to the impact a policy will have if implemented in their area, especially if it could be disruptive. These three factors often reinforce one another; however, we will treat them separately even though they may not be so easily separated in real life.

SOCIAL PRESSURES. Judges are social creatures with friendships and community relationships that long predate their ascension to the bench. Maintenance of these relationships is not affected by most of their decisions. But social relationships can be affected by rulings on certain economic issues (for example, pitting business against labor) and may be even more endangered when emotional issues such as school prayer or abortion come to court.

The strongest social pressures were applied to southern judges who desegregated schools. Segregation by race was a way of life in the South; it permeated all community affairs. One scholar, Jack Peltason, vividly described the pressures on federal judges below the Mason-Dixon line:

> The District judge is very much a part of the life of the South. He must eventually leave his chambers and when he does he attends a Rotary lunch or stops off at the club to drink with men outraged by what they consider "judicial tyranny." A judge who makes rulings adverse to segregation is not so likely to be honored by testimonial dinners, or to read flattering editorials in the local press, or to partake in the fellowship at the club. He will no longer be invited to certain homes; former friends will avoid him when they meet him on the street.[60]

These social pressures can be strong. Federal district Judge J. Waites Waring of South Carolina was cut off from Charleston society, into which he had been born, after making several desegregation decisions. He eventually felt so isolated that he resigned the judgeship and moved from the state.[61] Sometimes pressures were substantial even if there was some distance between the affected community and the judge. When he ordered widespread busing in the Louisville, Kentucky, school system (after a court of appeals reversed his earlier, less pervasive order), Judge James F. Gordon found that "an awful lot of white people didn't talk to me," even though he lived in a community over 100 miles from Louisville.[62] There were other southern judges like Judge Waring, and as desegregation and other racial clashes spread beyond the South, some judges elsewhere have made highly unpopular decisions.[63] As we might expect, however, most judges do not act boldly in applying Supreme Court decisions that are unpopular in their communities.

Race relations is not the only issue that produced different environmental pressures depending upon which side of the Mason-Dixon line the judge was on. For example, until the Supreme Court interpreted Title VII of the 1964 Civil Rights Act to cover same-sex harassment (*Oncale v. Sundowner Offshore Inc.,* 1998), federal courts in the South generally held that Title VII did not make such behavior actionable, while northern federal courts generally ruled that it was actionable.[64]

Other issues, too, can create social unpleasantness for judges. When federal district Judge William Overton struck down Arkansas's law requiring that "creation science" be taught in the public schools (if evolution was taught), he was urged to "repent" and was asked, "How many monkeys do you have in your family tree?"[65] Some judges are also subject to social pressures from their racial, ethnic, or gender groups. (Indeed, pressures from whites on southern judges in desegregation disputes were just the other side of this coin.) A significant number of African Americans, Hispanics, and women have been named federal judges by Presidents Jimmy Carter and Bill Clinton. Some people see such judges as "representatives" of their group and expect them to interpret Supreme Court policies consistently with the group's (or the NAACP's or National Organization of Women's, and so on) policy preferences.[66]

POLITICAL PRESSURES. Judges are also political creatures. They come to the bench through a political process. State judges may be elected by the voters or appointed by a governor to whom they are politically close. Appointment to the federal bench is a political process that involves senators, presidential advisers, and the president's political allies in the relevant state. Thus judges have some political contacts and allies that antedate their judicial service. These can create a vague sense of obligation, perhaps reinforced when the judge shares the policy preferences of his or her political cohorts. These are facts of judicial life. So it is not surprising when scholars find that federal judges appointed by Republican presidents make more conservative decisions than do Democratic appointees, or even that judges named by Presidents Ronald Reagan and George Bush have a more conservative jurisprudence than do those appointed by Presidents Richard Nixon and Gerald Ford.[67] For example, through 1987 Carter appointees supported abortion rights claims 88 percent of the time in their published opinions, while Reagan judges did so in only 23 percent of their opinions.[68]

Lower court judges who are interested in being named to a higher court may also be cautious about making enemies. For example, New Jersey federal district judge H. Lee Sorokin wrote in one case that the "tobacco industry may be the king of concealment and disinformation" and suggested that the industry's own research was "a fraud." When President Clinton nominated him to the court of appeals, these words came back to haunt Judge Sorokin at his confirmation hearings.[69] (He did win confirmation.)

Unlike federal judges, few state judges serve for life. They face the possibility of being opposed for reelection. Judges in merit selection systems face periodic retention elections. Probably less than 10 percent of judges are defeated or lose retention elections, but this is enough to make them aware of the consequences unpopular decisions can have on their judicial career. This realization can be especially sharp when they must apply Supreme Court civil liberties or defendants' rights policies. Research shows that state supreme court justices are reluctant to overturn death sentences challenged as violating U.S. Supreme Court safeguards, and a justice's reluctance increases as the end of his or her term draws closer.[70] The fear is realistic; California Chief Justice Rose Bird lost her seat after consistently voting against the death penalty. More broadly, Daniel Pinello finds evidence that state supreme courts whose members do serve for life are more likely to apply U.S. Supreme Court criminal justice policies liberally than are courts where the justices must face the voters in one or another manner.[71] Like elected officeholders, state judges have to keep different electoral constituencies in mind—as well as the U.S. Supreme Court policy rulings.

Occasionally political pressures can be quite direct. The Louisiana Supreme Court struck down a state law that set twenty-one as the minimum drinking age. After pressure from the legislature and temperance groups as well as a threat from the federal government to cut off the state's highway money, the court reconsidered its ruling and reversed it (*Manuel v. State,* 1996). Strong pressures can also be applied to federal judges. For instance, in March 1996, when federal district judge Harold Baer of New York invoked the exclusionary rule to deny the admission of eighty pounds of cocaine as evidence against a suspected drug dealer because the arresting officer lacked probable cause to search the defendant's car, prominent Republicans called loudly for the judge's impeachment. Then President Clinton let it be known that he was considering asking the judge (his own appointee) to resign. Shortly afterward, Judge Baer reversed his previous ruling and admitted the evidence.[72]

THE INFLUENCE OF POLICY CONSEQUENCES. If lower court interpretations of higher court policies mean that substantial changes are required in the community and if those changes are viewed negatively by the community, there is a considerable incentive for local judges to implement the policies minimally, if at all. We have previously noted the reluctance of southern judges to implement *Brown v. Board* in the 1950s and 1960s. A study by Micheal Giles and Thomas Walker found a relationship between location of a federal court and location of the school system under desegregation orders by the judge. If the court was in the city whose schools were under supervision, then levels of segregation were likely to be substantially higher than if the schools were in a different town. Giles and Walker concluded that judges are more concerned with a desegregation ruling's impact in their own community than in an outlying area.[73]

Even when a lower court judge is indifferent to a higher court policy, he or she may find staying with an existing policy easier than making changes. This can also be true for courts that have already adopted policies somewhat akin to the higher court's new policy. After studying state supreme courts' interpretations of *Miranda v. Arizona,* Neil Romans suggested that there was

> a feeling of institutional loyalty within the innovative courts—a strong spirit of independence and resistance to outside interference in their policy making. These courts had developed a commitment to the policies that they had been evolving on their own and seemed to resent attempted interference from the outside forces with what they felt were adequate procedural safeguards for criminal suspects.[74]

Alan Tarr's study of state supreme court reactions to U.S. Supreme Court decisions concerning religious exercises in the public schools (for example, *Abington School District v. Schempp*, 1963) found that the more Supreme Court decisions change ongoing practices, the greater the likelihood of minimal or noncompliant responses. Appellate courts in states where religious practices in schools were new or localized had a 96 percent compliance rate, while those in states with longstanding and pervasive religious practices in schools had only a 70 percent rate.[75] By contrast, Frank Sorauf's study of federal courts' interpretation of the Supreme Court's religion in public school decisions found almost complete compliance (although some judges expressed disagreement), regardless of state practices.[76]

SUMMARY

The interpreting population exists because judicial decisions almost always generate further questions or problems about their meaning as they are applied to particular circumstances. Thus the actions of this population constitute the first link in the chain of events that develops the impact of judicial policies. Lower court judges are the heart of this population, since lower court interpretations are authoritative. This chapter has focused on their responses to higher court decisions.

Several factors result in freedom for and constraints on lower court judges in their interpretive role. One important source of freedom is that most lower court decisions are final; only a minority of cases are appealed. Another factor is that higher court judges cannot fire lower court judges for incompetent or even deliberate misinterpretations. However, lower court judges usually feel constrained to make honest interpretive efforts out of a sense of professionalism, legal obligation, and regard for their own reputation. Moreover, they realize that the legal system would fall apart if lower court judges did not generally abide by higher court rulings.

A judge's willingness to accept a higher court policy depends a good deal on his or her attitude toward the policy. Most judges are sufficiently professional to interpret the great majority of judicial policies with reasonable fidelity. But when it comes to policies in emotion-laden areas such as desegregation or religion, judges' attitudes may override their professional commitment. In such cases the judge can interpret a higher court decision extremely narrowly, can try to avoid having to acknowledge or interpret the decision at all, or, in rare instances, can engage in overtly defiant behavior. On the other side of the coin, a judge who is highly enthusiastic about a higher court decision can expand its meaning or coverage well beyond its original parameters.

Several factors affect lower court interpretations. First, clarity of the decisions that set forth the policy is an important factor. Ambiguous or vague statements, multiple opinions, inconsistent precedents, and the like make the task of interpretation difficult and leave more room for discretion. Second, there is no systematic method for communicating higher court policies; at times they are not accurately communicated to the lowest judicial levels. Third, a lower court is less likely to abide by a policy that appears in light of subsequent decisions to have lost higher court support or that had only ambivalent support on the higher court.

Lower court interpretations often respond to actual or perceived pressures from the local political and social environment. Concerns about reelection or promotion, adverse publicity, and reactions from social peers affect lower courts' interpretations of unpopular higher court policies. This is particularly true when there are marked political and cultural differences between the higher court's environment and that of the lower court—as occurred in the desegregation cases in the 1950s and 1960s. Lower court interpretations are also affected by the judges' own perceptions of the consequences of higher court policies on their communities. Courts already committed to prior policies of their own making are often more reluctant to accept different policies wholeheartedly than are courts with no preexisting policies.

NOTES

1. Lynne M. Ross, *State Attorneys-General: Powers and Responsibilities* (Washington, D.C.: Bureau of National Affairs, 1990), chap. 5.

2. Jack Peltason, *Fifty Eight Lonely Men: Southern Judges and School Desegregation* (Urbana: University of Illinois Press, 1961), 21.

3. See "Batson Protection Extended to Jews," *National Law Journal,* April 28, 1997, A-10.

4. These figures are for the federal courts. See C. K. Rowland and Robert A. Carp, *Politics and Judgment in Federal District Courts* (Lawrence: University of Kansas Press, 1996), 8.

5. "Foolish and Unnecessary," *National Law Journal,* June 30, 1997, A-8.

6. Robert Satter, *Doing Justice: A Trial Judge at Work* (New York: Simon and Schuster, 1990), 227.

7. See, for example, "Eleventh Circuit Slams Judge J. R. Elliott," *National Law Journal,* September 29, 1997, 6.

8. "Gus J. Solomon: 'On the Side of God,'" *National Law Journal,* April 27, 1987, 13.

9. "Alabama Governor Defends Prayer and Ten Commandments in Courtroom," *USA Today,* February 6, 1997, 3A.

10. See "9th Circuit–Supreme Court Fight Escalates," *National Law Journal,* July 5, 1993, 6. For cases, see *Brewer v. Lewis,* 997 F.2d 550 (9th Cir., 1993); *Mazurek v. Armstrong,* 94 F.3d 566 (9th Cir., 1996), and 138 L.Ed.2d 162 (1997); and *Calderon v. Thompson,* 120 F.3d 1045 (9th Cir., 1997), and 118 S Ct. 1489 (1998).

11. *Gomez and Vasquez v. U.S. District Court for Northern California,* 503 U.S. 653 (1992).

12. Lawrence Baum, "Specialization and Authority Acceptance: The Supreme Court and Lower Federal Courts," *Political Research Quarterly* 47 (1994): 693–704.

13. *Yang v. Sturmer,* 750 F.Supp. 558 (D.R.I., 1990), at 558–559.

14. Frank Sorauf, *The Wall of Separation* (Princeton: Princeton University Press, 1976), 217.

15. *Sojourner T. v. Roemer,* 772 F.Supp. 930 (E.D.La., 1991).

16. *State v. Harp,* 457 P.2d 800 (Okla. Crim., 1969), at 806.

17. *LeBlanc v. Henderson,* 259 So.2d 557 (La., 1972), at 566.

18. See Donald Songer, Jeffrey A. Segal, and Charles M. Cameron, "The Hierarchy of Justice: Testing the Principal-Agent Model of Supreme Court–Circuit Court Interactions," *American Journal of Political Science* 38 (1994): 673–696; Donald R. Songer and Reginald Sheehan, "Supreme Court Impact on Compliance and Outcomes: *Miranda* and *New York Times* in the United States Courts of Appeals," *Western Political Quarterly* 43 (1990): 297–319; Donald A. Songer, "The Impact of Supreme Court Trends on Economic Policy-Making in the United States Courts of Appeals," *Journal of Politics* 49 (1987): 830–841.

19. The research is summarized in Jeffrey Segal and Harold J. Spaeth, *The Supreme Court and the Attitudinal Model* (New York: Cambridge University Press, 1993).

20. James Gibson, "From Simplicity to Complexity: The Development of Theory in the Study of Political Behavior," *Political Behavior* 5 (1983): 8.

21. Charles A. Johnson, "Law, Politics and Judicial Decision-Making: Lower Court Uses of Supreme Court Decisions," *Law and Society Review* 21 (1987): 325–342.

22. See Peltason, *Fifty Eight Lonely Men.*

23. See Richard L. Pacelle and Lawrence A. Baum, "Supreme Court Authority in the Judiciary: A Study of Remands," *American Politics Quarterly* 20 (1992): 169–191.

24. *Stanton v. Stanton,* 552 P.2d 112 (Ut., 1976), at 114, a remand of the U.S. Supreme Court's decision in *Stanton v. Stanton,* 421 U.S. 7 (1975).

25. See *U.S. v. Haley,* 371 U.S. 18 (1962).

26. *Jaffree v. Board of School Commissioners of Mobile County,* 554 F.Supp. 1104 (S.D.Ala., 1983), at 1128.

27. "22 Negroes Fined in Bus Bias Case," *New York Times,* March 22, 1957, 14.

28. See Jeffrey A. Segal and Harold J. Spaeth, "The Influence of *Stare Decisis* on the Votes of United States Supreme Court Justices," *American Journal of Political Science* 40 (1996): 971–1003, and Saul Brenner and Harold J. Spaeth, *Stare Indecisis: The Alteration of Precedent on the Supreme Court, 1946–1992* (New York: Cambridge University Press, 1995).

29. "Man's Dress Was Simply Stunning," *Louisville Courier Journal,* March 12, 1988, 13.

30. "Sobriety Checkpoints Violate Michigan Constitution," *National Law Journal,* November 8, 1993, 30.

31. Barry Latzer, *State Constitutions and Criminal Justice* (Westport, Conn.: Greenwood Press, 1991). Similarly, John C. Kilwain and Richard A. Brisbin Jr. found that 24.2 percent of 1,040 state constitutional law cases decided between 1969 and 1993 involved claims of "strict scrutiny" in all civil liberties issues were decided more broadly than U.S. Supreme Court doctrine required. Strict scrutiny requires the state to show compelling evidence that a law limiting rights is necessary. See their "Policy Convergence in a Federal Judicial System: The Application of Intensified Scrutiny Doctrines by State Supreme Courts," *American Journal of Political Science* 41 (1997): 122–148.

32. For a thorough discussion of the new judicial federalism in state courts, see Jennifer Friesen, *State Constitutional Law,* 2d ed. (Charlottesville, Va.: Michie, 1996), chap. 1.

33. "A Patchwork of Rulings on Free Speech at Malls," *New York Times,* February 10, 1986, A-10.

34. See, for example, *Millikin v. Bradley,* 418 U.S. 717 (1974), and *Freeman v. Pitts,* 503 U.S. 467 (1992).

35. Susan Fino, "Judicial Federalism and Equality Guarantees in State Supreme Courts," *Publius* 17 (1987): 51–67.

36. Henry R. Glick, "The Impact of Permissive Judicial Policies: The U.S. Supreme Court and the Right to Die," *Political Research Quarterly* 47 (1994): 207–222.

37. *Flemming v. South Carolina Gas and Electric Co.,* 128 F.Supp. 469 (D.S.C., 1956), at 470.

38. See Bradley C. Canon, "Organizational Contumacy in the Transmission of Judicial Policies: The *Mapp, Escobedo, Miranda* and *Gault* Cases," *Villanova Law Review* 20 (1974): 50–79.

39. *American Federation of State, County and Municipal Employees v. Washington,* 578 F.Supp. 843 (D.Wash., 1983), reversed at 770 F.2d 1401 (9th Cir., 1985). The case was settled shortly afterward and thus never appealed to the Supreme Court.

40. "Polygraph Ban Relaxed by 9th Circuit," *National Law Journal,* Jan. 20, 1997, 8.

41. James T. Richardson, Gerald Ginsburg, Sophia Gatowski, and Shirley Dobbin, "The Problems of Applying *Daubert* to Psychological Syndrome Evidence," *Judicature* 79 (1995): 10–16.

42. Traciel V. Reid, "Judicial Policy-Making and Implementation: An Empirical Investigation," *Western Political Quarterly* 41 (1988): 509–527.

43. *Delosenko v. Brandt*, 313 N.Y. S.2d 827, at 830 (1970).

44. Quoted in Gerald N. Rosenberg, *The Hollow Hope: Can Courts Bring About Social Change?* (Chicago: University of Chicago Press, 1991), 90.

45. *Chicone v. Chicone*, 479 N.W.2d 891, at 896 (S.Dak., 1992).

46. A good investigation of lower court judges' role perceptions can be found in J. Woodford Howard, *Courts of Appeals in the Federal Judicial System: A Study of the Second, Fifth and the District of Columbia* (Princeton: Princeton University Press, 1981).

47. Bob Woodward and Scott Armstrong, *The Brethren* (New York: Simon and Schuster, 1979), 112.

48. Dissenting in *Metromedia Inc. v. City of San Diego*, 453 U.S. 490 (1981), at 569.

49. "Supreme Court Turns Down Appeal of Case on Affirmative Action in College Hiring," *Chronicle of Higher Education*, March 20, 1998, A-35.

50. John Gruhl, "The Supreme Court's Impact on the Law of Libel: Compliance by Lower Federal Courts," *Western Political Quarterly* 33 (1980): 518.

51. Bradley C. Canon, "Reactions of State Supreme Courts to a U.S. Supreme Court Civil Liberties Decision," *Law and Society Review* 8 (1973): 109–134.

52. *Rawlings v. Kentucky*, 448 U.S. 98 (1980) and *U.S. v. Leon*, 468 U.S. 897 (1984), respectively.

53. Thomas C. Dalton, *The State Politics of Judicial and Congressional Reform* (Westport, Conn.: Greenwood Press, 1985), 110.

54. "Chief Justice Burger Proposes First Steps Toward Certification of Trial Advocacy Specialists," *American Bar Association Journal* 60 (1974): 173–174.

55. Segal and Spaeth, "The Influence of *Stare Decisis* on the Votes of United States Supreme Court Justices." Several scholars take issue with Segal and Spaeth on the degree to which the Court follows stare decisis. See the November 1996 issue of the *American Journal of Political Science*.

56. *Podbersky v. Kirwan*, 38 F.3d 147 (4th Cir., 1994).

57. "More 'Hopwood' Fallout," *National Law Journal*, June 9, 1997, A-6. See also "The Color Bind," *Newsweek*, May 12, 1997, 58–60.

58. See S. Sidney Ulmer, "Earl Warren and the Desegregation Cases," *Journal of Politics* 33 (1971): 689–701.

59. Charles A. Johnson, "Lower Court Reactions to Supreme Court Decisions: A Quantitative Examination," *American Journal of Political Science* 23 (1979): 802.

60. Peltason, *Fifty Eight Lonely Men*, 9.

61. Ibid., 10.

62. "The Busing Judge: A Reminiscence," *Louisville Courier Journal*, September 21, 1980, 17.

63. See Jack Bass, *Unlikely Heroes* (New York: Simon and Schuster, 1981), and Phillip J. Cooper, *Hard Judicial Choices: Federal District Court Judges and State and Local Officials* (New York: Oxford University Press, 1988).

64. "Employment Rulings Show Local Slant," *National Law Journal,* January 26, 1998, B-1.

65. Robert A. Carp and Ronald Stidham, *The Federal Courts,* 2d ed. (Washington, D.C.: CQ Press, 1991), 151.

66. See, for example, Abraham L. Davis, *Blacks in the Federal Judiciary* (Bristol, Ind.: Wyndham Hall Press, 1989), and Elaine Martin, "The Representative Role of Women Judges," *Judicature* 77 (1993): 166–173. Empirical studies show little representational effect. See Thomas G. Walker and Deborah Barrow, "The Diversification of the Federal Bench: Policy and Process Ramifications," *Journal of Politics* 47 (1985): 596–617, and Donald Songer, Sue Davis, and Susan Haire, "A Reappraisal of Diversification in the Federal Courts: Gender Effects in the Courts of Appeals," *Journal of Politics* 56 (1994): 425–439.

67. The findings are summarized in Rowland and Carp, *Politics and Judgment in Federal District Courts,* chap. 2. See also Randall D. Lloyd, "Separating Partisanship from Party in Judicial Research: Reapportionment in the U.S. District Courts," *American Political Science Review* 89 (1995): 413–420.

68. Steve Alumbaugh and C. K. Rowland, "The Links Between Platform-Based Appointment Criteria and Trial Judges' Abortion Judgments," *Judicature* 74 (1990): 153–162.

69. "Appellate Nominee Tones Down Words," *National Law Journal,* August 15, 1994.

70. See Melinda Gann Hall, "Constituent Preference in State Supreme Courts: Conceptual Notes and a Case Study," *Journal of Politics* 49 (1987): 1117–1124, and "Electoral Politics and Strategic Voting in State Supreme Courts," *Journal of Politics* 54 (1992): 427–446; Craig Emmert and Carol Ann Traut, "The California Supreme Court and the Death Penalty," *American Politics Quarterly* 22 (1994): 41–61.

71. Daniel R. Pinello, *The Impact of Judicial-Selection Method on State Supreme Court Policy* (Westport, Conn.: Greenwood Press, 1995).

72. See "Gingrich Asks Judge's Ouster for Ruling Out Drug Evidence," *New York Times,* March 7, 1996, B-4; "Clinton Pressing Judge to Relent," *New York Times,* March 22, 1996, 1; and "Judge Assailed Over Drug Case Issues Reversal and Apology," *New York Times,* April 2, 1996, 1.

73. Micheal Giles and Thomas Walker, "Judicial Policy-Making and Southern School Desegregation," *Journal of Politics* 37 (1975): 917–936.

74. Neil Romans, "The Role of State Supreme Courts in Judicial Impact Analysis," *Western Political Quarterly* 27 (1974): 51.

75. G. Alan Tarr, *Judicial Impact and State Supreme Courts* (Lexington, Mass.: Lexington Books, 1975).

76. Frank Sorauf, *The Wall of Separation: The Constitutional Politics of Church and State* (Princeton, N.J.: Princeton University Press, 1976).

CHAPTER THREE

The Implementing Population

Political scientists pay a great deal of attention to the antecedents of public policies as well as to the policies themselves. In recent years researchers have broadened their interests to include the consequences of these policies as well. The results of their analyses are striking. No matter what type of policy we examine—executive, legislative, or judicial—the implementation is never straightforward, and the actual impact of a policy is rarely what its makers intended.

In our discussion of the aftermath of the Supreme Court's 1973 abortion decision, we touched on the wide range of events that may follow a judicial decision. In Chapter 2 we explored the role of lower courts in the impact of judicial decisions and found that lower courts—which, in theory, are obliged to follow the policies of higher courts—do not necessarily interpret policies faithfully. This chapter concerns the actors who are one step further removed from the sources of judicial policy. We call these actors the implementing population because members of this population usually carry on the day-to-day tasks of translating judicial policies into action.

The membership of the implementing population is quite diverse. Although it is a mistake to dismiss the influence of individuals acting alone in implementing public policy, in most cases implementation is a group effort by a bureaucratic organization. Implementing groups range from major departments of the federal government to local school officials. The population is largely composed of institutions, and the individuals within them have different motivations and preferences from those of the legislators, executives, and judges who originated the policies. In addition, the implementors are subject to a variety of pressures that may not affect the original policy makers.

Since these groups implement legislative, executive, and judicial policies, statements about their behavior regarding judicial policy may also apply to their reactions to legislative and executive policies. School boards, for example, must respond on a variety of issues to demands from state education offices, state legislatures, the U.S. Departments of Education and Justice, and occasionally a state or federal court. Although there has been little research on the matter, there is reason to believe that school boards, and perhaps more generally any implementing group, respond differently to different superior policy makers.

THE JUDICIARY AND THE IMPLEMENTING POPULATION

Variations in the implementation of public policies and differences between the intended and the actual consequences of a policy may be the result of several factors. The capacity of the court to shape the implementation process is one factor that is particularly relevant to the relationship between the judiciary and the implementing population. Using an implementation model proposed by Paul Sabatier and Daniel Mazanian, Lawrence Baum argues that the courts are in a weak position to influence the behavior of implementors. He points out that, first, "courts are imprisoned within the adjudicative process," and second, "courts lack some very important legal powers . . . the judiciary does not control the sword or the purse."[1] The effects of these two factors are substantial and underscore the tenuous nature of the relationship between judicial bodies and implementing groups.

Legislatures and executive officials may initiate a policy and investigate its implementation at their discretion. However, courts must wait until a case is filed before they can render a policy announcement in the first place, and then they must wait for additional cases to review a policy's implementation. For example, the Supreme Court announced in several decisions (such as *Abington School District v. Schempp,* 1963, and *Lee v. Weisman,* 1992) that religious activities in public schools must be curtailed.

BOX 3-1
Religious Activities in Public Schools

Although a series of landmark decisions have sought to limit religious activities in public institutions, especially in public schools, some members of the implementing population continue to seek ways of avoiding or challenging the judiciary's decisions in this area. On many of those occasions, no action is taken by the judiciary simply because the public schools are not challenged in the courts. Defiance can be widespread at times and in some places; a federal district court in Alabama had to enjoin prayer in schools throughout the state.[a] Reports from the First Amendment Center at Vanderbilt University (http://www.fac.org) often include actions by state or local officials that appear to test implementation of the Supreme Court's religious decisions, but go unchallenged and unchanged.

For example, a high school in DeKalb County, Georgia, reportedly held a revival-style assembly in its gymnasium "to listen to a religious lecture and participate in a church-style service led by a local Baptist minister." This assembly followed by several weeks the violent deaths of two students on school grounds. The DeKalb public safety commissioner (and member of the church whose minister led the assembly) reportedly told the students "Here we are in defiance of the Supreme Court, calling the name of Jesus Christ." The chairman of the county school board told the *Atlanta Journal-Constitution* that he hoped the assembly would not be seen as an unconstitutional religious service.[b] As a one-time memorial service for the two students, the assembly did not lend itself to legal action by opponents of religious activities in schools. In this instance, as in many others, the implementing organization was fully in control of how Supreme Court decisions were interpreted and followed.

Activities or events with religious overtones that are planned well in advance may also be met with complacency or silence if students or parents are disinclined to challenge activity. By way of illustration, a public high school march-

---

However, many school systems continued these exercises simply because no one brought suit to stop them. Local courts could not order schools to stop the religious activities in the absence of a properly initiated suit. If the implementing group is not challenged or if it is successful in keeping the issue out of the courts, then court influence on the group is quite limited. The continuing nature of difficulties in challenging local policies on religious matters is illustrated in Box 3-1.

ing band in Trenton, Tennessee, reportedly practiced extensively for and presented a halftime program in which the band formed a giant cross on the field; depicted the life, death, and resurrection of Jesus; and included several Christian hymns. Although some parents were upset by the display, the band's director commented that parents and students knew about the program for months and that he had received no complaints. The program was scheduled for all halftime football games and various band competitions during the year.[c] The program evidently remained unchallenged.

Robert S. Alley reports another important reason that court challenges to religious practices remain uncommon: community sentiment. In 1994 a parent objected to a school policy that encouraged prayers after physical education classes in an East Baton Rouge Parish, Louisiana, high school. Students were evidently sanctioned for refusing to participate. After the parent's protest of the activity was turned aside by the school, the ACLU wrote to the school on the parent's and student's behalf. The school board refused to alter the policy, and the principal publicly criticized a student whom he thought had initiated the complaint. At that point, the student's parent decided not to bring suit because of the criticism mounting in the community.[d]

[a] "Alabama Judge Issues Final Federal Order in School Prayer Case," *First Amendment Legal Watch,* vol. 2, no. 47 (November 26, 1997).

[b] "Revival-Style Gathering at Georgia High School Raises Church-State Concerns," ibid., no. 36 (October 13, 1997).

[c] "Public High School Marching Band Performs Religious Halftime Routine," ibid., no. 35 (September 2, 1997).

[d] Robert S. Alley, *Without a Prayer: Religious Expression in Public Schools* (Amherst, N.Y.: Prometheus Books, 1996), 210–212.

Another source of difficulty in the relationship between implementing groups and the judiciary is that a policy itself may be incomplete, unclear, or contradictory. Judicial policies stemming from a court decision are usually limited by the facts of a case and the applicable case law; rarely will a single decision completely outline a policy for implementing groups to follow. Also, because of the norms of the judicial process—especially the requirement that only real cases in controversy will be decided by the courts—implementing groups cannot easily return to a court for clarification of a policy. Therefore, these agencies must frequently interpret a judicial policy before carrying it into action. Of course, unlike the interpretations of judicial policies rendered by lower courts, interpretations by implementing groups do not have authoritative force. Even so, in order to be reversed an implementing group's interpretation must first be challenged in court, something that does not occur in many policy areas. If the original statement of a judicial policy is unclear or ambiguous—which as we noted in Chapter 2 is the case with many court decisions—implementing groups are more or less free to interpret and implement the policy as they wish, until their actions are challenged and reversed in court.

A further difficulty that is unique to judicial policies is that the institutional powers of the judiciary usually limit the court's selection of who implements a judicial policy, how it is done, and with what resources. Thus courts must work with existing implementing groups—they cannot fire unenthusiastic implementors and hire new ones. To compound the problem, the groups that immediately implement the policies are frequently parties to the decision. If the implementing group loses its case, then it must immediately execute a decision which it fought against for months or even years. Other implementing groups are often similarly situated and may have commitments to a policy similar to that of a participant in the original lawsuit. For example, the implementors of *Texas v. Hopwood* (1996), which prohibited an affirmative action policy at the University of Texas (see Chapter 2), were university officials who obviously favored the policy; when *Hopwood* was applied to other universities, it would likely be administered by their officials who supported affirmative action programs. Similarly, Adarand Constructors, the plaintiff in *Adarand Constructors v. Pena* (1995), which struck down federal affirmative action programs, complained two years later that it was still "losing out because of advantages minority firms enjoy in the government contract bidding process."[2] In short, the judiciary frequently has no choice except to rely on implementing groups that have vigorously opposed the policy the court has adopted.

While courts may not select implementing groups or appoint their personnel, they do have the power to impose fines and jail sentences. If an implementing group is ordered to carry out a particular policy but fails to do so, its members may be cited for contempt of court. Being convicted of contempt could result in daily fines or in jail sentences for the offending parties. For example, in 1988 a federal district judge ordered Yonkers, N.Y., to build public housing projects in white neighborhoods. The city council refused. The judge then fined the resisting council members $500 a day and the city $1 million a day. Even at these confiscatory rates, the council held out for three months, but then the specter of municipal bankruptcy increased public pressure for compliance and enough council members changed their votes to insure compliance.[3]

Although contempt powers are substantial, courts are reluctant to use them. Most judges explore all other alternatives first. The size and diversity of some implementing groups encourage caution—citing numerous members of a department of government for contempt is difficult logistically. Moreover, issuing contempt citations to officeholders may be problematic—for example, citing a governor or a legislature for contempt is difficult politically for a judge. He or she may anticipate career damage if politicians are cited for contempt, because doing so may inflame public opinion against the court or the policy, and there is always a risk that the contempt citation will not be honored by higher courts. Federal and state courts sometimes faced this dilemma when enforcing civil rights policies in the South during the 1960s.

From time to time, judges do decide to use their contempt authority. For example, a federal district judge cited Mississippi Governor Ross Barnett when he openly resisted black applicant James Meredith's admission to the University of Mississippi in 1962, although the action was later overturned by the Supreme Court (*Barnett v. United States,* 1964). Likewise, Carter administration Attorney General Griffin Bell was held in contempt by a federal district judge when he refused to turn over a list of informers in the course of a Socialist Workers Party suit against the FBI, only to see the citation overturned. Still, implementors do not treat the prospect of contempt citations lightly. In all but the most extreme situations, officials will seek to avoid them through at least minimal compliance and tacit compromises.

The relationship between any policy-making group and any implementing group is likely to be tenuous. But the procedural constraints of the judicial process and the limited powers of the judiciary make the relationship between the judiciary and relevant implementing groups especially tentative. It is wrong to infer that few judicial policies are ever implemented; most are, at least to some extent. The fact is that implementation varies from group to group and from policy to policy. The remainder of this chapter is devoted to understanding why these variations occur.

IMPLEMENTING GROUPS AS ORGANIZATIONS

Some judicial policies do not require much implementation (as we will discuss in Chapters 4 and 7). They simply allow people to do something if they want to, but do not require them to do it (examples include advertising by attorneys or seeing an X-rated movie). But most decisions require that implementation be carried out by some type of group. This is particularly true of judicial policies regarding desegregation, the administration of criminal justice, the environment, and health and safety. Commonly, the implementing groups are formal organizations, regardless of the policy area involved, the number of implementing groups affected, or the size of the groups expected to respond to the judicial policy. Most are governmental bureaucracies—federal, state, or local agencies—but a few are private organizations, as were some of the hospitals that responded to the Supreme Court's abortion decision. In our efforts to understand implementing groups, the work of organizational theorists and researchers about how these groups respond to demands for change is especially relevant.

Organizational responses to judicial decisions arise out of a series of complex factors, including an organization's commitment to existing programs and policies and its wish to conserve resources for agency-defined goals.[4] These factors often constitute inertial forces that undercut attempts to change policies and practices. However, agencies also want to avoid sanctions for failure to change programs and policies. Hence, if a court decision requires change, it is likely to meet some resistance, unless the effects of inertial forces are overcome or unless the change furthers the organization's pursuit of its own goals.

Organizational theorists tell us that organizations faced with demands for change engage in at least three activities: (1) they interpret demands for change and decide whether to accept or reject them; (2) they search for ways to meet those demands as well as for ways to circumvent them; and (3) if necessary, they change policies and practices in ways that satisfy the demands for change while retaining as many of their original goals as possible.

Interpreting Judicial Decisions

An agency's acceptance of a judicial decision is a function of what the agency believes the court is requiring, that is, of the agency's interpretation. Studies of local school officials' reactions to the Supreme Court's decisions concerning prayers in schools provide good illustrations of how interpretations influence organizational responses. One study of rural and small town public school administrators by Kenneth Dolbeare and Phillip Hammond found that officials interpreted the *Abington School District v. Schempp* (1963) decision as banning the *establishment* of religion in schools, but not as limiting the *free exercise* of religion. Because their schools did not coerce students to say prayers, these officials took no action to ensure compliance with *Schempp*.[5] By contrast, separate studies of different school systems by William K. Muir and Richard Johnson found that *Schempp* was interpreted as banning all religious activities in schools. As a consequence, virtually all religious activities in these school systems were ended.[6]

The significant factor to emerge from these studies is the importance of interpretations by authoritative figures in organizations. In general, when a judicial decision receives an incorrect or narrow interpretation, it is likely that no leader in the implementing organization is in agreement with the policy; when a decision receives a generally correct or broad interpretation, we would expect to find one or more authority figures who are in fundamental agreement with the policy, or at least who see implementation as costless to the organization. Except for a few officials who came to their positions after the Court had acted, no officials in Dolbeare and Hammond's study had accepted the school prayer decisions. In several school systems studied by Muir and by Johnson, however, many officials were sympathetic with the Court's actions to remove religion from the public schools. Even in these compliant systems, however, if the school superintendent in one system and the school board's attorney in the other system had not given *Schempp* an accurate and supportive interpretation, those systems probably would not have discontinued prayers. It is significant that both of these officials dealt with their systems from a position of strength and thus were able to persuade and cajole others in the systems to accept their interpretations.

The Search Process

An integral part of adjusting to a judicial policy, except in the few instances when an agency rejects a decision at the very outset, is obtaining information about the policy and about alternative courses of action for the agency. This information-gathering process is often called the search process. Not surprisingly, the search process is influenced by the goals and preferences of agency officials, sometimes to the extent that an incomplete picture of the demands and alternatives emerges. But no matter how imperfect the process, it affects the implementation of policy in concrete ways, and we need to understand how the search is conducted.

Since administrative officials usually wish to conserve resources as well as to avoid sanctions, one of their first considerations is to determine whether the court-mandated change conflicts with agency goals or compromises agency preferences. If, in the agency's judgment, the mandates of the court do not significantly alter existing policies, then the agency may continue its activities much as it did before the court decision, making only minor changes in policies or procedures. The agency's decision concerning whether the court's demands are acceptable will depend on at least two factors: the perceived difference between its existing program and that suggested by the court, and the commitment of the agency to the existing program. The less compatible the existing policies are with those suggested by the court, the greater the change that will probably be required by the judicial policy. In such a situation, compromise in agency goals and preferences will be called for. An agency that is faced with an incompatible court decision, rather than adopting the court's policy immediately, will initiate a search for alternatives.[7]

In searching for alternatives, agency officials must consider the threat of sanctions and their potential severity. If a court policy is not immediately acceptable to an agency and if the probability of enforcement is low, then the agency is not likely to engage in an extensive search because any search draws on limited time and money. On the other hand, if officials believe the probability of enforcement to be high, then the search will be wider and will cover a full range of interpretations and alternatives. The severity of sanctions would have a similar impact on any decision to institute a search for alternatives—the greater the probability of severe sanctions, the greater the search activity.

This process is shown in Neal Milner's study of differences in the search behavior of four Wisconsin police departments in reaction to *Miranda v. Arizona's* (1966) mandate that criminal suspects be informed of their rights. He reported that since the departments believed that *Miranda* would result in major changes in the rules governing police behavior, each of them sought out information from legal sources or law enforcement organizations regarding the implications of *Miranda*. Which and how many information sources a department consulted were influenced by the professionalism of the department, but the diligence of the search was also affected by how strictly a department believed local criminal defense attorneys would enforce the *Miranda* standards. The departments in cities with an aggressive defense bar gathered more information.[8]

Sometimes agency searches produce schemes that largely continue an existing policy and yet avoid sanctions. For example, in the Reagan years, the Social Security Administration (SSA) adopted fiscal conservatism as a major goal. In consequence, the agency changed its policies to deny many more disability claims than it had in previous administrations. Lower federal district courts often overturned the denials, accompanied by opinions holding that the agency's policy was contrary to law. In such cases, Social Security administrators would pay the particular claim, thus avoiding any sanctions. But they would continue denying similar claims. An SSA official explained, "Circuit court decisions are written to decide individual cases, not to provide instructions to decision-makers."[9] Thus only claimants who had the resources and fortitude to carry a long appeal to the courts would get their money. The agency saved money and avoided sanctions. Ultimately SSA was reined in when it lost a large class action suit (*Hyatt v. Heckler,* 1989) relating to how it evaluated pain; the SSA is now adjudicating claims in compliance with this decision.[10]

Not unexpectedly, researchers have also found that attorneys tend to dominate the search process within most agencies. Attorneys provide interpretations of the court decision and help shape alternative responses to its mandate. In most instances, the search process produces narrow interpretations and a limited number of alternatives, usually as consistent as possible with existing policy preferences and agency practices—thus minimizing the need for changes.

PROGRAM ADJUSTMENTS AFTER JUDICIAL DECISIONS

Adjustments by an agency after an adverse court decision may involve a variety of changes in policies, procedures, and practices. An agency's response to such a decision usually falls into one of three categories: (1) *noncompliance,* evidenced by the lack of change in policies, procedures, or practices; (2) *evasion,* which may include minor or cosmetic changes in policies, procedures, or practices; and (3) *compliance,* characterized by adjustments that conform wholly or largely to the decision. Of course, as we noted in Chapter 2, categorizing such responses is not always an easy matter, especially if there is some ambiguity about what precisely the court expects an agency to do after the decision. Nevertheless, although the categories are rough, they serve at least as useful reference points in discussing the responses of organizations to judicial policies.

Our explanation of the adjustments made by agencies must be considered in the context of their decision to agree or disagree with a decision—their acceptance decision. Presumably, an agency that agrees with a decision is likely to be compliant, as is one that decides to abide by an adverse decision. But other factors affect their responses as well, so that even when they make similar acceptance decisions organizations may adopt different behavioral responses. Explanations by social scientists of organizational responses tend to emphasize one or more of the following features: the communication and clarity of the judicial decision, the policy setting within which the implementing group is expected to respond, and the internal dynamics of the organization implementing the decision.

Communication of the Decision

Just as the clarity and transmission of a judicial policy affect lower court interpretations of that policy, so do they affect the behavior of implementing groups. In examining the implementation of judicial policies, scholars usually focus on two aspects of the communication process: the *clarity* of the decision itself and the *sources of information* used by the implementing agencies to understand the judicial policy.

Ambiguities in the U.S. Supreme Court's *Brown v. Board of Education* decisions in 1954 and 1955 substantially affected the progress of school desegregation in the 1950s. This case involved two separate opinions, sometimes referred to as *Brown I* and *Brown II. Brown I* held that separate but equal educational facilities were unlawful; the implementation issues associated with that decision were addressed in *Brown II,* announced one year later. Here the Court used the phrase "all deliberate speed" to guide the implementation of desegregation.[11] Assessing the impact of *Brown I* and *Brown II,* Stephen Wasby, Anthony D'Amato, and Rosemary Metrailer argue that the *Brown II* decision did not provide specific instructions, was not persuasive, and indicated how *Brown I* could be evaded, at least in the short term. Adding to the problem of *Brown's* ambiguity, for almost a decade the Court did not issue any other general rulings regarding the implementation of *Brown I* to guide lower courts or school boards in this issue area.[12]

A similar lack of clarity can be found in some of the Court's criminal justice decisions, especially in the search and seizure area. The problem is not so much that particular decisions are ambiguous (although some are), but that taken collectively, the Court's decisions do not offer very clear guidance and sometimes seem contradictory. To some extent this ambiguity occurs because courts by their nature take a case-by-case approach to balancing the constitutional protection against unreasonable searches with society's need to address crime. But the scattershot cases and apparent contradictions also make it difficult for police departments and officers to know how to adjust their behavior. A New York district attorney remarked, "If the Chief Justice of the United States sat in the back of a squad car in Manhattan, I doubt he could counsel the officer, within a legal degree of certainty, on the constitutionality of the police action."[13] Law professor Wayne LaFave, a leading scholar of the Fourth Amendment, and one sympathetic to its requirements, wrote:

> Fourth Amendment doctrine . . . ought to be expressed in terms that are readily applicable by the police. . . . A highly sophisticated set of rules that is qualified by all sorts of ifs, ands, and buts and requiring the drawing of subtle nuances and hairline distinctions, may be the sort of heady stuff upon which the facile minds of lawyers and judges eagerly feed, but they may be literally impossible of application by the officer in the field.[14]

Indeed, one scholar, Craig Bradley, argues that the absence of straightforward judicial mandates is primarily responsible for police and prosecutorial indifference in carrying out the major criminal justice reforms announced by the Supreme Court under Chief Justice Earl Warren.[15]

James F. Spriggs's analysis of the reactions of all major federal agencies to Supreme Court decisions from 1953 to 1990 also underscores the importance of clarity in accounting for variations in agency responses to judicial decisions. Judicial decisions reversing agency policies varied considerably during this period—some were quite specific in outlining actions that agencies were to take, and others gave little direction to agencies about what they were to do. Spriggs found that where change requirements were set forth explicitly in the Court's opinion, 95.5 percent of the responses were classified in the "major compliance" category; where the expectations were not specified by the Court, only 3.4 percent of the decisions fell in this category. Fully 59 percent of the court's non-specific decisions did not lead to changes by the agencies. [16]

If the original decision leaves implementors confused, so too may the communication process by which the message is transmitted from the

Supreme Court to the implementing agencies. Agency officials rarely read the full opinion of the Court; instead they rely on interpretations of the opinion by others, on an excerpt of the opinion distributed by someone inside or outside of the agency, or on summary information supplied by coworkers or the news media. The communication of criminal justice decisions, for example, appears to be a haphazard, multistage process, which according to some critics inadequately informs police officers of judicial decisions and expectations. Stephen Wasby found that police officers learn of judicial decisions from a variety of sources, including friends and the general media as well as training sessions and bulletins from law enforcement agencies. He notes that although the local prosecutor is another source of information, the degree to which prosecutors actually inform the police of current due process standards varies considerably. Even where local prosecutors were the dominant source of information, Wasby found that police officers often felt that prosecutors gave them too little information.[17]

Research suggests that media reports about Supreme Court decisions can mislead readers and viewers. Elliot Slotnick and Jennifer Segal's analysis of television news coverage found it infrequent, brief, usually incomplete, and sometimes just plain wrong. For example, denials of certiorari were at times reported as decisions on the merits.[18] While newspaper coverage is more frequent and more thorough, it, too, often has misleading emphases.[19] Implementors (and others) who get their information about Court policies from the media may well end up misunderstanding the Court's policies.

The Policy Setting

Members of the implementing population must consider the impact of the judicial policies they carry out, including how their own operations are affected. The police, for example, are naturally concerned about court decisions that limit or expand their powers to make arrests, conduct searches, or otherwise deter crime. Similarly, federal court involvement in defining the rights of prisoners substantially affects the ways that prisons are administered. (See Box 3-2 for a discussion of reactions by prison officials to a major court decision in Texas.)

Generally, the political and social environment into which a decision is announced as well as the reactions of affected individuals constitute what we call the policy setting for the implementation of a judicial decision. The policy setting of a court decision may influence the responses of implementing groups, regardless of how the decision is communicated or how the implementing groups are affected. Three aspects of the policy setting are most often examined by judicial impact researchers: the community's policy preferences based on prevailing traditions, norms, or functions; the pressure from external forces to make changes or to retain the status quo; and the levels of coercion from the judiciary faced by the implementing group.

COMMUNITY POLICY PREFERENCES. It stands to reason that a community's policy preferences, which are based on existing norms, traditions, and functions, will have a direct effect on how a judicial decision is received and implemented. (Communities are usually geographic, but occasionally occupational or institutional communities that transcend geographic boundaries are affected by Court decisions.) If the policy preference is reinforced by a judicial decision, the community is likely to react positively; if a judicial policy runs counter to a community's traditional preferences, reactions will be negative.

The early reactions of local officials to the Supreme Court's decisions limiting school prayers and other religious activities in public schools illustrate the importance of community traditions, as several analyses suggest. Survey data reported by John H. Laubauch reveal that changes in behavior and policies were minimal in the South, where religious exercises and education were traditionally mixed. By contrast, areas of the country where such a tradition was weak underwent more dramatic change after the prayer decisions.[20] Donald Reich compared religious practices in the 1960s in Ohio, where schoolhouse religion was common, and in Minnesota, where it was not; he found little policy change in Ohio and widespread approval of the decision in Minnesota. Reich suggests that the particular histories of these two states account for differences in the responses of local school boards.[21]

Perceptions of community norms can be as important as the reality. Dolbeare and Hammond's study of five Indiana communities found that local school officials essentially did nothing in response to the Schempp decision—they did not announce a new policy, call for changes in behavior, or even endorse the status quo. Most believed that making program changes such as banning religious exercises would raise the ire of the community, thus jeopardizing other school district projects. The threat or fear of community retaliation was sufficient to deter compliance with the Supreme Court's policy. Interestingly, although school board officials

---

Box 3-2
Responses to Court-Ordered Reforms in Prisons

The 1970s and 1980s saw a rising number of lawsuits by prisoners in state and federal prisons who were claiming that terrible prison conditions and harsh treatment by prison officials were unconstitutional. Many of these suits resulted in orders from state and federal judges to change the way prisoners were housed and treated. A widely publicized case occurred in Texas, *Ruiz v. Estelle* (1980), in which federal district judge William Wayne Justice issued a series of rulings that made substantial demands on the Texas Department of Corrections and led to massive changes in Texas prisons.

Sociologists Ben M. Crouch and James W. Marquart studied the implementation and impact of Judge Justice's intervention in the Texas prison system and concluded that every aspect of prison operations was affected by the decision. But they also noted that the reforms were resisted by prison officials and, initially, by state officials; that they cost the state millions of dollars in legal fees, not to mention the costs of the changes; and that they contributed to changes in prison policies and practices that caused hundreds of injuries and some deaths.[a]

Crouch and Marquart characterize governance of Texas prisons as going through three stages during this time: a "repressive order" before litigation, a "legalistic order" during the immediate post-litigation time period, and a "bureaucratic order" following organizational adjustments to the judicially imposed standards. The "repressive order" emphasized a system of control and discipline, and in which guards had a great deal of authority. In this setting, "law [was] subordinate to order in prison."[b]

Ruiz challenged this form of social control and sought to impose constitutional standards for the treatment of prisoners. These changes required massive adjustment in prison policies, and especially in the behavior of prison personnel. Reaction to Justice's orders is characterized by the comments of a veteran officer: "The judge says an inmate can spit in your face. I won't have it. That's no good for the inmate! What does that teach him but to misbehave the way he's always done?"[c] Because of their commitment to the previous policies, Judge Justice's decision was resented by all and resisted by most prison guards and administrators. But as the judge's orders became more insistent and as top

---

believed that the community was heavily committed to certain religious practices in the local schools, Dolbeare and Hammond found little evidence that such a commitment existed or that retaliation for compliance with the Supreme Court's decisions would have been likely.[22] Nonetheless, state prison officials agreed to court settlements under increasing judicial and political pressures, prison officials accepted the formalization of many prison routines. These new routines circumscribed the authority of prison guards and imposed a system of accountability that, in turn, led to lower officer morale, higher turnover, and less contact with prisoners. Faced with uncompromising orders to change, prison officials either sullenly adopted the new policy or left the system.[d]

By most accounts, the prison officials' adoption of a legalistic order resulted in much greater turmoil in the prisons, more prisoner-on-prisoner attacks, and the emergence of prison gangs. Reactions to prison disruptions led to the third phase—bureaucratic order. As Crouch and Marquart noted, prison officials learned to use "constitutional means to achieve official ends (especially control)," which resulted in increased stability in the prisons. In this new order, prison officials "learned how to use sanctions legally available to them for inmate control. . . . By varying the degree to which they apply the rules, by threatening, frustrating, and harassing prisoners with the multiplicity of rules, officers [could] intimidate and control most prisoners."[e] Thus the original goals in the repressive policy setting emerged as the working priorities in spite of the due process–oriented policies and procedures required by Judge Justice's orders. Although prison conditions improved, the new prison regime clearly underscored order and control as central features of the prison system.

[a] Ben M. Crouch and James W. Marquart, "*Ruiz:* Intervention and Emergent Order in Texas Prisons," in *Courts, Corrections, and the Constitution: The Impact of Judicial Intervention on Prisons and Jails,* ed. John J. DiIulio Jr. (New York: Oxford University Press, 1990), 94–95.

[b] Crouch and Marquart, "*Ruiz,*" 97.

[c] John J. DiIulio Jr., "The Old Regime and the *Ruiz* Revolution: The Impact of Judicial Intervention on Texas Prisons," in *Courts, Corrections, and the Constitution,* 63.

[d] Crouch and Marquart, "*Ruiz.*"

[e] Ibid., 105.

even if community preferences are more perception than reality, they can be effective constraints on implementing groups.

Even when judicial policies have been in place for a long time, community values can constrain judicial policies. Robert Alley, for example, reports that thirty years after the Supreme Court banned religious activities in public schools, many schools in highly religious communities continued religious practices such as distributing Bibles, putting on Christmas programs dominated by Christian songs, and leading prayers over the schools' public address systems.[23]

EXTERNAL SUPPORT FOR OR OPPOSITION TO CHANGE. Another critical feature of the policy setting is whether other groups or affected individuals that support or oppose judicially mandated changes apply pressure on an organization to change. If, for example, local groups oppose a judicial policy and those groups are particularly influential or important to an implementing organization, change might be less likely than if there are no relevant groups bringing pressure or if such groups support the judicial policy. The impact of external groups has been documented in studies about several policy areas, but perhaps the best illustrations come from the studies of the implementation of school desegregation decisions by southern school boards in the 1950s and early 1960s.

Resistance to desegregation was both widespread and intense. While some cities in border areas, such as Baltimore and St. Louis, moved to desegregate swiftly—at least in policy if not in practice—the Deep South simply refused to consider changing.[24] As noted above, there was little real pressure to desegregate from the U.S. Supreme Court and from local courts, while influential leaders in southern communities loudly, frequently, and in no uncertain terms, demanded continued segregation. Legislatures in several states passed laws that would overrule the school boards or close the schools in the state if segregation should be abandoned. In Texas, for example, state funds were to be withheld from school systems where desegregation was planned unless approval for desegregation was obtained in a popular referendum.[25] And in New Orleans, after the school board prepared to abide by court-ordered integration, it had to fight to retain control of the school system, a fight it lost temporarily to the state legislature and governor. In another nationally known case of opposition, local officials controlling funds in Prince Edward County, Virginia, forced the closing of public schools, over the school administrators' objections, rather than allowing desegregation.[26]

Another source of support for the status quo came from the "Southern Manifesto"—a document signed in 1956 by ninety-six U.S. senators and representatives from the South, which says, in part:

> We pledge ourselves to use all lawful means to bring about a reversal of this decision [*Brown v. Board of Education*] which is contrary to the

Constitution and to prevent the use of force in its implementation. In this trying period, as we seek to right this wrong, we appeal to our people not to be provoked by the agitators and trouble makers invading our states and to scrupulously refrain from disorder and lawlessness.[27]

For many southern officials the Southern Manifesto legitimized opposition to the *Brown* decision. One scholarly study of *Brown*'s impact suggested that the Manifesto "was probably the single most influential document defying desegregation in the South. It provided important approval of and support for the plan of 'massive resistance' and made such resistance 'socially acceptable' by giving [it] the blessing of the Southern Establishment."[28]

The first decade after *Brown* did not see a great deal of change in policies or behavior. However, the rate of desegregation increased dramatically in the mid-1960s. By then the pressures on southern school boards from external forces had changed from overwhelming support for segregation to substantial support for desegregation. The Supreme Court abandoned its hands-off policy and required local boards to take "positive steps" to desegregate (*Green v. School Board of New Kent County*, 1968). Many lower federal courts followed suit.

Perhaps a more important agent of change was the passage of the 1964 Civil Rights Act, which ushered in what Harrell Rodgers and Charles Bullock call the administrative-judicial era of the civil rights movement.[29] Title VI of the act provided that the Department of Health, Education and Welfare (HEW) could terminate funds to public schools that practiced racial discrimination. With this provision the slow, case-by-case approach using the courts was replaced by administrative guidelines establishing particular requirements for school districts in progressing toward desegregation. Also, the law required that the districts report their progress to HEW, thus placing them in the position of having to defend the current racial distributions in the schools. Soon after the passage of the law, HEW moved to terminate funding in several districts, and a small number did lose their federal funds in 1967. The net effect of these measures was sufficient to overcome community pressures to maintain segregation, largely bringing about an end to dual school systems in the South by the mid-1970s.[30]

When civic leaders changed their views about desegregation, local school boards often reconsidered their resistance. The U.S. Commission on Civil Rights reported that "even where political leaders have actually opposed the specifics of a court order, . . . if they take a position of 'obedience to the law,' the result is a positive contribution to the desegregation process."[31] Economic considerations often led southern elites to drop their resistance as major industries refused to locate in communities where the schools were closed or filled with tension, or where black employees could not get decent treatment.

More recently this scenario has been repeated with the Supreme Court's sexual harassment policies. In cases such as *Meritor Savings Bank v. Vinson* (1986), *Harris v. Forklift Systems* (1993), and *Ellerth v. Burlington Industries* (1998), the Court held that Title VII of the 1964 Civil Rights Act outlawed "hostile working environments" for women. This means that employers can be sued if they tolerate crude remarks, innuendoes by other employees, or unwanted sexual propositions. Nonetheless, many workplaces, especially those that were traditionally filled by men or where women have traditionally had a subordinate status, have norms that tolerate behavior ranging from sexual jokes to sexual propositions. Many employers make little effort to change these norms. Sexual harassment suits are common these days, and sometimes victims receive large awards. Because most employers are private organizations, the government cannot put the same pressures on them that it put on southern school systems. However, the Equal Employment Opportunities Commission can file lawsuits where harassment is systematic and egregious, as it did against Mitsubishi Motor Co. in 1996. Moreover, the high cost of losing lawsuits is inducing public agencies and private corporations alike to alter their behavior patterns in this area.

COERCION TO PRODUCE CHANGE. The level of coercion used by the courts to force changes in policies or behavior is the third feature of the policy setting that affects implementation. Of course, courts cannot initiate review of an implementing agency's responsiveness to a judicial policy; they must instead await a suit that charges violation of the policy. However, once a case is brought to court, a judge may pressure implementing agencies to change their policies or behavior (as we saw in the Texas prison case in Box 3-2), thus overcoming the effects of community traditions or organizational concerns.

Earlier in this chapter we discussed judges' ability to issue contempt citations against those who refuse obedience. Sometimes judges can assume the administrative powers of the agency itself as has occasionally happened in school desegregation or prison reform cases. But it can happen in other types of cases: in the 1990s a federal district court took over the administration of the Washington State Department of Fisheries to secure enforcement of the court's ruling that Native American fishermen could catch 50 percent of the harvestable fish as allowed by an 1854 treaty.[32] This alternative allows the judge to implement the policy from the courthouse.

The likelihood of a court's becoming involved in forcing an implementing group to make programmatic changes depends on a variety of factors, some of which we will discuss later. There is substantial evidence that as levels of coercion increase, the probability that program adjustments will be made also increases.[33] The reverse of this can also occur. Research by Gary Orfield and his associates provides evidence (see Box 2-2, and Chapter 4) that resistance to judicial policies re-surfaces when judicial pressures for change subside. Several school systems, for example, essentially resegregated in the late 1980s and 1990s after federal judges ended their supervision.[34]

Organizations involved in the criminal justice system—especially police and prison officials—are among the groups with a high probability that courts will review their work. Of course, the courts cannot review every police encounter to ensure the rights of the criminal suspect, but there is a reasonable likelihood of review after an arrest. The more likely departmental superiors or judicial officials are to review an officer's behavior, the more likely the officer will be to comply with due process standards.[35]

Several officials are in a position to review and supervise the implementation of criminal justice decisions. In theory, prosecutors look at the record and refuse to prosecute a suspect if they believe that the police have not conducted their investigation and made the arrest according to the requirements set down in various court decisions. Similarly, judges are in a position to rule certain evidence inadmissible if they believe the defendant's rights have been violated during earlier stages of the legal process. However, prosecutors' and judges' tolerance for police misbehavior has been widely reported.[36] In addition, some observers report that the police are unconcerned about the possibility of undercutting an investigation by violating a suspect's rights, except when the arrest is considered an important one.[37]

If prosecutors and judges do not ensure some measure of compliance with criminal justice decisions by the police, defense attorneys may be effective. David Neubauer's study of the criminal justice system in "Prairie City" indicated that "specialized defense attorneys" occasionally charged that rights had been violated by the police.[38] Milner found that one of the four Wisconsin cities he examined had a criminal lawyer who specialized in making constitutional challenges to the arrest procedures of local police.[39] Although the success rate for these claims usually is not high, police in jurisdictions with such attorneys tend to keep in line with judicial policies on criminal justice to a greater extent than do police where vigilant attorneys are not around.

Internal Dynamics of Responding Organizations

Forces within the implementing group may also compel program changes. We loosely refer to these forces as internal dynamics. A simple, straightforward, and obvious relationship is often observed by judicial impact researchers: barring other constraints or pressures, groups that support a judicial policy will implement the policy faithfully; those that do not will either ignore it or resist its implementation, wherever and whenever possible.

An agency's approval or disapproval of a judicial policy may be explained by several factors. One of these factors is the cost of the policy or program changes to the agency. Assuming that the decision is not generally beneficial to the agency and that the costs of implementation are not insurmountable, three other factors affect implementation: whether the policy conflicts with an agency's goals or mission, whether the policy conflicts with preferences of key agency personnel, and whether the agency can effectively resist judicial pressure to implement a policy.

COST OF CHANGE. The cost factors include the amount of time required to implement program changes and the loss of money and skills invested in the existing program. Sometimes the costs of compliance can be substantial. For example, the police commissioner of New York City reported that a great deal of money was spent in retraining police officers after the Supreme Court announced several decisions requiring new procedures for arrests, searches and seizures, and confessions.[40]

The implementation of massive changes in prisons required by U.S. federal courts was sharply limited by the resources for those changes. Researchers report that litigation eventually prompted budget increases for prison construction and operation, but that this was in many states a lengthy process requiring political compromises.[41] Some prison administrators, while resentful about adverse judicial decrees, found a silver lining when they were able to obtain greater funds from the state treasury. However, some scholars argue that these new expenditures were actually little more than what might be expected with the normal growth of state budgets.[42]

Other changes may involve only a minimal cost to an agency. For example, one of the immediate responses of many police departments to

Miranda was to start issuing "*Miranda* cards" from which a police officer had to read criminal suspects their rights. Relatively speaking, such a change was not very expensive, compared with massive retraining or major capital expenditures. Resistance in cases that incur major costs is more prevalent than it is in those cases where compliance is inexpensive.

ORGANIZATIONAL NORMS AND INDIVIDUAL ATTITUDES. In many instances, the organizational goals or mission may be the sum of the attitudes and preferences of agency personnel; but with some organizations the pervasive nature of an organizational ethos or set of norms overrides or reshapes individual attitudes. The field of criminal justice provides good illustrations of the impact of organizational norms and goals on the implementation of judicial decisions. Police as individuals did not readily accept the Supreme Court's criminal justice decisions in the 1960s and early 1970s, which imposed stricter due process standards. Jerome Skolnick's classic study of police behavior in the 1960s summarizes police attitudes toward the *Mapp* decision in 1962, which required that courts exclude illegally seized evidence from consideration:

> [Most officers believe] the impact of the exclusionary rule . . . has not been to guarantee greater protection of the freedom of "decent citizens" from unreasonable police zeal, but rather to complicate unnecessarily the task of detecting and apprehending criminals. From the pragmatic perspective of the police, the right to conduct exploratory investigations and searches ought largely to be a matter of police-supervisory discretion.[43]

Almost a decade later, Stephen Wasby found that attitudes had changed somewhat. His study of police officers in small communities in Illinois and Massachusetts revealed that officers were still "irritated when judges granted motions to suppress evidence," but generally seemed willing to "live within the new search rules." Wasby also reported that officers were more willing than they had been to follow judicial policies concerning a suspect's right to legal assistance early in the arrest process.[44]

Measuring compliance with Supreme Court decisions in the face of adverse norms and attitudes is problematical. This is illustrated by reaction to *Miranda*. Compliance with the letter of the law—as when a *Miranda* card is read—can be measured, but compliance with the spirit of the law is much harder to evaluate. For example, direct observation of police behavior in New Haven, Connecticut, shortly after *Miranda* found that many times the warnings were read in a "formalized, bureaucratic tone to indicate that his [the police officer's] remarks were simply a routine, meaningless legalism." Moreover, if a suspect expressed an interest in finding an attorney, the police frequently "offered him a telephone book without further comment, and that response was enough to deter him from calling a lawyer." [45] In a technical sense, the officer who reads a suspect his or her *Miranda* rights in a formalized tone of voice or who does not aid a suspect in securing an attorney is not disobeying *Miranda*. Nevertheless, such behavior could effectively dissuade a suspect from exercising his or her constitutional rights.

Observing police behavior nearly twenty-five years after *Miranda,* Richard Leo reports that the police have largely nullified the decision requiring that arrestees be informed of their rights to silence and to having an attorney present during questioning. Arguing that the police now employ a "confidence game" to interrogate suspects, Leo finds that "American police have responded to *Miranda's* legal requirements by becoming increasingly skilled at the use of manipulation and deception inside the interrogation room." [46]

A 1998 *New York Times* investigation noted various ways that the police circumvented *Miranda's* requirements. For example, detectives will invite suspects to the station house or go to the suspects' homes because *Miranda* applies only when suspects are being held in custody. Or a detective might diminish the importance of the warnings to someone in custody by casually saying something like, "We would like to discuss the evidence against you, but first we have to read your *Miranda* rights—you know, like on TV. Then we can talk." The *Times* also found that *Miranda* warnings are sometimes ignored. In Albuquerque and Los Angeles, for instance, detectives are told to continue an interrogation even if the suspect has invoked his or her *Miranda* right to request that a lawyer be present before any questions are asked. From the police perspective, there is little to lose and much to gain by ignoring (or delaying complying with) the suspect's request. Sometimes appellate courts have allowed statements taken under such circumstances to be admitted into evidence. Yale Kamisar, an authority on criminal justice law, lamented, "It's very discouraging. Very little [is] left of *Miranda*." [47]

In addition to skirting judicial decisions or implementing them passively, some police officers adjust their behavior so as to avoid the impact or consequences of due process policies. For example, sometimes the police conduct searches just to harass known prostitutes or drug dealers with no intent to arrest or prosecute a suspect. The New Haven study observed several instances of "aggressive" interrogations by the police, and these frequently resulted in confessions or useful incriminating evidence.[48] These aggressive interrogations may be marginally within the law—suspects were read their rights—but whether the aggressiveness bordered on coercion could not easily be subject to review or challenge before a judge.

Police resistance to judicial due process decisions may have a variety of causes, but one study after another suggests that the organizational expectations of police officers are a primary factor in explaining it. Of course, norms and expectations are not the same in every police department. Some are quite insulated from reform pressures while others have more professional leaders and training processes.[49] But in all cases, police departments will view with suspicion court decisions that seem to interfere with their core mission of controlling and solving crime.

ATTITUDES AND PREFERENCES OF KEY AGENCY PERSONNEL. Another important factor in accounting for an organization's responses to judicial policies is the collective attitude of key agency personnel. The attitudes of key agency personnel may on occasion differ from the prevailing attitudes among the rank and file within an organization. Nevertheless, some of the research regarding the reactions of school systems to judicial policies suggests that the preferences of top officials can be responsible for changing the policies and practices of the entire organization. The impact of organizational leadership is most clearly demonstrated when new leaders take over an organization. In their study of Georgia school systems, Rodgers and Bullock noted that most school superintendents were committed to segregation during the late 1950s and early 1960s; indeed, some were actually leaders of local segregationist forces. However, counties that changed superintendents were more likely to desegregate since the new superintendents were less committed to segregation than their predecessors had been, and they also "felt no need to continue resistance for the purpose of defending past recalcitrance."[50] The same phenomenon occurred regarding acceptance of *Mapp, Miranda,* and similar decisions when a new chief of police took over.[51]

The collective attitudes of an organization's governing board are also important, even if the required changes run counter to organizational routines or norms. Robert Crain's study of school desegregation in the first decade after *Brown* found that when a school board opposed desegregation it made no moves to change either policies or practices.[52] Studying desegregation in the 1970s, David Morgan and Robert England reported a positive correlation between board support for desegregation and changes in levels of segregation in fifty-two metropolitan school districts.[53]

If key members of an implementing organization do not signal clear acceptance or rejection of judicial policies, the influence of the attitudes and preferences of others in the organization increases substantially. That is, if boards or high-level administrators take no action, make unclear agency policies, or show little interest in enforcement, lower level persons are likely to exercise discretionary power. In such a situation, this diffuse response is less visible and less controllable. Sometimes this diffuseness is what agency leaders want, as happened in the school systems that did not direct or monitor individual schools' practices or individual teachers' actions after *Schempp*. But such laxness can also get organizations in trouble, as we noted in our discussion of sexual harassment decisions.

INTERNAL CAPACITY TO RESIST EXTERNAL PRESSURES. As we have discussed, pressures external to organizations often shape the responses to judicial policies. In some circumstances, however, implementing agencies are able to avoid external pressures and follow their own preferences in responding to judicial actions. For example, a federal or state agency may be politically insulated from a local community. This separation allows the agency to respond as it wishes, consistent with its organizational goals and preferences, and not as local people would have it respond.

Implementing agencies may be insulated from external pressures in a number of ways. For example, agency leaders may be appointed by Washington, D.C., or Sacramento or Springfield, rather than locally, or governing boards may be composed of persons who are not employees of the organization (for example, university trustees). Agency leaders such as school superintendents may be professionally oriented outsiders rather than home-grown types. Civil service protections and tenure for educators shield personnel in many agencies from external pressures. Corporate factories or offices are often managed from faraway headquarters. For example, sometimes local protests occur when a company adopts a policy of giving benefits to same-sex partners, but the protests may be of little avail if the company is not locally owned. Over the twentieth century, in fact, the clear trend is toward greater insulation of both public and private organizations from local community pressures. Thus organizations are better able to resist environmental pressures relating to whether they accept or resist changed judicial policies.

Resisting external pressures through insulating features does not work in all instances, so an agency may use other organizational resources to retain its autonomy. One resource is the agency's legal staff. A large and high quality legal staff can develop alternate responses to a court decision and help accelerate or delay implementation. Less tangible resources include an agency's prestige, political support, and expertise. Good relations with the legislative or executive branches or with influential interest groups can be translated into support for an agency's response, whether it is evasive of or compliant with a Court decision. For example, an analysis of desegregation in ninety-two northern cities by David Kirby, Robert Harris, and Robert Crain suggests that in many cities mayors were a liberal force, often shielding the school board from protests for or against desegregation, and otherwise minimizing conflict. The mayors acted "to clarify the situation, to encourage meetings, to reassure groups, to discourage the civil rights movement from demonstrating."[54] The prestige of the mayoral office also helped push the school board to do whatever was necessary to maintain peace in the community.[55]

Implementing agencies may also use the norm of professional expertise to enable their personnel to respond in a particular way. Professionalism is particularly relevant to agencies such as those involved in health care and education. This characteristic is becoming more common among police and welfare agencies. Indeed, hardly any implementing agency is without some sense of professionalism. An argument in favor of the professional handling of a policy may be used to limit external pressures: "Why not let the doctors (teachers, police) handle it? They're the experts!" While the issue of compliance with judicial policy usually extends well beyond questions of professional judgment, agencies with strong public images of professional expertise nonetheless can substantially reduce outside pressures on their behavior. Research by Charles A. Johnson and Jon Bond revealed that after *Roe v. Wade* (1973) hospitals were not particularly responsive to community pressure to make abortion services available or to pressures from religious or right-to-life groups to limit abortions. The authors concluded that "there is little that individuals or groups in the community can do to influence hospital policy, even on a highly salient, non-technical issue such as abortion."[56]

SUMMARY

Like all public policies, judicial policies are rarely implemented by the policy's originators. Presidents, legislators, and judges rely on others in the political and social system to put their policies into action. The implementing population for judicial policies is varied and sometimes includes private individuals or organizations. However, the most common and visible implementation occurs in government agencies that provide public

services or public protection. Most of the research on this population concerns two subpopulations—educators and police officers—because most
Supreme Court decisions mandating dramatic changes have affected these
areas.

Implementing agencies usually follow through on judicial policies independent of direct judicial supervision. A court cannot initiate a review of
whether and how an agency is implementing a judicial policy; instead, it
must wait until a consumer challenges the agency's manner of implementation. Moreover, while courts have an array of punitive powers to deal
with noncompliance, including contempt citations, they are reluctant to
use them except for the most flagrant violations. Courts do not have the
power of the purse in most cases, especially to order the expenditure of
money an agency does not have, although some decisions mandating
improved prison conditions seem to have affected state appropriations.
Courts usually have few supervisory or oversight powers and, with rare
exceptions, cannot supervise day-to-day agency operations.

Most organizations follow similar patterns when confronted by an
applicable judicial decision. The agency must first interpret the decision to
determine what the court says the agency ought to be doing or whether
changes might be required. This stage tends to be guided by the policy
preferences of agencies in that an adverse decision is interpreted more narrowly than one supporting the agency's goals or expanding its powers.
Then, if the decision requires some response, the agency will initiate a
search for alternative courses of action. Finally, if it is necessary, the organization will change some of its policies or behavior.

Three factors account for the extent to which implementing organizations change their policies or behavior in response to a policy-making
court's desires. First, the communication of the decision to relevant implementing groups may lack clarity or be distorted, and this may encourage
agencies to do more or less than is expected of them by the court. Second,
the environmental setting of the agency may be influential. If community
traditions are inconsistent with a judicial policy or if relevant interest
groups are opposed to it, then little change can be expected. The opposite
is true if the policy reinforces existing traditions or if it is supported by
interest groups. Another environmental factor is the level of coercion used
to compel change by an agency. As coercion increases, the benefits of noncompliance decline and greater adjustments in policy and behavior can be
expected. Third, organizational characteristics—such as commitments to
existing policies and the attitudes of organizational personnel—influence
an agency's responses. These forces operate from within an organization

much like environmental forces operate from outside. In addition, the resources of an organization may affect its responses to a judicial policy, regardless of the organization's acceptance of the policy itself.

Notes

1. Lawrence Baum, "The Influence of Legislatures and Appellate Courts over the Policy Implementation Process," *Policy Studies Journal* 8 (1980): 561.

2. "Federal Bill Seeks an End to All Affirmative Action," *National Law Journal,* July 21, 1997, A-10.

3. Henry R. Glick, *Courts, Politics and Justice,* 3d ed. (New York: McGraw-Hill, 1993), 398–399.

4. This discussion of these organizational responses to judicial decisions is drawn from Charles A. Johnson, "Judicial Decisions and Organizational Change: A Theory," *Administration and Society* 11 (May 1979): 27–51.

5. Kenneth Dolbeare and Phillip Hammond, *The School Prayer Decisions: From Court Policy to Local Practice* (Chicago: University of Chicago Press, 1971), 90.

6. William K. Muir, *Prayer in the Public Schools: Law and Attitude Change* (Chicago: University of Chicago Press, 1967), and Richard Johnson, *The Dynamics of Compliance* (Evanston, Ill.: Northwestern University Press, 1967).

7. Charles A. Johnson, "Judicial Policies and Organizational Change: Some Theoretical and Empirical Notes on State Supreme Court Decisions and State Administrative Agencies," *Law and Society Review* 14 (1979): 27–56.

8. Neal Milner, *The Court and Local Law Enforcement: The Impact of* Miranda (Beverly Hills, Calif.: Sage, 1971), chaps. 5–8.

9. "Agency Policy: To Break the Law?" *National Law Journal,* June 9, 1997, A-12.

10. Ibid.

11. *Brown v. Board of Education of Topeka,* 349 U.S. 294 (1955), at 301.

12. Stephen Wasby, Anthony D'Amato, and Rosemary Metrailer, *Desegregation from Brown to Alexander* (Carbondale: Southern Illinois University Press, 1977), 123–126.

13. Quoted in Craig M. Bradley, *The Failure of the Criminal Justice Revolution* (Philadelphia: University of Pennsylvania Press, 1993), 41.

14. Wayne LaFave, "'Case-by-Case Adjudication' Versus 'Standardized Procedures'," *Supreme Court Review* (1974): 141.

15. Bradley, *The Failure of the Criminal Justice Procedure Revolution.*

16. James F. Spriggs, "The Supreme Court and Federal Administrative Agencies: A Resource-Based Theory and Analysis of Judicial Impact," *American Journal of Political Science* 40 (1996): Table 3, 1140.

17. Stephen Wasby, *Small Town Police and the Supreme Court: Hearing the Word* (Lexington, Mass.: Lexington Books, 1976), 120–122.

18. Elliott E. Slotnick and Jennifer A. Segal, *Television News and the Supreme Court: All the News That's Fit to Air?* (New York: Oxford University Press, 1998).

19. Richard Davis, *Decisions and Images: The Supreme Court and the Press* (Englewood Cliffs, N.J.: Prentice Hall, 1994).

20. John H. Laubauch, *School Prayers: Congress, the Courts, and the Public* (Washington, D.C.: Public Affairs Press, 1969), 138.

21. Donald Reich, "The Impact of Judicial Decision-Making: The School Prayer Cases," in *The Supreme Court as Policy-Maker: Three Studies on the Impact of Judicial Decisions,* ed. David Everson (Carbondale: Public Affairs Research Bureau, Southern Illinois University, 1968).

22. Dolbeare and Hammond, *The School Prayer Decisions,* 95–128.

23. Robert Alley, *Without a Prayer: Religious Expression in Public Schools* (Amherst, N.Y.: Prometheus Books, 1996).

24. Robert Crain, *The Politics of School Desegregation* (Chicago: Aldine, 1968), chaps. 2 and 7.

25. Harrell R. Rodgers Jr. and Charles S. Bullock III, *Law and Social Change: Civil Rights Laws and Their Consequences* (New York: McGraw-Hill, 1972), 72.

26. Bob Smith, *They Closed Their Schools* (Chapel Hill: University of North Carolina Press, 1965).

27. "Text of 96 Congressmen's Declaration on Integration," *New York Times,* March 12, 1956, 19.

28. Wasby, D'Amato, and Metrailer, *Desegregation from* Brown *to* Alexander, 168.

29. Rodgers and Bullock, *Law and Social Change,* 81–88.

30. Micheal Giles, "HEW Versus the Federal Courts: A Comparison of School Desegregation Enforcement," *American Politics Quarterly* 3 (1975): 81–90.

31. U.S. Commission on Civil Rights, *Fulfilling the Letter and Spirit of the Law: Desegregation of the Nation's Public Schools* (Washington, D.C.: U.S. Government Printing Office, 1976), 180, 174.

32. "Court Rebuffs Challenge to Judge's Mental Status," *National Law Journal,* November 4, 1996, A-7.

33. Harrell R. Rodgers Jr. and Charles S. Bullock III, *Coercion to Compliance* (Lexington, Mass.: Lexington Books, 1976), and Laubauch, *School Prayers,* 104–111.

34. Gary Orfield, Susan Eaton, and the Harvard Project on School Desegregation, *Dismantling Desegregation: The Quiet Reversal of* Brown v. Board of Education (New York: New Press, 1996), 118.

35. Jerome Skolnick, *Justice Without Trial* (New York: Wiley, 1966), chap. 10.

36. Neubauer, *Criminal Justice,* 180–182, and Comment, "Effect of *Mapp v. Ohio* on Police Search-and-Seizure Practices in Narcotics Cases," *Columbia Journal of Law and Social Problems* 4 (1968): 101.

37. Skolnick, *Justice Without Trial,* 155–162.

38. Neubauer, *Criminal Justice*, 173–174.

39. Milner, *The Court and Local Law Enforcement*, 177–179.

40. Michael Murphy, "The Problem of Compliance by Police Departments," *Texas Law Review* 44 (1966): 939–964.

41. See, for example, M. Kay Harris and Dudley Spiller, *After Decision: Implementation of Judicial Decrees in Correctional Settings* (Washington, D.C.: National Institute of Law Enforcement and Criminal Justice, 1977); Linda Harriman and Jeffrey Straussman, "Do Judges Determine Budget Decisions," *Public Administration Review* 43 (1983): 343–351; and Malcolm Feeley, "The Significance of Prison Corrections Cases: Budgets and Regions," *Law and Society Review* 23 (1989): 273–282.

42. John Fliter, "Another Look at the Judicial Power of the Purse: Courts, Corrections, and State Budgets," *Law and Society Review* 30 (1996): 399–414. See also William Taggert, "Redefining the Power of the Federal Judiciary: The Impact of Court Ordered Prison Reform on State Expenditures for Corrections," *Law and Society Review* 23 (1989): 241–271.

43. Skolnick, *Justice Without Trial*, 227.

44. Wasby, *Small Town Police and the Supreme Court*, 217–218.

45. Michael Wald et al., "Interrogations in New Haven: The Impact of *Miranda*," *Yale Law Journal* 76 (1967): 1519–1648.

46. Richard A. Leo, "Miranda's Revenge: Police Interrogation as a Confidence Game," *Law and Society Review* 30 (1996): 259–288, 261. See also Richard A. Leo and George C. Thomas III, eds., *The Miranda Debate: Law, Justice, and Policing* (Boston: Northeastern University Press, 1998).

47. "Some Officials Are Skirting Miranda Restraints to Get Confessions," *New York Times*, March 29, 1998, 1.

48. Wald et al., "Interrogations in New Haven," 1562.

49. See James Q. Wilson, *Varieties of Police Behavior* (Cambridge, Mass.: Harvard University Press, 1968).

50. Rodgers and Bullock, *Law and Social Change*, 44; see also David Morgan and Robert England, *Assessing the Progress of Large City School Desegregation: A Case Survey Approach* (Norman: Bureau of Government Research, University of Oklahoma, 1981), 68, and R. Johnson, *The Dynamics of Compliance*, 106–108.

51. Wilson, *Varieties of Police Behavior*.

52. Crain, *Politics of School Desegregation*.

53. Morgan and England, *Assessing the Progress of Desegregation*, 67.

54. David J. Kirby, T. Robert Harris, and Robert L. Crain, *Political Strategies in Northern School Desegregation* (Lexington, Mass.: Lexington Books, 1973), 107–108.

55. See also R. Johnson, *The Dynamics of Compliance*, 113–114.

56. Charles A. Johnson and Jon Bond, "Policy Implementation and Responsiveness in Nongovernmental Institutions: Hospital Abortion Services after *Roe v. Wade*," *Western Political Quarterly* 35 (September 1982): 403.

CHAPTER FOUR

The Consumer Population

The concept of consumers is familiar to all of us. To the question, "Who buys and uses American products and services?" the answer is, "We all do." The entire population is a consumer population. We can expand the concept of a consumer population beyond the use of products and services; we can think in terms of consuming judicial policies. Everybody is a consumer of judicial policies.

The composition of the consumer population varies according to the product. Laundry detergent, for example, has a fairly universal consumer population, whereas electrical generators are used by a small, specialized group of people. Court decisions likewise have different consumer populations. A judicial decision imposing higher taxes affects all taxpayers, one establishing to what extent people have a right to die affects all persons with a terminal illness (perhaps a lot of people over time), a decision relating to the patentability of new life forms affects a few commercial enterprises, while a ruling on who is at fault in an automobile accident may affect only the drivers and their insurance carriers.

Thus, while we can talk about the people of the United States as consumers of judicial policies in general, only persons who are affected by a particular decision constitute the consumer population for that decision. Consequently, our discussion of the consumer population will include a greater variety of actors than did previous chapters.

CHARACTERISTICS OF CONSUMERS AND CONSUMPTION

At the outset of this chapter, we must make a few conceptual distinctions with respect to the consumption of judicial policies. First, we distinguish the consumer population from the implementing and secondary populations, which may be in some instances related or similar. Second, we discuss the nature of judicial policies and whom they benefit. The remaining sections of this chapter discuss the responses of consumers to judicial policies.

Distinguishing the Consumer Population

Persons who use judicial policies—that is, who actually engage in acceptance and adjustment behavior (or who may have it forced upon them in the case of disadvantageous policies)—constitute the core of the consumer population. But often people are *potential* rather than actual users of a judicial policy: it is available to them but they choose not to use it. For example, many pregnant women decide to have babies although they could choose abortion. Nonetheless, such women must be considered as part of the consumer population for *Roe v. Wade.* A judicial policy has given them the choice; the availability of the choice puts them in the consumer population.

A more difficult problem in identifying the consumer population occurs when the use of judicial policies is contingent upon some prior happening. For example, a woman has to conceive before she can use the abortion decision. Do all fertile women constitute *Roe*'s consumer population? Or, to take another decision, one has to undergo police questioning in order to use *Miranda v. Arizona* (1966). Anyone might be arrested and questioned at some time in the future. Does that make all of us part of *Miranda*'s consumer population?

By and large, in the absence of the contingency that makes the judicial policy available to them, we will treat such persons as part of the secondary population, not the consumer population. However, we recognize that there are gradations of potential consumption and will not be dogmatic. Clearly, large numbers of women will become pregnant at some time in their lives, whereas only a minuscule proportion of the general public will ever be subject to police interrogation. Generally, the more likely a contingency is to occur, the more reasonable it is to include a large number of people in at least the periphery of the consumer population.

CONSUMERS AND IMPLEMENTORS. The consumer population differs from the implementing population, but in one sense implementors are often consumers. The police may be as disadvantaged by *Miranda* as suspects are advantaged by it. A busing order may inconvenience school administrators almost as much as it does the pupils who dislike being bused across town. But the implementors are affected in their official capacity and so remain in the implementing population for the policy. We should note, however, that nongovernmental consumers sometimes perform implementation functions. Realtors, for instance, are key players in making fair housing decisions (such as *Jones v. Mayer Co.*, 1968) and laws work. During the 1960s, however, the National Association of Real Estate Brokers along with many local realtors' associations advised their members to ignore fair housing decisions and laws.[1]

CONSUMERS AND SECONDARY GROUPS. It is similarly useful to distinguish the consumer population from the secondary population. Members of the latter are not personally affected by a judicial policy. They receive no real benefits, and no real disadvantages are imposed upon them. Of course, they may be interested in the policy—at times more intensely than those actually affected. But their interest is motivated by ideological or religious values or perhaps simply by sympathy toward friends who are actually affected by the policy. It is not an interest based upon a sense of gain or loss to one's own life. For example, a Catholic priest will never consume the Court's abortion policy personally, although he may be vitally interested in it, counsel women about it, and perhaps engage in public protest or political opposition.

Once again, it is not always possible to separate the populations neatly. For instance, it is difficult to specify in which population the parents of a woman considering an abortion should be placed. Obviously, the possibility of a grandchild is of more immediate concern to them than it is to the priest. Generally, however, the impact of the woman's decision will not be nearly as great on her parents' lives as it will be on that of the father—to say nothing of the woman herself. In short, there are gray areas between the populations; for us, the degree to which a judicial policy affects a person's life directly is the crucial element distinguishing the consumer from the secondary population.

For some judicial policies, everyone is a consumer and there is no secondary population. The Supreme Court's reapportionment decisions of the 1960s provide a prime example. While the Court's orders were directed to state legislators, the true consumers were the voters whom the legislators represented. Urban and suburban residents gained political power; rural voters lost it. Several scholars have concluded that state expenditures for such urban concerns as education and welfare rose more rapidly as state legislatures were reapportioned.[2] Similarly, research by Mathew McCubbins and Thomas Schwartz shows that a reapportioned national House of Representatives spawned policy changes that reallocated benefits to urban and suburban residents.[3] More recently, it has been argued that the policy of creating a number of black majority congressional districts in the South has enhanced Republican chances in many other districts because they now contain fewer African Americans. The Supreme Court's rejection of oddly shaped black majority districts in *Shaw v. Reno* (1993) and subsequent cases may reduce Republican strength among southern representatives in Congress.[4]

Judicial decisions that impose economic gains or losses on nearly everyone can have an all-encompassing consumer population, as did, for example, the New Jersey Supreme Court decision virtually establishing a state income tax (*Robinson v. Cahill,* 1975) or the 1982 federal district court ruling breaking up the Bell Telephone System, which increased the cost of local telephone service and decreased the cost of long-distance service. In some cases, however, the temptation to say that society as a whole constitutes the consumer population must be resisted. Politicians sometimes claim, for instance, that everyone is adversely affected by decisions upholding defendants' rights such as *Miranda v. Arizona* because fewer criminals will be brought to justice. But this linkage is too remote and speculative to justify putting the whole public into such cases' consumer population.

In the remainder of this chapter, we will consider the acceptance and adjustment behavior of the consumer population. We will focus on the degree to which individuals and organizations accept relevant policies and alter their thinking and patterns of behavior or institutional arrangements to accommodate the policies. Since the reactions of consumers to judicial policies that benefit them are likely to be quite different from the reactions of consumers to policies that are disadvantageous, we will consider the acceptance and adjustment behavior for each circumstance separately.

Compared with members of the interpreting, implementing, and (to some extent) secondary populations, members of the consumer population are more diverse and their behavior is more difficult to assess because it is less visible. Consequently, researchers have more difficulty probing their thinking and behavior. This deficiency is unfortunate because knowledge about consumption is crucial to understanding the ultimate impact of judicial policies; like a business executive, we are trying to find out how the product "sells." Because "sales" data on judicial policies are sparse, this chapter at times relies on speculation or inference.

Types of Consumption

ADVANTAGEOUS AND DISADVANTAGEOUS CONSUMPTION. We normally think of economic consumption as a beneficial activity. We don't buy an item unless we believe that it will make a contribution to our well-being. In classical economic theory there are no losers in such transactions; everyone benefits.

The consumption of judicial policies, however, can be disadvantageous as well as advantageous. Lawsuits are adversarial by their nature and thus require losers as well as winners; they are zero sum games—what one party gains the other loses. Often suits pit consumer against consumer; medical malpractice or auto accident victims gain while physicians, hospitals, or other drivers (and their insurers) lose. Some state court decisions are landmarks because they empower actual consumers to sue producers who were previously protected by law. For example, the classic *MacPherson v. Buick Motor Co.* (1916) case undercut the ancient doctrine of privity (requiring a direct sales relationship between the plaintiff and defendant), thus allowing purchasers to sue manufacturers (rather than retailers) for unsafe products. *Sindell v. Abbott Laboratories* (1980) apportioned liability by market share when the specific manufacturers of products that were found harmful (chemicals, medicines, and the like) could not be identified.

But in many suits involving public policy, one side is not a part of the consumer population and the other is. Cases in which the government or one of its agencies is a party often pit the interests of an implementing population against those of a relevant group of consumers. *Miranda,* for instance, broadened the rights of criminal suspects (the consumers) by regulating the behavior of the police (an implementing agency). By contrast, in *U.S. v. Salerno* (1987) the Supreme Court upheld the Bail Reform Act of 1984, which allows judges to deny bail to a defendant when there is reason to believe that he or she might commit a crime while free on bail. In these cases, members of the affected consumer population either universally benefited from a judicial policy or universally suffered disadvantages from it.

At times, however, consumers who are similarly affected by a decision can feel quite differently about it. Some high school athletes might be nervous or offended by the Court's decision in *Vernonia School District v. Acton* (1995) allowing random drug tests of players, while others might be gratified to know that their teammates were drug free. Likewise, children who were glad to say prayers in school would see *Abington School District v. Schempp* (1963) as disadvantageous, while those who were uncomfortable reciting prayers in school would welcome it.

Sometimes when a government agency is a party to a suit, it is not so much an implementor as it is a representative of one element of the consumer population. Here, too, the zero-sum-game situation prevails. Good examples of such representation can be found in regulatory agencies, which often try to protect the interests of the industry they supervise. When the Supreme Court struck down the Virginia Board of Pharmacy's rule prohibiting pharmacists from advertising drug prices (*Virginia State Board of Pharmacy v. Virginia Citizens Consumer Council*, 1976), the real losers were pharmacists. The main purpose of the rule had been to discourage competitive pricing and thus keep pharmacy profits up. But consumers may also pay a price; nowadays large pharmaceutical companies advertise products to lower cholesterol, grow hair, relieve allergies, and so on, directly to the public. As a consequence, physicians may feel pressured to prescribe what the patient asks for even though more effective or less expensive alternatives may exist. [5]

For that matter, affirmative action policies are like zero sum games. When a government agency encourages or mandates more hiring (or university admissions) for minorities or women, it means that fewer white males will get the jobs or places. Thus affirmative action decisions such as those discussed in Chapter 2 have two sets of consumers, white males and other persons. This helps explain why both public debate and litigation concerning affirmative action is so intense.

Gains or losses are not always strictly economic. In decisions involving environmental regulation, for example, profits may be at stake for corporations, but other considerations motivate nature lovers. (Of course, environmentalists can also argue that a community may suffer long-term economic loss from poor air quality, coastal erosion, or the like.)

DIRECT AND INDIRECT CONSUMPTION. Returning to our products and services analogy, we can see that there may be more than one level of consumption. As we mentioned, most of us purchase laundry detergents but almost never buy electric generators. The latter are purchased by utility companies. But the capacity and efficiency of the generators will affect all of us in terms of the reliability and cost of electricity. Thus a larger set of consumers may be *indirectly* affected by the choices of a smaller population that consumes more directly.

Some judicial policies have both direct and indirect consumer populations. For example, in *Bates v. Arizona Bar* (1977) the Supreme Court ruled that lawyers could advertise their legal services. Presumably, competitive advertising benefits the public's ability to find the most appropriate services and prices. But separate research by Lauren Bowen and Carroll Seron revealed that only about a third of attorneys with many short-term clients (such as divorce or auto accident cases) actually advertise (and then mostly in the phone book), and only a handful list prices for routine services.[6] When large numbers of attorneys choose not to advertise, they minimize the advantages of *Bates* to the public.

The same is true of abortion providers. For reasons of conscience, status, or avoidance of controversy, fewer hospitals and gynecologists perform abortions than did in the 1970s. Abortions are now largely obtained at specialized women's clinics. These are located almost exclusively in urban areas, so that rural women may have to travel a long distance to have an abortion.[7] Moreover, pro-life groups try to discourage abortion by protesting at the clinics, some extreme ones through blockades and other semi-violent tactics (see Chapter 1). (In fact, there have been numerous clinic bombings and some murders.) While the number of abortions has fallen by 7 or 8 percent in the 1990s, it is not at all certain that the protests have caused the decline. But it is clear that pressures on and the responses of the direct consumer population can minimize the impact of an advantageous judicial policy.

Disadvantageous judicial policies may also have an indirect consumer population. An example of one that affected college faculty and students occurred in 1990, when a federal district court ruled that the copyright law required copy shops to obtain permission before making multiple copies of parts of books or articles (*Princeton University Press v. Michigan Documents Service,* 1996). Because obtaining permission required payment to publishers as well as considerable paperwork, instructors (indirect consumers) often no longer bothered to put their own "texts" on sale in copy shops, and students (also indirect consumers) spent more time in library stacks or reserve rooms reading the assigned articles in their original journals.

RESPONSES TO BENEFICIAL DECISIONS

The responses of consumer populations may depend heavily on whether particular decisions are seen as beneficial or as adverse. Some judicial decisions improve consumers' lives; others can be detrimental. In our discussion of each type of decision, we distinguish between situations where consumers need not take any action to receive the advantages or disadvantages of a judicial decision and those where some action is necessary to secure a decision's benefits or avoid its inconveniences.

Automatic Consumption

Often benefits accrue to consumers automatically. No action—that is, no acceptance decision or behavior—on the part of the consumer is necessary. All necessary adjustments are performed by the implementing population. Put another way, there is no choice about being a consumer; everyone in the affected population consumes the policy.

One type of automatic consumption occurs when court decisions restrain government officials or agencies from behaving in unlawful ways or require them to engage in new behavior patterns in certain situations. Courts especially do this in the criminal justice area. Perhaps the most notable example is *Gideon v. Wainwright* (1963) and *Argersinger v. Hamlin* (1972), in which the Court held that indigent defendants in felony cases and in misdemeanor cases where a jail sentence is likely are entitled to be represented by counsel at trial. Also, in the 1970s and 1980s numerous lower federal courts ruled that state and local prisons had to meet minimum provisions for space, sanitation, and medical care.[8] A more recent example comes from two Supreme Court cases, *Batson v. Kentucky* (1986) and *Georgia v. McCullom* (1992), holding that potential jurors in criminal cases could not be peremptorily challenged (removed without cause) because of their race. Defendants who believe that jurors of their own race will be more sympathetic to them automatically benefit from these cases.

We must note that automatic benefits are sometimes more impressive on paper than in practice. Heavy caseloads impair the quality of indigents' defense and the low compensation of public defenders does not attract the most competent attorneys.[9] (These factors prolong death penalty cases when "inadequate representation by counsel" claims are raised on appeal.) Court orders have improved the worst prison conditions, but they cannot prevent prison officials from mistreating their charges in less visible ways.[10] *Batson* and *McCullom* give little guidance to judges in detecting racially motivated peremptory challenges; one researcher has charged that

Batson and its progeny have proven less an obstacle to discrimination than a road map to it. Parties now have a good idea of what they can and cannot get away with in eliminating jurors and adjust their means to suit the desired end.[11]

Illustrating this, a training video for new prosecutors in Philadelphia gave specific advice on how to get around *Batson*.[12]

Automatic benefits can affect public expenditures also. Prison reform decisions, for example, have contributed to state tax increases.[13] An even greater fiscal impact occurred in the dozen or so states whose supreme court has ruled that unequal per pupil spending between poorer and wealthier school districts violates their state constitution. In most of these states, the legislature has revised the school taxing and expenditure system to allot more money to poorer districts. Presumably pupils in these districts will benefit. However, the additional spending usually requires additional taxes. Several state supreme courts have rejected claims that unequal per pupil spending violates the state constitution; perhaps these courts were reluctant to impose the new costs on the state's residents.[14]

Economic benefits accrue automatically when a court decision confers advantages on a group of people in the form of lower prices or higher quality goods and services. For example, in *Quill Corp. v. North Dakota* (1992), the Supreme Court halted states' attempts to apply sales taxes to mail order items purchased outside the state.

Sometimes economic benefits are given to indirect consumers at the discretion of the direct consumer population. For example, in 1975 the Supreme Court held that bar association minimum fee schedules violated the Sherman Antitrust Act (*Goldfarb v. Virginia State Bar*). Similarly, in 1980 the Court held that so-called fair trade laws establishing minimum prices for liquor were illegal (*California Liquor Dealers v. Midcal Aluminum*). Presumably these cases led some attorneys and liquor stores to charge lower prices, although the impact of the cases has not been systematically studied.

Consumption by Choice

Many judicial policies are structured so that members of the consumer population have to act in order to take advantage of them. That is, the consumer is given an option or choice that previously did not exist or that was much more difficult to exercise. However, the direct benefits of the policy are gained only when the person makes the newly available choice. In contrast to the automatic consumption of actual benefits, these policies create only a *potential* consumer population. Potential consumers must become actual consumers on their own volition.

Quite often members of the potential consumer population are not interested in taking advantage of a particular judicial policy. This is particularly true when the policy addresses behavior that has little direct or personal benefit. Supreme Court decisions expanding the meaning of the First Amendment's freedom of speech and press clauses are a good example. Not many of us take our soapbox down to a city park or distribute pamphlets at the airport, even though courts have held that we have the right to do so.

Some potential consumers may reject a policy, believing it to be harmful or immoral rather than beneficial. For instance, a study by James Levine revealed that following a series of liberal Supreme Court decisions, many bookstore proprietors refused to stock salacious material because of personal objections to it or fear of offending their customers.[15] National boycotts called by "family values" groups against stores displaying or even carrying *Playboy* or *Hustler* have pressured many stores into not selling "adult" magazines. Likewise, many women who are unhappy at finding themselves pregnant will reject the abortion alternative because it violates their strongly held religious or ethical beliefs.

Even when consumers have no principled objection to a judicial policy, other factors may convince them not to take advantage of it. As noted earlier, a pregnant woman might not get an abortion for reasons such as cost or the absence of a local clinic. Family, church, or community counseling or pressures or the receipt of emotional or economic support from Birthright or similar pro-life groups may lead her to carry the fetus to term. Indeed, the whole purpose behind laws that restrict access to abortion by such means as refusing Medicaid funds or requiring parental permission (see Chapter 1) is to discourage women from choosing the abortion option.

Other people may make no acceptance decision at all. For example, some people may not be offended by the availability of X-rated videos, but they may have no personal interest in viewing them. Similarly, a person may lack the motivation or temperament to engage in picketing or door-to-door canvassing even though he or she has no objections to others doing so.

Of course, many people do actually consume the benefits conferred on the public by broad-scope decisions. Millions of customers do rent adult videos, and some R-rated films of the 1990s like "Basic Instinct" (which thirty years earlier would have been banned as obscene almost everywhere) are nationwide hits with millions of viewers. Some people do picket or pass out material on behalf of political, social, or economic causes. Such activity, in turn, can draw attention to societal grievances and become a cutting edge of change—as happened with the civil rights and anti–Vietnam War demonstrations of the 1960s. As for abortions, about 1.4 million are performed each year in the United States.[16] This compares with approximately 3.9 million births annually. Although the total number of pregnancies is unknown due to miscarriages, as many as one-quarter of all pregnancies in this country terminate in abortion. Obviously, many women are taking advantage of this Supreme Court policy. And the Court, of course, never intended or believed that all pregnant women would choose abortion; it only intended that they have a choice.

Nevertheless, at times, real impediments can make seemingly advantageous options hollow. For example, in the decade following *Brown v. Board of Education* (1954), exceedingly few African Americans tried to enroll their children in previously all-white schools.[17] Many believed that the personal disadvantages of taking such action outweighed its benefits. Negative considerations might include the probable loss of employment or income, the disruption of existing relationships with the white community (and perhaps part of the black community also), harassment of their children in school, and the possibility of injury or even death—to say nothing of the cost in time, energy, and perhaps money of litigating a desegregation suit for several years. Because of these impediments, Congress (in the 1964 Civil Rights Act) empowered the Justice Department to file integration suits itself and shortly afterward mandated that local school boards adopt desegregation plans as a condition for receiving federal aid. The courts overcame another impediment when they ordered cross-district busing to get around segregated housing patterns in urban areas. Thus, instead of remaining potential consumers who had to overcome barriers in order to actually consume *Brown*'s benefits, African Americans became actual consumers when the courts automatically conferred benefits.

Of course, impediments are not always alleviated. The Supreme Court has held that subdivision developers cannot discriminate on the basis of race (*Jones v. Alfred H. Mayer Co.,* 1968). But African Americans generally make less money than whites, and no programs exist to assist them in particular in meeting the costs of purchasing a home. This discrepancy helps explain why housing remains largely segregated. Indeed, the absence of money can be a major impediment to anyone's enjoying a great many of the benefits allowed by law.

Habitual community behavior patterns can also rob advantageous decisions of actuality. Despite the complete abolition of legal segregation, many rural areas in the South retain racial separation in such things as funeral homes, barber and beauty shops, restaurants, bars, and even restrooms. As an African American woman explaining her presence in a dentist's separate waiting room put it, "This is where we always went, so that's where we go." A black undertaker put it more generally, "It's more difficult to change a habit than a law."[18] By contrast, there is much less segregation in the urban South. The distance between small southern towns and cities like Charlotte or Atlanta may be better measured in decades than in mileage.

Even decisions that seem to bring a direct economic advantage may not always be accepted by consumers. As we have noted, only a comparative handful of attorneys advertise their services beyond the telephone book despite the Supreme Court's *Bates* decision. While some attorneys believe that the probable returns from advertising are not worth the energy and expense, others do not accept the legitimacy of professional advertising.[19] Indeed, powerful figures in the legal profession, including the late Chief Justice Warren E. Burger, have denounced such advertisements.[20] Of course, those in the public who need legal services—the indirect consumers—receive few benefits if the direct consumer population rejects the policy.

Miranda v. Arizona (1966) is one judicial policy that has been the subject of some fairly systematic research. In this famous case, the Supreme Court required that suspects undergoing in-custody police interrogation be informed that they have the right to remain silent, that anything they say can be used against them in court, that they may have an attorney present during the questioning, and that if they cannot afford one, an attorney will be provided for them before questioning begins. Following *Miranda* some researchers examined arrest/interrogation/charge records, and a few even observed police interrogations or interviewed suspects in about a dozen cities.[21]

Legal scholar Paul Cassell analyzed these studies. He determined that there were 16 percent fewer confessions following *Miranda*. He further estimates that confessions were absolutely necessary for conviction in nearly one-quarter of the cases where they were obtained. Thus, he concludes, *Miranda* costs society almost 4 percent fewer convictions than would otherwise occur.[22] Cassell's figures can be disputed. Law professor Stephen Schulhofer analyzed the same data but used different assumptions (for example, that the police are better adjusted to *Miranda* in the 1990s than

---

BOX 4-1
Consumer Reaction to a Beneficial Decision: *Miranda v. Arizona*

Even after *Miranda* warnings have been given, a substantial proportion of suspects—from 40 to 50 percent—in all the cities that have been studied readily answered questions, did not request to have a lawyer present, and gave incriminating statements to the police despite the *Miranda* warnings. Moreover, of those who did not give incriminating statements, a sizable proportion were nonetheless willing to talk with police.

Observations and interviews revealed that a communication problem explained as much as 25 percent of the cooperation; the suspects simply did not understand the meaning of the warning.[a] The following are typical of the misinterpretations made by suspects regarding their right to have a lawyer present:

- "The police had some lawyer of their own who was working with them."
- "It means that I would have to pay for a lawyer."
- "They planned to appoint someone at court."

Similarly, the right to silence was misunderstood:

- "If I . . . like tried to bribe them they would use it against me in court."
- "I should . . . say something so they could use it in evidence in court.[b]

Even when the warnings were adequately understood, some suspects refused to take them at face value. They cynically believed that the warnings were only a formality, a card read by the police because they had to, and that the police would not really forgo interrogation or allow an attorney to be present. For these suspects no meaningful choice existed.

But the largest group of suspects who failed to take advantage of *Miranda* rejected it not out of misunderstanding or cynicism but because they believed it was better to cooperate with the police. Suspects might come to such a decision for several reasons. One, of course, might be conscience: "I did it and I'm sorry." Or a suspect might perceive that he or she could not hide guilt any

---

they were immediately following the decision), and concluded that less than 1 percent fewer convictions resulted from *Miranda*.[23]

The Supreme Court justices expected that most suspects would take advantage of their *Miranda* rights.[24] And many of them did. But Box 4-1

way—witnesses would testify or damning evidence was already available. Perhaps cooperation would get a shorter sentence.

Most suspects quite naturally believed that refusing to talk or insisting upon the presence of an attorney would be a tacit admission of guilt. Such behavior would only intensify police suspicion and investigation. The best course, then, would be to deflect suspicion from oneself by appearing to be cooperative—to take the risk of lying or telling less than the whole truth.

The most rational course for most suspects (assuming they want to avoid prosecution) is to remain silent and request an attorney. However, the interrogation atmosphere is not conducive to rationality.

> The suspect arrested and brought downtown for questioning is in a crisis-laden situation. The stakes for him are high—often his freedom for a few or many years—and his prospects hinge on decisions that must be made quickly: To cooperate and hope for lenience, to try and talk his way out, to stand adamantly on his rights . . . the likely consequences of the alternatives open to him are unclear—how much lenience cooperation may earn, how likely fast talk is to succeed, how much a steadfast refusal to talk may contribute to a decision by the police, prosecutor or judge to "throw the book" at him.[c]

In such situations many people can't act rationally. Thus, they do what many of us do when we find ourselves alone in a strange situation: take the path of least resistance, which under the circumstances means cooperating with the police.

[a] A later test survey showed that less than half of ordinary adults understood the *Miranda* warnings in their entirety. See Thomas Grisso, "Juveniles' Capacity to Waive *Miranda* Rights: An Empirical Analysis," *California Law Review* 68 (1980): 1152.

[b] Richard J. Medalie et al., "Custodial Police Interrogation in Our Nation's Capital: An Attempt to Implement *Miranda*," *Michigan Law Review* 66 (1968): 1375, 1378.

[c] Michael Wald et al., "Interrogations in New Haven: The Impact of *Miranda*," *Yale Law Review* 76 (1967): 1613–1614.

makes it clear that consumer behavior in response to *Miranda* does not fulfill the rational model contemplated by the Court. Consumers of judicial decisions do not always adopt rational self-interested behavior even when much is at stake.

The consequences of judicial policies that are disadvantageous to members of the consumer population are analogous to those of advantageous policies. Disadvantageous decisions tend to be imposed much more automatically upon the consumers; one rarely chooses to accept and adjust to a detrimental situation. Often there is no way for the consumer to avoid the imposition of an undesirable policy. But at times at least some members of the consumer population have a choice. They can choose whether to accept and adjust to the adverse decision or whether to engage in some type of alternative behavior with fewer negative consequences.

Automatic Imposition

For some disadvantageous judicial policies, acceptance behavior is simply an irrelevant concept and defiance is not an option. For example, in *Missouri v. Jenkins I* (1989) the Supreme Court upheld a desegregation decree that led to a substantial increase in Kansas City area school taxes. If your tax rate is increased, you must pay whether you like it or not. So you must adjust your budget by spending less money on other things.

Judicial policies in zero-sum-game disputes will leave losing segments of the consumer population little choice but to live with the policy. For instance, in the classic cases of *Lochner v. New York* (1905) and *Adkins v. Children's Hospital* (1923), where the Supreme Court struck down maximum-hour and minimum-wage legislation, a considerable economic disadvantage was imposed on large groups of workers. Although the rare worker may have quit as a result of one of these decisions, in the aggregate the workers had no choice but to suffer the consequences of the employers' imposition of long hours and low wages. The same holds true for the Court's negation of laws regulating child labor (*Hammer v. Dagenhart,* 1918; *Bailey v. Drexel Furniture Co.,* 1922). When the Court reversed these policies in *West Coast Hotel Co. v. Parrish* (1937) and *U.S. v. Darby Lumber Co.* (1941), it imposed an automatic disadvantage on companies that were profiting from long hours, low wages, and child labor.

Environmental law often involves zero-sum litigation. Courts are sometimes called on to settle disputes between environmentalists and growth-oriented businesses. Victories for the former often have considerable adverse economic consequences for the business community, while decisions favoring business may have a less quantitative but no less significant detrimental impact upon many persons' quality of life. The Supreme Court, however, has resisted efforts to find environmental guarantees in the Constitution. Thus the Court's role in these clashes involves interpreting statutes such as the Endangered Species or the Toxic Substances Control acts.[25] In such cases, when Congress feels strongly that the outcome is not good public policy, it can reverse the Court's action, as it did to allow the construction of an oil pipeline across Alaska and a dam in Tennessee that wiped out a species of snail darters.[26]

Choosing Alternative Adjustment Behavior

When a disadvantageous judicial policy is not automatically imposed upon its consumer population, consumers accept or reject the policy in accordance with their assessment of the situation. One form of acceptance occurs when people come to believe that the policy, though disadvantageous to them personally, is a legitimate one: that it may be required by the Constitution or that it may serve the overall public interest. Political scientists have found that such adjustments can occur after a Supreme Court ruling.[27] But people can also accept a disadvantageous policy without coming to believe in its legitimacy. They accept it in the sense that they decide that their best option is simply to live with the policy and adjust their behavior accordingly. Most people do in fact live with many policies, judicial or otherwise, that they perceive as disadvantageous; if this were not so, we would not live in an ordered society.

At times, however, members of the consumer population will decide not to accept a judicial policy. In such situations they have essentially two choices: they can refuse to alter their behavior, thereby defying the policy; or they can adjust their behavior so as to avoid the policy's impact without being defiant.

DEFIANCE. On rare occasions, defiance is outright and confrontational. Radicals in so-called militia groups have refused to recognize the legitimacy of judicial policies (as well as those of other government institutions).[28] On a less violent note, journalists have occasionally defied subpoenas or refused to testify in court despite a Supreme Court ruling that they have the same obligation as other members of the public in this regard (*Branzburg v. Hayes,* 1972). This holding is disadvantageous to journalists, as it makes it less likely that persons who want anonymity will talk to them. A classic act of defiance took place in 1978, when *New York Times* reporter Myron Farber spent forty days in jail and the *Times* was fined heavily for refusing to give the trial judge notes he made while investigating a murder case.[29] In general, however, defiant acts of consumers are less dramatic and visible than those of implementors.

AVOIDANCE. Often consumers can avoid the full impact of a disadvantageous judicial policy by engaging in behavior that minimizes or evades the policy's consequences. Such adjustment behavior usually incurs a cost. Sometimes the cost is not burdensome. For example, in recent years some state and local school systems have adopted a moment of silence at the beginning of each day to reduce the impact of the school prayer decision. Similarly, when the Supreme Court found school-sponsored baccalaureate service prayers unconstitutional (*Lee v. Weisman,* 1992), students in some schools organized private services with prayers. Often, however, the costs are considerable. Pregnant poor women who want an abortion might have to pay several hundred dollars for one following the Supreme Court's 1980 *Harris v. McRae* decision upholding Congress's cutoff of Medicaid payments for this purpose (the Hyde Amendment). The cost is considerable but perhaps not insurmountable for a poor woman.

Banning organized prayers or cutting off abortion funds are examples of prohibitive judicial policies. These policies tell consumers that they cannot do something they want to do or have been doing, or at least that they cannot do it in the most habitual or effective manner. They tell the consumer: "Thou shalt not. . . . " Courts are reluctant to issue "thou shalt" commands to consumers because they are difficult to enforce and they generate a high degree of resentment. However, the courts have had to impose "thou shalt" commands in developing desegregation policies that a large number of whites perceived as being to their disadvantage, particularly with regard to busing, equal employment opportunities, and fair housing.

Let us look at how white consumers reacted to court-ordered busing, an area where there has been a fair amount of social science research. Busing required thousands of white children, often in elementary schools, to be transported to classes some miles away rather than being assigned to the nearest school. White parents and pupils found the long rides and their consequences for home life inconvenient. (Many African Americans were also inconvenienced by busing, but in general they felt that busing was more beneficial than disadvantageous to them.) Also, many whites perceived a disadvantage in attending formerly all-black, inner-city schools, which they felt were intellectually and physically inferior to the predominantly white schools. Many also wanted to avoid black-majority schools.

Avoidance is possible and legal. One method of evading busing is for parents to place their children in a private school. Another is for the family to move to a different area, perhaps in the suburbs, that is unaffected by the busing order. These two forms of avoidance behavior are often termed white flight. Obviously, there are considerable costs in money and inconvenience to white flight. Tuition at a private school is expensive, and the school may be inconveniently located. A house in the suburbs may be high priced and may not be convenient to the parents' jobs. But avoidance can be motivated by emotion at least as much as by calculation.

Moving to the suburbs and sending children to private schools also occur for reasons independent of racial considerations. Researchers explored to what extent this pattern was motivated by busing plans. Some found that busing contributed significantly to white flight, while others found virtually no relationship. This disparity in findings has been accompanied by much controversy between the researchers, reflecting in part different data bases and focuses and in part the researchers' own opinions about busing. Perhaps the chief proponent of a linkage is sociologist James Coleman, who studied sixty-six large and mid-sized school districts. He concluded:

> The extremely strong reactions of individual whites in moving their children out of large districts engaged in massive and rapid desegregation suggests that in the long run the policies that have been pursued will defeat the purpose of increasing overall contact among the races in the schools. . . . Thus a major policy implication of this analysis is that in an area such as school desegregation, which has important consequences for individuals and in which individuals retain control of some actions that can, in the end, defeat the policy, the courts are probably the worst instrument of social policy.[30]

Some federal courts have accepted Coleman's thesis.[31]

Political scientist Christine Rossell reached the opposite conclusion after analyzing data from eighty-six school districts. She found that only two of them showed significant white flight above and beyond normal out-migration patterns and that even in those two cities the flight was "minimal and temporary." Desegregation, she concluded, was not substantially related to white flight.[32] In a more recent study, Gary Orfield and Susan Eaton, also political scientists, second Rossell's finding, noting that the decline in white enrollment in cities like New York, Chicago, and Houston—which did not have mandatory busing—paralleled those in Detroit and Atlanta, which did have mandatory busing orders in effect.

Orfield and Eaton also attribute the decline to a considerable fall-off of the white birth rate compared with that of minorities.[33]

These scholars based their findings on inferences drawn from changes in school enrollment data. Three political scientists at Florida Atlantic University, Micheal Giles, Douglas Gatlin, and Everett Cataldo, used another approach: interviewing white parents in seven Florida counties subject to court-ordered busing about their attitudes and behavior.[34] Although a large number of parents did not agree with or want to accept the busing order, only about 15 percent actually avoided busing by sending their children to private schools or by moving away. (As the entire county was included in the busing order, moving was not as easy to do as it might have been in some other locales.) Parental income was the strongest explanation for avoidance. Ironically, the intensity of white racism was negatively associated with avoidance behavior. This is because racism was greatest among lower-income parents who could not afford private schools. Higher-income parents, although they were less racist and less bothered by busing for other reasons, more often avoided the busing policy because they had the capacity to do so.

The findings we have outlined suggest the general proposition that attitudes have a far greater effect on acceptance decisions than upon adjustment behavior. Behavior is more affected by the magnitude of the inconvenience and the consumer's capacity to avoid compliance.[35] Nonetheless, attitudes sometimes lead to avoidance activities. Existing research gives no precise answer about the degree to which busing—or other forms of court-ordered desegregation—cause white flight. But clearly some parents acted to avoid busing or other significant desegregation. Private and largely all-white schools proliferated throughout the South in the 1970s and early 1980s. And busing has certainly been one of several factors that have induced families to move to the suburbs.

SUMMARY

The consumer population is more varied than the interpreting or implementing populations. For some judicial policies it consists of the general public while for others it is composed of only a handful of persons.

Consumption is advantageous when affected persons perceive themselves as benefiting from the judicial decision. Consumption is disadvantageous to persons who believe they are adversely affected by a policy.

Moreover, consumption can be direct or indirect. Individuals who are directly affected by a policy take part in direct consumption. Those who receive benefits or disadvantages depending upon consumption choices made by another group are indirect consumers.

Some judicial policies are consumed automatically: benefits or disadvantages accrue to individuals without any action on their part. Automatic consumption occurs when a court constrains an implementing agency from granting an advantage or imposing a disadvantage upon a group, or, conversely, when the court requires such a response of the agency. Automatic consumption also occurs when a judicial policy leads to an increase or decrease in the price of goods or services or when it affects the quality of persons' lives, as does a decision regarding safety conditions in the workplace.

Other judicial decisions are consumed by choice. Decisions to consume beneficial policies are affected by such things as a person's temperament, interest, beliefs, or knowledge; the availability of opportunities; and the monetary and social costs involved. For combinations of these reasons, many people do not take advantage of judicial policies. For example, many video store customers do not rent sexually explicit films; many arrested persons do not exercise their *Miranda* rights; and many African Americans do not buy homes in the suburbs.

When disadvantageous consumption is not automatic, members of the consumer population have the choice of accepting the disabilities imposed or of engaging in alternative adjustment behavior. The choice depends upon two main variables: their perception of the legitimacy of the judicial policy and their assessment of the monetary and psychological costs of abiding by the policy versus not abiding by it. One alternative form of adjustment behavior is defiance, which is uncommon and is usually followed only as a matter of principle. Another is avoidance, which is more common; avoidance occurs when people take steps to get away from the situation covered by the judicial policy. Sometimes avoidance can be simple; at other times it can be costly, as when parents send their children to private schools to avoid a busing order.

Notes

1. Gerald N. Rosenberg, *The Hollow Hope: Can the Courts Bring About Social Change?* (Chicago: University of Chicago Press, 1991), 83.

2. See, for example, H. George Frederickson and Yong Hyo Cho, "Legislative Apportionment and Fiscal Policy in the American States," *Western Political Quarterly* 27 (1974): 5–37, and Michael Maggiotto et al., "The Impact of Reapportionment on Public Policy: The Case of Florida, 1960–1980," *American Politics Quarterly* 13 (1985): 101–121. However, see Timothy O'Rourke, *The Impact of Reapportionment* (New Brunswick, N.J.: Transaction Books, 1980), who concludes that reapportionment's effects "are generally quite weak" (141).

3. Mathew McCubbins and Thomas Schwartz, "Congress, the Courts and Public Policy: Consequences of the One Man, One Vote Rule," *American Journal of Political Science* 32 (1988): 388–415.

4. See Kevin Hill, "Does the Creation of Black Majority Districts Aid Republicans? An Analysis of the 1992 Congressional Elections in Eight Southern States," *Journal of Politics* 57 (1995): 384–401.

5. See Justice Rehnquist's prediction of this in his dissent in *Virginia Pharmacy,* 425 U.S. 748 (1976).

6. Lauren Bowen, "Do Court Decisions Matter?" in *Contemplating Courts,* ed. Lee Epstein (Washington, D.C.: CQ Press, 1995), 376–389; "Attorney Advertising in the Wake of *Bates v. State Bar of Arizona* (1977): A Study of Judicial Impact," *American Politics Quarterly* 23 (1995): 461–484; and Carroll Seron, *The Business of Practicing Law: The Work Lives of Solo and Small Firm Attorneys* (Philadelphia: Temple University Press, 1996).

7. For a fuller discussion, see Gerald N. Rosenberg, "The Real World of Constitutional Rights: The Supreme Court and the Implementation of the Abortion Decision," in *Contemplating Courts;* see also Rosenberg, *The Hollow Hope,* 191ff.

8. See, for example, *Ruiz v. Estelle,* 503 F.Supp. 1265 (S.D., Tex., 1980) and *Ramos v. Lamm,* 639 F.2d 559 (10th Cir., 1980).

9. See Anthony Lewis, "The Soul of Justice," *New York Times,* January 4, 1993, A-15, and "Lawyers Shunning Death Row Cases," *New York Times,* September 22, 1986, 1.

10. See, for example, James W. Marquart and Ben W. Crouch, "Judicial Reform and Prison Control: The Impact of *Ruiz v. Estelle* on a Texas Penitentiary," *Law and Society Review* 20 (1985): 557–586. Considerable discussion of the impact of prison reform decisions can also be found in *Courts, Corrections and the Constitution: The Impact of Judicial Intervention on Prisons and Jails,* ed. John I. DiIulio Jr. (New York: Oxford University Press, 1990).

11. Karen M. Bray, "Reaching the Final Challenge in the Story of Peremptory Challenges," *U.C.L.A. Law Review* 40 (1992): 554–555. The Supreme Court seems unenthusiastic about distiguishing criteria offered as a pretext from genuine race-neutral criteria. See *Purkett v. Elem,* 514 U.S. 765 (1995).

12. "Former Prosecutor Accused of Bias in Election Year," *New York Times,* April 3, 1997, A-10.

13. See William A. Taggert, "Redefining the Power of the Federal Judiciary: The Impact of Court Ordered Prison Reform on State Expenditures for Corrections," *Law and Society Review* 23 (1989): 241–271; and Linda Harriman and Jeffrey D. Straussman, "Do Judges Determine Budget Decisions? Federal Court Decisions in Prison Reform Cases and State Spending," *Public Administration Review* 43 (1983): 343–351.

14. Kentucky, for example, increased its taxes by over $1 billion following *Rose v. Council for Better Education,* 790 S.W. 2d 186 (Ky., 1989). The U.S. Supreme Court rejected an argument that unequal spending violates the Fourteenth Amendment's equal protection clause in *San Antonio Independent School District v. Rodriguez* (1973). For a discussion of the issue, see Christopher E. Smith, *Courts and Public Policy* (Chicago: Nelson-Hall, 1993), chap. 5, and G. Alan Tarr, *Judicial Process and Judicial Policymaking* (St. Paul, Minn.: West, 1996), 369–380.

15. James P. Levine, "Constitutional Law and Obscene Literature: An Investigation of Bookseller Censorship Practices," in *The Impact of Supreme Court Decisions,* 2d ed., ed. Theodore L. Becker and Malcolm Feeley (New York: Oxford University Press, 1973); "Adult Magazines Lose Sales as 8,000 Stores Forbid Them," *New York Times,* June 16, 1986, 1.

16. Rosenberg, "The Real World of Constitutional Rights," in *Contemplating Courts.*

17. See Reed Sarrett, *The Ordeal of Desegregation* (New York: Harper, 1966); Jack Peltason, *Fifty Eight Lonely Men: Southern Judges and School Desegregation* (Urbana: University of Illinois Press, 1961), 99ff.; and Rosenberg, *The Hollow Hope,* 83–93.

18. The quotes are in "Across the Rural South, Segregation as Usual," *New York Times,* April 27, 1985, 1, 7.

19. Bowen, "Attorney Advertising in the Wake of *Bates v. State Bar of Arizona.*"

20. "Burger Condemns Some Lawyer Ads," *New York Times,* July 8, 1985, 1.

21. The studies are summarized in Paul G. Cassell, "*Miranda*'s Social Costs: An Empirical Reassessment," *Northwestern University Law Review* 90 (1996): 387–499.

22. Ibid., 437–438.

23. Stephen J. Schulhofer, "*Miranda*'s Practical Effect: Substantial Benefits and Vanishingly Small Societal Costs," *Northwestern University Law Review* 90 (1996): 500–563. See also Peter Nardulli, "The Societal Costs of the Exclusionary Rule: An Empirical Assessment," *American Bar Foundation Research Journal* 1983 (1983): 585–609.

24. *Miranda v. Arizona,* at 468–473.

25. See Rosenberg, *The Hollow Hope,* 271–293, for a summary of the courts' impact on environmental policy. Also see Lettie M. Wenner, *The Environmental Decade in Court* (Bloomington: Indiana University Press, 1982).

26. The cases are *Wilderness Society v. Morton,* 479 F.2d 842 (D.C., Cir., 1973) and *Tennessee Valley Authority v. Hill,* 437 U.S. 153 (1978).

27. See William K. Muir Jr., *Prayer in the Public Schools: Law and Attitude Change* (Chicago: University of Chicago Press, 1971); Larry Bass and Dan Thomas, "The Supreme Court and Policy Legitimation," *American Politics Quarterly* 12 (1984): 335–360; Jeffrey J. Mondak, "Perceived Legitimacy of Supreme Court Decisions: Three Functions of Source Credibility," *Political Behavior* 12 (1990): 363–384; and Valerie J. Hoekstra, "The Supreme Court and Opinion Change: An Experimental Study of the Court's Ability to Change Opinion," *American Politics Quarterly* 23 (1996): 109–129.

28. See, for example, "For Radical Freemen, All Courts Are Stages," *New York Times,* March 26, 1997, A-10.

29. See *In re Farber,* 394 A.2d 330 (N.J., 1978). Farber was released from jail when the defendant was acquitted.

30. James S. Coleman et al., *Recent Trends in School Desegregation* (Washington, D.C.: Urban Institute, 1975), 21–22.

31. For example, *Riddick v. School Board of Norfolk,* 627 F.Supp. 814 (E.D., Va., 1984).

32. Christine H. Rossell, "School Desegregation and White Flight," *Political Science Quarterly* 90 (1976): 675–695.

33. Gary Orfield, Susan Eaton, and the Harvard Project on School Desegregation, *Dismantling Desegregation: The Quiet Reversal of* Brown v. Board of Education (New York: New Press, 1996), chap. 3 and 93–96.

34. See Micheal Giles, Douglas Gatlin, and Everett Cataldo, "White Flight and Percent Black: The Tipping Point Reexamined," *Social Science Quarterly* 54 (1976): 85–92; Douglas Gatlin, Micheal Giles, and Everett Cataldo, "Policy Support within a Target Group: The Case of School Desegregation," *American Political Science Review* 72 (1978): 985–995; and Micheal Giles and Douglas Gatlin, "Mass Level Compliance with Public Policy: The Case of School Desegregation," *Journal of Politics* 42 (1980): 722–746.

35. For a similar finding regarding energy conservation, see David Sears et al., "Political System Support and Public Response to the Energy Crisis," *American Journal of Political Science* 22 (1978): 56–82.

CHAPTER FIVE

The Secondary Population

The secondary population is composed of those who are not in the other populations; it is a residual category. As we discussed briefly in Chapter 4, the distinctions between the secondary population and the consumer population are not always sharply drawn. Some policies with universal impact (for example, those relating to income taxes) may have virtually no secondary population. But for most judicial policies there are numerous individuals whose lives are not directly affected, and some of them will react. For instance, many members of the clergy are vitally concerned with abortion decisions, and many persons without children in public schools have reacted vigorously to school prayer decisions. There is nothing wrong with their concern. Citizens in a democracy should be interested in public policies beyond ones that may directly affect them.

In this chapter we examine how the secondary population reacts to judicial policies. To do so, we divide the secondary population into four categories. First we consider public officeholders such as members of Congress, the president, and state legislators. For some judicial policies, of course, officeholders will be implementors or consumers and not members of the secondary population. But more often than not, officeholders fall within the secondary population. Officeholders form a particular kind of secondary population. They are the public's elected representatives in government, and it is through them that the public voices its reactions to judicial policies. Officeholders are part of institutions that can bring pressure, both on the courts to maintain or change their policies and on the interpreting and implementing populations to reinforce or constrain the impact of judicial policies. These officials are a major conduit by which the consumer population and other members of the secondary population send feedback to the courts.

Second, we discuss interest groups whose members are not part of the consumer population, for example the American Civil Liberties Union. On many occasions interest groups are responsible for bringing cases to the judiciary; we will review how interest groups react to preferred and to disliked decisions of the judiciary. In some instances, these groups may effectively influence either follow-up decisions by the judiciary or implementation decisions by government agencies. These groups may, therefore, be potent forces that affect the aftermath of a judicial decision.

Third, we consider the impact of the media on judicial policies. We have occasionally mentioned aspects of communications in discussing how other populations react to judicial decisions, and we will discuss communications theory more extensively in Chapter 6. In this chapter we review some of the research on the attention given the judicial policies by the media as well as the impact of that attention on efforts to implement judicial policies.

Finally we discuss the reactions of the other members of the secondary population, which we shall call the public at large. It is divided into two categories, the attentive public and the mass public. Much of our discussion centers on how well informed these groups are: Who knows and cares about judicial policies? We also discuss what impact these publics have on efforts to implement judicial policies. Unfortunately, research in this area is scattered, and our remarks are largely speculative.

PUBLIC OFFICIALS AND JUDICIAL POLICIES

Congress

More than any other public agency, Congress tends to be the focal point for public reaction to judicial policies. As a political body, Congress cannot ignore any sizable or prominent group of constituents. Some groups become especially agitated when they are unhappy with some judicial decision or doctrine, and they make their dissatisfaction known to members of Congress. If the pressure is great enough and is not counterbalanced by pressure from groups that support the judicial policy, Congress will, if feasible, take action. At the very least, numerous members of Congress will score political points by showing righteous indignation on behalf of the disaffected groups.

Clashes between Congress and the courts are virtually as old as the two branches. *Marbury v. Madison* (1803) was a political finesse of a hostile Congress by the Supreme Court. Constitutional crises have been provoked by such decisions as *Dred Scott* (*Scott v. Sandford*, 1857) and several anti–New Deal decisions in the 1930s. Strained relationships just short of crises have developed from numerous other decisions. Of course, not all differences between the courts and Congress are emotionally charged. Many of the differences arise over mundane issues such as pension or admiralty law. Either way, almost every year Congress reacts to judicial decisions.[1]

Two matters are worth examining at this point. First, what options does Congress have in reacting to a Supreme Court decision? Second, what factors influence Congress's choices of action? We discuss these questions in turn. In doing so, we distinguish between Court decisions that interpret congressional statutes and those that interpret the Constitution.

STATUTORY INTERPRETATION. When court decisions involve statutory interpretation, Congress can override them by rewriting the statute. Sometimes the Court will even invite this.[2] A study by William Eskridge found that Congress changed 121 Supreme Court interpretations between 1967 and 1990, with 92 of them occurring in less than ten years after the decision. A quarter of the overrides occurred when the United States lost directly or as an amicus curiae in a case. In another 16 percent, business interests asked Congress to alter the interpretation. During this period, Congress also overrode 220 lower federal court statutory interpretations that were never reviewed by the Supreme Court.[3]

We should emphasize that the great majority of statutory interpretations are not changed by Congress. Congress finds most interpretations acceptable and sometimes ratifies them by incorporating them into statutory revisions. *Silent ratification*—where Congress does nothing to alter a judicial interpretation—is also quite common. Many attempts to override never make it through the legislative process. However, there have been two eras of considerable Congress-Court interpretive conflict in the last fifty years. One came during the 1950s when the Court, interpreting various laws fairly liberally, made it more difficult to question, prosecute, or deport persons suspected of subversive activity. A more conservative Congress overrode two such interpretations and came close to overriding several others; the Court eventually backed away from such confrontations.[4]

In the 1980s, the shoe was on the other foot, with Congress changing about twice as many conservative Court interpretations as liberal ones. A disproportionate number of pro-business decisions (compared with the number of civil rights and civil liberties cases) were overridden as Congress sided with groups such as disabled airline passengers, mental patients, retired employees, and environmentalists who had lost to bureaucrats or business interests in the Court.[5] When Congress did react to civil rights cases, its most notable actions reversed several narrow interpretations of the 1964 Civil Rights Act. For example, *Grove City College v. Bell* (1984) held that only particular college programs that received federal aid had to abide by the act's nondiscrimination requirements, not the college as a whole. Likewise, *Wards Cove Packing Co. v. Atonio* (1989) interpreted the act to require proof of intent in employment discrimination; statistical analyses of hiring patterns would not suffice. Both holdings were contrary to longstanding practices in applying the act (for *Wards Cove,* practices based upon the Court's opinion in *Griggs v. Duke Power Co.,* 1971). Congress reversed these decisions in 1988 (over President Reagan's veto) and 1991, respectively.[6]

CONSTITUTIONAL LAW. Constitutional law decisions, such as those involving school prayer or abortion, more often arouse widespread and intense emotions than do statutory interpretations. Unlike statutory interpretations, however, constitutional interpretations are far more difficult to reverse. An obvious way to do so is to pass a constitutional amendment. Yet changing the Constitution to allow what the Supreme Court forbade is not easily accomplished. A constitutional amendment requires a two-thirds vote in each house of Congress, followed by ratification by three-quarters of the states. Only four Supreme Court decisions in U.S. history have been overruled by constitutional amendment.[7]

In the last four decades, Congress has considered several proposed amendments that would negate or severely modify the Court's decisions in such controversial areas as reapportionment, abortion, busing to achieve racial balance, school prayers, and flag burning. A couple of proposals have been approved by one house or the other, but despite repeated attempts and the unpopularity of some of the Court's policies, no "overcoming" amendment was ever submitted to the states. The amendment route can be used to overcome a Supreme Court interpretation of the Constitution only when there is a general consensus that the Court's policy should be altered.

Occasionally Congress will try to negate a Court decision through ordinary legislation that contradicts the decision. For example, after the Court struck down state laws against burning the U.S. flag (*Texas v. Johnson,* 1989), Congress passed such a law. The Court promptly found the federal law unconstitutional (*United States v. Eichmann,* 1990). After the Court rejected Native American Church claims that its members had a free exercise right to ingest peyote despite state drug laws (*Oregon Employment Division v. Smith,* 1990), Congress passed the Religious Freedom Restoration Act, which purported to nullify *Smith.* In 1997 the Court held the act unconstitutional as a violation of separation of powers and the Tenth Amendment (*City of Boerne v. Flores*). However, there are certain situations where Congress can informally negate a Court ruling. One is discussed in Box 5-1.

Congress can pass legislation that minimizes the impact of court decisions with which it disagrees. We noted in Chapter 1 that following the abortion decision Congress passed the Hyde Amendment and other laws restricting the use of federal funds for elective and therapeutic abortions. The power of the purse can be a formidable weapon for blunting judicial policies. On one occasion, for example, the House of Representatives came within one vote of refusing to appropriate money to provide back pay for a government official who had won a Supreme Court decision entitling him to the money (*United States v. Lovett,* 1946).[8] In 1980 President Jimmy Carter vetoed the Justice Department appropriations bill because it contained a rider prohibiting any federal spending on efforts to obtain court decisions favoring busing. However, among the Supreme Court's policies that are regarded most negatively by Congress, many involve civil liberties issues that are not associated with appropriations.

Article III of the Constitution gives the Supreme Court appellate jurisdiction "with such Exceptions and under such Regulations as the Congress shall make," so in theory Congress could withdraw the Court's jurisdiction to hear certain types of cases. Congress has done so only once in constitutional cases: during the Reconstruction Era it prohibited the Court from hearing habeas corpus appeals from southern civilians detained by military authorities (*Ex parte McCardle,* 1869). Since World War II proposals to withdraw the Court's jurisdiction in such areas as congressional reapportionment, school prayers, U.S. internal security matters, the interrogation of criminal suspects, busing to achieve school integration, and

---

Box 5-1

A "Landmark" Curb on Congress Ends Up a Paper Tiger

In the 1983 case of *Immigration and Naturalization Service v. Chadha,* the Supreme Court ruled that the so-called legislative veto was unconstitutional because it violated the separation of powers. Laws allowing executive branch officials discretion in such areas as spending funds often contained such provisions. The legislative veto allowed Congress—or sometimes one house or even a particular committee—to veto the discretionary action within a certain time period. Chadha, for example, was an illegal alien subject to deportation. The Immigration and Nationality Act allowed the attorney general to suspend deportation subject to a legislative veto. Congress had vetoed the attorney general's suspension of Chadha's deportation. Over 200 laws, some going back to the administration of President Herbert Hoover in the early 1930s, had legislative veto provisions.

Chadha was widely regarded as a landmark decision at the time. Justice Lewis Powell, cautiously concurring, said, "the breadth of this holding gives one pause," and dissenting Justice Byron White noted that more laws were struck down in *Chadha* than in all of the Court's earlier history. Several members of Congress along with some journalists and political scientists predicted that *Chadha* would profoundly affect government.

But Congress largely ignored *Chadha*. It continued to pass laws containing legislative veto provisions, doing so over 200 times since 1983. The presidents,

---

women's right to abortion have all been defeated in Congress, although bills in the first two areas did pass in one house.[9] One problem with Congress's use of this weapon is that withdrawal of jurisdiction would not invalidate the Court's previous decision. Rather the interpretation of the decision would be entirely in the hands of other federal and state appellate judges. If the Supreme Court were not the final authority in these areas of law, confusion would reign.

Despite the obstacles, Congress does not play dead when the Supreme Court strikes down legislation. A study by James Meernik and Joseph Ignagni examined the 569 Supreme Court decisions declaring a federal or state law or an executive order unconstitutional between 1954 and 1990. Congress considered in a roll call vote some type of overcoming legislation in response to 125 (22 percent) of the decisions and approved the law in 41 instances (7 percent of the cases—33 percent of the considerations).[10]

while sometimes saying publicly that the veto provisions had no legal force, signed these laws because they needed the executive branch discretion written into them.

The problem is that federal agencies are very reluctant to challenge legislative vetoes. All agencies try to keep good relations with Congress, the source of their funds and authority. Challenging a veto can sour the relationship. Moreover, Congress can simply deny an agency discretion, even forcing the agency to spend all its money exactly as the budget stipulates regardless of how circumstances may change. What happens, instead, is that agencies enter into formal or informal agreements with relevant congressional committees to inform them of anticipated discretionary actions and to implement them only after some time period, say, 90 days. The agency also agrees that if the committee objects during that time period, the agency will not act or will seek a compromise with the committee.

So the legislative veto survives in practice if not in constitutional law and the Court's "landmark" curb on Congress's power has become largely a paper tiger.

Sources: Jessica Korn, *The Power of Separation* (Princeton: Princeton University Press, 1996), 33–35, and Louis Fisher, "The Legislative Veto: Invalidated, It Survives," *Law and Contemporary Problems* 56 (1993): 273–292.

FACTORS AFFECTING CONGRESSIONAL REACTION. Public opinion is usually a catalyst to congressional reaction. Meernik and Ignagni found that the likelihood of a roll call vote was related to public controversy over a decision. Numerous polls show, for instance, that large majorities favor school prayers, would outlaw flag burning, and believe criminal suspects have too many rights. However, the intensity of feelings can sometimes be more important than majority support. For example, while a nationwide majority favored school desegregation following *Brown v. Board of Education* (1954), the intensity of southern opposition kept Congress from taking any supportive action for a decade. Only when strong northern support had coalesced in the wake of the 1960s sit-in demonstrations did Congress pass civil rights legislation. Likewise, polls have consistently shown that there is majority support for a woman's right to obtain an abortion; yet many opponents of abortion are so intensely active that they use the question as the major, or even the sole, determinant of their vote in congressional elections. By contrast, the pro-choice public feels less strongly about the issue. Consequently, Congress has passed some laws curbing access to abortion.

When emotions run high on both sides, there may be little reaction from Congress. Congress has largely ignored the Court's affirmative action decisions regardless of who benefited. While feelings are strong, Congress is not unified. Indeed, many members from divided constituencies would probably rather let the judiciary handle the matter.

What explains congressional approval of bills that would overcome or limit a judicial policy? Meernik and Ignagni found that presidential opposition to a decision was by far the strongest factor; passage was 89 percent more likely when the president opposed a decision than when he took no position on the issue. Majority opinion, as reflected in polls, increased the probabilities of congressional action by 22 percent.[11]

GENERAL RETALIATION. Congress can also respond negatively to judicial policies through general punitive actions or through actions designed to change decision rules or judicial personnel. Punitive actions are basically symbolic and sometimes involve the refusal of Congress to appropriate sufficient funds for the Supreme Court. For instance, in the 1970s Congress had not seen fit to appropriate funds for an automobile to take the Supreme Court's associate justices to and from work or on other official business, despite the fact that every federal district judge is provided such a vehicle. One southern senator responded to the justices' request for automobiles, "Couldn't we get a bus to bus the judges? I learned about busing from reading the *Swann* case."[12] Congressional punishment of the Court is nothing new: in 1816 Congress refused to appropriate one thousand dollars for a court reporter because of its displeasure with the decision in *Martin v. Hunter's Lessee* (1816).[13]

Another retaliatory tactic involves the judges' salaries. Article III prohibits reductions in judges' salaries by Congress; it was intended to prevent fiscal punishment for unpopular decisions. In an inflationary era, however, the failure to increase salaries is tantamount to a reduction. In 1964 Congress raised the salaries of all federal judges except those on the Supreme Court by $7,000; the justices received only a $4,500 raise. In debating the issue, several members of Congress made it clear that dissatisfaction with the Supreme Court's decisions motivated their action. Republican Rep. Robert Dole of Kansas (later senator and the 1996 GOP presidential nominee) was quite blunt about the connection, virtually to the point of suggesting blackmail. He said:

> Whenever thinking of the Supreme Court I think of last June 15, 1964,
> and reapportionment decisions handed down in *Reynolds against Simms*
> [*sic*] and the related cases. It has been suggested that perhaps Section 2 of
> the Bill might be amended whereby the effective date of the pay increase
> if adopted by this House, would be the date the Supreme Court reverses
> the decision in *Reynolds against Simms* [*sic*].[14]

Although it is unlikely that the justices can be "bought" for $2,500, such congressional actions, in conjunction with other forms of pressure, may have a long-term influence on the Court.

In the nineteenth century Congress changed the number of justices on the Supreme Court seven times to achieve its policy goals. After the Civil War, for instance, the radical Republican Congress decreased the number so that President Andrew Johnson could not appoint any justices. A later increase is considered to be directly responsible for reversing the Court's position on the constitutionality of paper money.[15]

This tactic was tried only once in the twentieth century, in President Franklin D. Roosevelt's famous "court-packing" plan. Frustrated by the Court's declaring many New Deal laws unconstitutional, Roosevelt proposed enlarging the Court from nine to as many as fifteen justices (the proposal would allow a new justice to be named for each one over seventy who did not retire, with a maximum of six new justices). Although Congress eventually defeated the plan, the Court evidently got the message and, in what one wag described as "the switch in time that saved nine," never again declared a piece of New Deal legislation unconstitutional. Any attempt to change the Court's size these days would be met with widespread public hostility. But Congresses, past and present, have created or refused to create new lower federal judgeships depending on who was president and the probable political ideology of the judges he would appoint.[16]

The Senate, in particular, can also influence the composition of the courts through its confirmation powers. Confirmation hearings and votes usually center on a nominee's political and legal philosophy. Senators can use the hearings to criticize or defend current judicial policies—to fire warning shots across the Court's bow, so to speak. Sometimes hearings provoke a major public discussion about the Court's policies, as happened when the Senate rejected Robert Bork in 1987 and narrowly confirmed Clarence Thomas in 1991. Indeed, nearly one-fifth (27 of 148) of the nominees to the Supreme Court have been rejected by the Senate.

Only five of the rejections occurred in the twentieth century; perhaps fear of rejection leads modern presidents to nominate less partisan and ideological types to the Court.[17] Direct retaliation can play a part in a Senate rejection. When President Lyndon Johnson nominated sitting justice Abe Fortas to the chief justiceship in 1968, the nomination was defeated by a filibuster motivated largely by Fortas's liberal votes and opinions as an associate justice and, beyond that, by the general liberalism of the Warren Court.[18] Historically the Senate has paid little attention to the ideology of appointees to lower federal judgeships. But in 1997 its Republican majority began a serious ideological scrutiny of President Clinton's nominees, to the point where large numbers of vacancies went unfilled and even conservative Chief Justice William Rehnquist chastised the Senate.[19]

Finally, a federal judge can be removed through the impeachment process, but it is cumbersome and time-consuming. In 1804 the Jeffersonian House of Representatives impeached Supreme Court Justice Samuel Chase, a blatant Federalist partisan both on and off the bench, but failed to secure a conviction in the Senate. Since then, the House has impeached judges only in cases of severe malfeasance in office. In 1997, however, a group of House Republicans, including majority leader Dick Armey of Texas, sought impeachment of several lower court federal judges (including Judge Harold Baer; see Chapter 2) who had made what the group considered outrageously liberal decisions.[20]

C. Herman Pritchett and Walter Murphy have independently advanced what might be termed the *sacrosanctity theory* to explain why Congress so seldom uses its big weapons to retaliate against the Court.[21] This theory holds that the public will not tolerate a congressional invasion of the Supreme Court's territory of constitutional interpretation. It stems in part from the unsophisticated public's sense of the Supreme Court's "nonpolitical" role, analogous to the norm that ball players should not physically attack the umpire even when he makes a bad call. Still, as we will discuss later in this chapter, the empirical evidence that the public as a whole views the Supreme Court as an impartial institution is quite mixed.

There is probably some truth to the sacrosanctity theory. Many congressional supporters of the New Deal opposed President Roosevelt's court-packing plan in 1937, and many conservatives opposed measures to retaliate against the Warren Court in the 1950s and 1960s. Current Republican efforts to force draconian changes in the federal judiciary are opposed by many conservatives.[22] Many members of Congress, especially those on the judiciary committees, may themselves believe that they will do serious damage to the constitutional balance of powers if they overreact to what they consider erroneous decisions.[23]

The Court may or may not stand up to intimidation. In the 1950s, it backed away from some of its national security decisions, as when *Barenblatt v. U.S.* (1959) virtually restored congressional committees' investigative power, which the Court had limited in *Watkins v. U.S.* (1957). By contrast, the Court refused to backtrack on busing in the 1970s and 1980s, despite repeated congressional signals of displeasure with the Court's policies.

State Legislatures

Researchers have directed most of their attention to congressional reactions to Supreme Court policies; they have seldom examined how state legislatures react to judicial policies. Thus our discussion of state legislatures is relatively brief. It is divided into two subsections: (1) legislatures' reactions to U.S. Supreme Court policies, and (2) their reactions to decisions of their own state supreme court.

STATE LEGISLATURES' REACTIONS TO THE U.S. SUPREME COURT. The U.S. Supreme Court strikes down state laws far more often than it does federal laws, but state legislatures have a much more limited ability than Congress to express displeasure meaningfully. The states' relative lack of power is inherent in the nature of the Union. Justice Oliver Wendell Holmes once said: "I do not think the United States would come to an end if we lost our power to declare an act of Congress unconstitutional. I do think the Union would be imperiled if we could not make that declaration as to the laws of the several states."[24] Nonetheless, state legislatures are not reluctant to protest and even to try thwarting the impact of a U.S. Supreme Court decision when they feel strongly about it. Desegregation provides the most notable examples. Following *Brown v. Board of Education* (1954), the Virginia legislature required the closing of public schools in any district subject to an integration order, while the South Carolina and Mississippi legislatures repealed their compulsory education laws. In 1960 the Louisiana legislature was repeatedly convened in special session to pass a series of laws in a last-ditch effort to forestall court ordered desegregation in New Orleans. In the end, as we know, southern legislative resistance was unsuccessful.

Resistance occurs in other areas. Recently the New York legislature has fought the Court's decision in *Kiryas Joel School District v. Grumet* (1994), which struck down the state's establishment of a special school district for a Jewish sect. The legislature has twice passed new and slightly altered laws to reestablish the district, only to be stymied by the courts.[25] In 1998, Alabama Governor Fob James told the Supreme Court that the Bill of Rights did not apply in Alabama. James was leading an effort to restore Christian prayers to the state's public schools in defiance of a federal judge's cease and desist order.[26] When the Court held that a state could not impose term limits on its representatives in Congress (*U.S. Term Limits v. Thornton,* 1995), several states adopted laws that would put words like "Disregarded Voter Instructions on Term Limits" beside the name of incumbents who wished to serve longer.[27] Sometimes legislatures resist decisions for financial reasons. A number balked at complying with *Davis v. Michigan Department of Treasury* (1989) and its follow-up decisions because it meant that hundreds of millions of dollars had to be paid out in state income tax refunds. *Davis* held that state taxes on pensions of retired federal employees were unconstitutional if (as was true in twenty-three states) the pensions of retired state employees were not subject to state taxes.[28]

More often, state legislatures try to minimize the impact of a decision. In Chapter 1 (Table 1-1), we noted several legislative attempts to limit the circumstances when a woman could obtain an abortion. In recent years, several states adopted laws requiring a minute of silence for meditation at the beginning of each school day. Others tried to limit busing. Following *University of Texas v. Hopwood's* (1996) ban on considering race as an admissions criterion, Texas legislators provided that the top 10 percent of graduates from any high school in the state would automatically be admitted to any state college or university (presumably assuring that there would be admittees from largely African American and Hispanic high schools). Minimization efforts are more successful if the new law does not seem to directly conflict with the Court's policy. In the abortion area, for example, laws that required the father's consent or even his notification have been struck down by federal courts, but state laws requiring a twenty-four-hour waiting period or not allowing payment for abortions for women on welfare were upheld (see *Harris v. McRae,* 1980, and *Casey v. Planned Parenthood,* 1992).

Occasionally widespread reaction to a decision by state legislatures will influence the Court's development of policy. Following *Furman v. Georgia* (1972), which left the constitutional status of the death penalty uncertain, thirty-seven legislatures repassed death penalty statutes—a phenomenon that did not go unnoticed by the Court when it eventually held the death penalty constitutional (*Gregg v. Georgia,* 1976).

Again we want to note that attempts by state legislatures to block or minimize U.S. Supreme Court decisions are the exception and not the rule. Most commonly when the Supreme Court voids a state law, the legislature either does nothing in reaction or revises its legislation in accordance with the Court's opinion.

STATE LEGISLATURES' REACTIONS TO STATE SUPREME COURTS. State legislatures relate to state supreme courts in much the same way as Congress relates to the U.S. Supreme Court. Thus their power to respond to state high courts' interpretations of the state constitution and statutes is similar to Congress's ability to respond to Supreme Court policies. There is one notable exception: in all but a handful of states, legislatures have no input in the selection of state judges. Legislatures occasionally propose constitutional amendments, reverse statutory interpretations, or adopt new statutes in response to common law decisions. Most legislatures, however, meet for limited periods and have small staffs, so their ability to oversee, modify, or reverse court decisions is not as great as that of Congress. In general, state supreme courts are more deferential to legislative policies and public opinion than the U.S. Supreme Court is. Thus state decisions arouse anger or resistance less intensely or frequently.

Nonetheless, clashes do occur. In 1993 the Hawaii Supreme Court broadly hinted that it would interpret the state's constitution to authorize same-sex marriages as well as heterosexual ones (*Baehr v. Lewin,* 1993), leading the state legislature to propose a constitutional amendment precluding this interpretation. In Nevada, the legislature refused to repair the state supreme court's roof (rain poured in during storms) in retaliation for some of that court's criminal justice decisions.[29] In several states, the supreme courts has made "right to die" policies in frustrated response to legislative inaction.[30]

Perhaps the most important clashes have occurred in the school financing area. Since 1970 over fifteen state supreme courts have made decisions requiring state legislatures to equalize funding so that per pupil spending is approximately the same in poor school districts as it is in wealthy ones. Implementation has gone more smoothly in states such as California and Kentucky where the court has not engaged in close supervision, but in others, including New Jersey and Texas, legislative compliance with greater court detail has been grudging and angry feelings have followed.[31]

The President

Like Congress, the president can stand in any of several relationships to judicial policies. He is charged by the Constitution to "take care that the laws be faithfully executed," so he becomes an important part of the implementing population for federal court decisions. In a constitutional system that emphasizes limited authority and separation of powers, the actions of the president (or his subordinates acting for him) are often subject to challenge; therefore he is frequently a consumer of court decisions. And, of course, as a politician, national leader, and head of state, he must have a keen interest in judicial policies that may not affect him directly. In such cases, he is in the secondary population. Here we treat the president primarily as part of the secondary population, but his roles are not easily differentiated and our discussion will deal with other aspects of the presidential–Supreme Court relationship.

ENFORCEMENT AND INFLUENCE. On rare occasions, federal courts may have to call upon the president himself to enforce their policies, and some presidents have refused to do so. Recall that we opened this book with President Andrew Jackson's famous (though perhaps apocryphal) remark, "John Marshall has made his decision, now let him enforce it." This followed *Worcester v. Georgia* (1832), where the U.S. Supreme Court held that Georgia's courts lacked jurisdiction over crimes committed on Indian lands within the state; Worcester remained in jail when federal authorities did not enforce the decision. And on occasion President Abraham Lincoln ordered his military commanders to refuse obedience to several writs of habeas corpus during the Civil War, including one from Chief Justice Roger Taney. Usually presidents do obey court orders: following a Supreme Court decision (*Youngstown Sheet and Tube Co. v. Sawyer,* 1952), President Harry S. Truman returned steel mills, seized during the Korean War, to their owners; Richard M. Nixon sealed his own fate after *U.S. v. Nixon* (1973) by surrendering seventeen audiotapes recorded in his White House office to the special prosecutor investigating the Watergate scandal. Presidents Dwight D. Eisenhower and John F. Kennedy sent federal troops to Arkansas and Mississippi, respectively, to enforce federal courts' desegregation rulings.

Even when enforcement is not in question, the president can influence the impact of a judicial policy. More than anyone else, he has access to the public; his words and deeds, even subtle or casual ones, can do much to encourage people to cooperate with or to resist judicial policies. President

Franklin D. Roosevelt used some of his famous "fireside chats" to label the justices as the "nine old men" and inform the public how their anti–New Deal decisions were hurting economic recovery. President Eisenhower was not enthusiastic about *Brown v. Board of Education,* and his unwillingness to support it in more than a pro forma fashion encouraged southern resistance. President Kennedy's attitude toward the school prayer decision provides an illustrative contrast with Ronald Reagan's. Kennedy obliquely supported the decision by remarking that perhaps Americans should emphasize religion more in the church and home; Reagan, on the other hand, repeatedly said he believed the decision was in error and that there ought to be prayer in the public schools.

The president can use his powers more specifically. He can use the machinery of the federal government to minimize a decision's impact. For example, after *Adarand Constructors v. Pena* (1995) scuttled affirmative action programs, President Bill Clinton directed that such federal programs be revised to comply perhaps with *Adarand'*s letter but not its spirit. A president can propose new legislation to limit or overturn a court policy. President George Bush, for example, pushed legislation and then a constitutional amendment to outlaw the burning of the U.S. flag following the Court's *Texas v. Johnson* (1989) decision. Of course, such presidential proposals are not always successful. Presidents Nixon, Reagan, and Bush all proposed that parents receive a federal tax credit for tuition they paid to send their children to religious schools, though the Supreme Court had held that such aid was unconstitutional (*Committee for Public Education and Religious Liberty v. Nyquist,* 1973); Congress never gave the proposals serious consideration.

Using another of his powers, the president can veto legislation either that would overturn or hinder the implementation of a judicial policy or that would help in the implementation of a policy. Both presidents Reagan and Bush vetoed congressional acts overriding the Supreme Court's narrow interpretations of the 1964 Civil Rights Act in the *Grove City College* and *Wards Cove* cases discussed earlier in this chapter. Congress overrode Reagan's veto, but it had to compromise with Bush in order to get him to sign another such law.

THE APPOINTMENT POWER. The policy importance of the president's power to appoint federal judges—especially to the Supreme Court—is enormous. Obviously, major judicial policies cannot survive the appointment of several justices dedicated to different policies. We will examine the long-term implications of the appointment power in Chapter 7. In the short run and on narrower issues, the ability of a president to affect judicial decisions through appointments depends on factors such as the ideological division of the Court and the number of vacancies that he gets to fill. When President Nixon was able to name four justices within three years, the Court's five- or six-member majority bloc of liberals in the area of defendants' rights was reduced to a minority of three. The Court became more conservative in general after Ronald Reagan named three justices, and it almost overruled *Roe v. Wade* in 1989 (*Webster v. Reproductive Health Services*). President Clinton's appointments of Ruth Bader Ginsburg and Stephen Breyer to the Court have restored a more even ideological balance to Supreme Court policies; current abortion policies, for example, will not be seriously altered until a more conservative president appoints some justices.

Some presidents think quite seriously about the policy implications of their appointments. The Reagan administration, for example, was said to screen candidates for all federal judgeships for their attitudes toward abortion.[32] President William Howard Taft (1909–1913), believing that the Supreme Court was the most important policy maker in government, chose his six appointees with great care, and they imposed their economic conservatism on the country for over two decades. But not all presidents have been as concerned about judicial policy. President Truman filled his four Court vacancies with some of his friends, and President Eisenhower's five appointees certainly had a mixture of ideological approaches. For that matter, not all judges vote as their appointing president would like. Eisenhower later believed that appointing Chief Justice Earl Warren, who became more liberal the longer he served on the Court, was his "biggest damnfool mistake."[33] Likewise, Nixon appointee Harry Blackmun, initially a believer in judicial restraint, became a judicial activist in such areas as abortion and the death penalty.

THE JUSTICE DEPARTMENT. Through the Department of Justice the president has a unique ability to influence the courts—particularly the Supreme Court. The department initiates federal criminal prosecutions and civil suits; thus it can advance novel legal propositions that are likely to go to the Supreme Court for final adjudication. In other words, the department has some ability to shape the federal judiciary's agenda of policy issues. In fact, the Court takes about 75 percent of the cases for which the solicitor general (the department's chief lawyer) seeks certiorari.[34] Moreover, the government is victorious before the High Court in 63 percent of its cases.[35] The Justice Department's influence has been particularly telling in the area of civil rights cases: for over a half century the Justice Department has urged—usually successfully—the Supreme Court to expand statutory and constitutional interpretations to give minorities greater federal protection from local abuse and repression.

When the government is not a party, the Justice Department can file an amicus curiae ("friend of the court") brief with the Supreme Court. While almost any interested group can do this, the solicitor general's briefs are always well prepared and traditionally accorded great weight.[36] Indeed, the Court sometimes invites the solicitor general to submit an amicus brief "expressing the views of the United States." In these briefs the administration communicates warnings, encouragements, and policy considerations to the justices.

Most Justice Department actions are taken without direct consultation with the president; President Clinton was politically embarrassed by his solicitor general's "soft" stand in a pornography case.[37] On rare occasions, a president will directly influence the solicitor general's position.[38] Regardless, the president's attitude on major issues is usually known. When President Reagan said that he thought tax exemptions for private schools that racially discriminated should be continued, the Justice Department withdrew at the last minute from a case it had brought to deny an exemption to such a school.[39]

INTEREST GROUPS AND JUDICIAL POLICIES

Even the casual observer of American politics knows that interest groups play an important role in the constant development and redevelopment of public policy. This is true of judicial policies as well as those made by other branches, although the approach of interest groups to judges may differ from how they deal with policy makers in other branches. In this section we examine the behavior of interest groups in the implementation process, especially when they try to change judicial policies. This chapter focuses on the secondary population, so we are particularly interested in those interest groups that are not part of the implementing or consumer populations, those not directly affected by a judicial decision. For example, the American Civil Liberties Union, Right-to-Life, and Friends of the Earth are groups more interested in judicial policies for their own sake than for any occupational or financial advantage a policy may bring. Even so, groups such as the National Association for the Advancement of Colored

Persons (NAACP), the U.S. Chamber of Commerce, or the American Bar Association often approach judicial policies with a mixture of personal and public concern. In other words, the same interest groups may function sometimes as implementors or consumers and sometimes as part of the secondary population.

Scholars have paid considerable attention to the role of interest groups in judicial policy making.[40] Their research shows that the judiciary is one of many forums for organized interests and that in the late twentieth century groups have increasingly turned to courts to achieve policy objectives. Most of this research considers the effects of interest groups on judicial policies *before* the decisions are rendered by the courts. Recently, however, researchers have examined policies through the entire process, so that they also consider the role and influence of interest groups on the implementation and impact of judicial policies.

In this section, we focus on the ways interest groups help or hinder the interpretation, implementation, or consumption of judicial policies. Interest groups often ask courts to broaden or to limit their interpretation of a policy; they may attempt to have implementation narrowed or delayed, or applied more broadly or effectively; they may try to persuade courts to uphold or overturn other branches' acts that encourage or discourage a policy's use. In addition, interest groups will often turn to other branches of the government to enhance or block the implementation or consumption of a judicial policy. We will examine the responses of interest groups from three perspectives: first, how they are activated or organized in response to a judicial decision; second, how these groups are able to enhance implementation; and third, how groups can obstruct the implementation of judicial policies.

Activation of Interest Groups

Stuart Scheingold suggests that judicial decisions often create rights that are best understood as "political resources" and that are "best viewed as the beginning of a political process. . . ." Thus, Scheingold asserts that in the American political system a judicial victory won by an interest group actually results only in additional support for its policy demands; a favorable judicial decision may enable an interest group to "alter the balance of power" in the government, but it seldom guarantees overall success.[41] Or, as Sarah Weddington, the attorney who argued for Jane Roe in *Roe v. Wade* (1973), put it years later, "The day the Supreme Court decision was announced, I thought it was written in granite. Now I know it was written in sandstone." [42] Ultimately, then, a court decision merely serves as another tool for persuading others to behave in ways preferred by an interest group.

Judicial decisions can sometimes mobilize their beneficiaries to take political action, something we will discuss further in Chapter 7. Scheingold refers to this function as "a dual process of activating a quiescent citizenry and organizing groups into effective political units." [43] Scheingold's theory is that "perceptions of entitlement" are associated with rights and that these perceptions serve to activate and organize interests in the political system. Thus, "insofar as court decisions can legitimate claims and cue expectations, litigation can contribute to both activation and organization; to the building of new coalitions; and, in the long run, to a realignment of forces within the political arena." [44]

Scheingold, in observing that rights may activate interest groups, assumes that the groups winning new rights or benefits will mobilize. However, losing rights, benefits, or services may provoke similar activities. For example, when the fifth circuit overturned affirmative action admission procedures for the University of Texas Law School (*Texas v. Hopwood,* 1996; see Chapter 2), several Hispanic and African American groups held rallies in the state capital, supported appeals to the Supreme Court, and sought alternative state policies to further their interests. [45]

Groups on both sides may be activated while others may withdraw. This is illustrated in Box 5-2, which reports the results of a study by Joseph Kobylka on the reactions of interest groups to *Miller v. California* (1973), the case that reversed the Supreme Court's increasing liberalization of obscenity law during the 1960s.

Although winning a judicial decision often activates interest groups, there are a few notable exceptions. Some organizations appear to be more content with winning judicial decisions than with following through on their implementation. Some researchers have noted, for example, that the ACLU does not always initiate the follow-up cases that would be necessary to implement judicial policies nationwide. Karen O'Connor found that cases were accepted by the Women's Rights Project of the ACLU only if they met such criteria as being "novel and nationally important," being likely to end in victory if handled correctly, taking the law to its next logical step, benefiting a large number of women, and having no other attorney available to the client. [46] Stephen Halpern also discusses the law production orientation of the ACLU. He found that a sizable percentage of the cases brought to the local chapters of the ACLU in his study were

---

Box 5-2
Interest Groups and an Obscenity Decision

During the 1950s and 1960s the U.S. Supreme Court rendered a number of decisions that increasingly limited state and national governmental powers to censor or prosecute publications or films that authorities considered obscene. In all these decisions, however, the Court acknowledged that some forms of expression were obscene and thus not protected by the First Amendment. In 1973, with four Nixon appointees on the Court, the justices ceased shrinking the definition of obscenity and changed the course of law by broadening the definition somewhat. *Miller v. California* accomplished this by substituting local for national community standards of what constitutes obscenity, and discarding the previous standard that obscene material would have to be *utterly* without redeeming social value, saying instead that protected work must have *serious* literary, artistic, political, or scientific value.

The American Civil Liberties Union reacted to the *Miller* decision by largely exiting the obscenity policy arena. According to Joseph Kobylka, "ACLU officials saw little point in pursuing its obscenity goals though the judiciary." Calculating that the Court was now hostile to arguments used successfully in previous cases and having limited resources, the ACLU believed that there was little to gain for the organization or its policy goals by continuing to press obscenity litigation.

Groups that were supportive of *Miller* pursued a continuance strategy, continuing and expanding their efforts to proscribe what they saw as obscene films

---

enforcement cases; but the chapters rarely took action on such cases. In fact, most cases were either rejected, referred elsewhere, or deferred. Halpern concludes that "by emphasizing test cases, the ACLU has overvalued achieving official, public declarations of changes in policy and minimized the value of monitoring whether and how rights are enforced." [47] By contrast, interest groups with a more direct economic or occupational interest in expanding a judicial policy usually followed through with suits or other activities demanding implementation.

Enhancing the Implementation of Judicial Decisions

Interest groups may engage in several activities to enhance the impact of a favorable decision, thereby increasing the probability that the intended con-

and publications. One group, the Citizens for Decency through Law, developed a plan to assist local prosecutors to "offset" the expertise of "well-schooled defense counsel" who often represented publishers and filmmakers. Another group, Morality in Media, advanced the cause of a national database and reference library on the law of obscenity to provide assistance to obscenity prosecutions. These groups recognized that *Miller's* emphasis on local standards in prosecutions gave them an opening to limit the range of expression in morally conservative communities, and they sought to support efforts of local prosecutors that advanced their policy agenda.

But *Miller* also mobilized a variety of groups, including associations representing the motion picture industry, adult filmmakers, publishers, and libraries, which had a material interest in obscenity law. In contrast to the ACLU, whose commitment was seen as largely symbolic, new groups were organized to protect commercial interests. One group, the Media Coalition, participated in obscenity litigation by sponsoring "litigation testing the constitutionality, under *Miller,* of obscenity statutes." This group and others "mobilized to meet [*Miller's*] potential dangers by litigating more frequently and vigorously, changing the types of arguments they presented in courts, and broadening their activities to include lower court proceedings."

Source: Joseph F. Kobylka, *The Politics of Obscenity: Group Litigation in a Time of Legal Change* (Westport, Conn.: Greenwood Press, 1991), 86, 114–115, 134.

sumers actually benefit. Among these activities are returning to the courts for clarification, extension, or enforcement of the decision; finding and supporting consumers who will benefit from the policy; and enlisting the aid of other groups and institutions in their efforts to secure favorable policies.

Interest groups may return to the courts with two objectives in mind. They may ask the original policy-making court to expand the policy's nature and scope through subsequent clarifications and interpretations. Interest groups may also go to lower courts to seek enforcement of a judicial policy. A fairly standard procedure in the civil rights movement, for example, was for civil rights groups to file suits to force desegregation of schools after the *Brown* decision. Jack Greenberg, an attorney in the NAACP Legal Defense and Educational Fund (LDF) in the 1950s and 1960s, reported that

[by] the end of the 1950s LDF had commenced more than sixty elementary and high school cases. . . . The issues under litigation included flat refusals to desegregate (Louisiana and Virginia), outright violence (Little Rock), lower courts' reluctance to enforce the law vigorously (Maryland, South Carolina, Texas, and Virginia), pupil placement rules (Maryland, North Carolina, and Tennessee), and other stratagems to subvert integration.[48]

A key factor in predicting success for such moves is the longevity of the interest group. Citing several studies of the success of the NAACP in the civil rights field, O'Connor notes, "Interest group longevity appears to be critical if an organization sets upon a course of litigious activity that calls for it to systematically whittle away adverse precedent to attain its goals."[49]

Of course, interest groups do not always bring litigation in their own name or sponsor it by representing a nominal consumer. They often make their arguments through amicus curiae—friend of the court—briefs. These briefs supplement the briefs of the parties in a case. Interest groups file them at all judicial levels, but they are particularly numerous in U.S. Supreme Court cases. Over a hundred have been filed in a few recent affirmative action and abortion cases.

Interest groups may also enhance implementation (and consumption) by informing and mobilizing consumers of the policy. Indeed, interest groups are often invaluable in telling potential consumers of their rights and opportunities. Joel Handler points out that national civil rights groups were instrumental in alerting the local black population to registration opportunities after passage in 1965 of the Voting Rights Act and subsequent litigation. The litigation, Handler argues, was especially useful because it was "consciousness raising . . . [and] good press."[50] Joseph Stewart Jr. and James F. Sheffield Jr. provide even stronger evidence that interest group activities enhanced the implementation of civil rights policies in the South. Their study showed that activities in Mississippi during the 1960s and 1970s by the Lawyer's Committee for Civil Rights Under Law, the Lawyer's Constitutional Defense Committee, and the NAACP Legal Defense Fund led to an increase in the number of African Americans who registered to vote and in the number of black candidates who ran for local office. Mobilization had less of an impact, however, on victories by black candidates.[51]

Finally, interest groups may enhance the implementation of judicial policies by turning to other groups or institutions for assistance. As we discussed in Chapter 1, both pro-choice and pro-life groups have turned to state governments, Congress, and the federal executive branch to advance their policy objectives. In addition, these groups have allied with other liberal and conservative interest groups, respectively, in political battles. This type of alliance is not uncommon. As we saw in Box 5-2, distributors of sexually oriented material were allied with groups representing respectable publications, filmmakers, and distributors to work against restrictive interpretations of the Constitution's freedom of speech and press guarantees.

Restricting the Implementation of Judicial Decisions

On many occasions, interest groups opposing a judicial policy can be as intent on blocking or minimizing its implementation as others are on advancing it. To a large extent, groups promoting restrictions on a policy use strategies that are similar to those used by groups promoting compliance with it. For example, a group that has lost in court may return to the judiciary in hopes of obtaining either a limited interpretation or a policy reversal based on a different principle. While interest groups may recognize that having lost in a court means that the likelihood of their winning in the same court is low, they may be more successful in another court. Interest groups favoring change in the way school systems are financed, for example, lost in the U.S. Supreme Court (*San Antonio Independent School District v. Rodriguez,* 1973), but many carried on their fight in state courts, making arguments based on state constitutions. A review of such actions by the *New York Times* noted that school finance policies have been successfully challenged in more than fifteen states, despite *Rodriguez's* holding that the federal constitution does not require such changes.[52]

Interest groups that oppose a particular policy may also generate information about how a decision might be narrowly applied or interpreted. As we noted in Box 5-2, groups representing the movie and publishing industries mobilized resources to assist defendants in local trials to minimize the effect of local obscenity prosecutions following the *Miller* decision. Opposition may spread. When Alabama circuit judge Roy Moore refused to remove the Ten Commandments from his courtroom despite a court order to do so (Chapter 2), movements to post the commandments in public places soon sprung up in other states.[53]

Groups opposed to a court decision may also try to convince government officials to help block or limit the impact of the decision. For example, as we discussed in Chapter 1, pro-life groups were effective in lobbying Congress to limit drastically the federal funding of abortions for poor women. Congress's adoption of the Hyde Amendment in the mid-1970s and its acceptance by the Supreme Court constituted a major victory for those opposed to abortion (*Harris v. McRae,* 1980).

Perhaps the most unusual attempt to forestall a change in policy by the U.S. Supreme Court occurred in a 1997 case challenging affirmative action. A white teacher in Piscataway, New Jersey, won lower court decisions supporting her claim of discrimination when a school board dismissed her instead of a black teacher who had been hired on the same day. The board cited maintenance of racial diversity as the reason to keep the black teacher. As the Supreme Court seemed hostile to affirmative action programs (based on decisions such as *Adarand Constructors v. Pena,* 1995), supporters of these programs were fearful that the case would be used by a conservative Court to reverse most affirmative action programs in the country. To remove the case from the Court's docket, several civil rights groups got together and generated funds for a $433,500 settlement for the white teacher who had brought the original suit. This move by interest groups represented a novel but effective way of maintaining the implementation of an existing judicial policy by terminating a case that might have resulted in a reversal of that policy.[54]

MEDIA COVERAGE OF JUDICIAL POLICIES

Although the media sometimes are consumers of judicial decisions, they are usually observers—members of the secondary population. Newspapers, general and specialized magazines, and radio and television all report governmental affairs; yet covering the courts presents distinct challenges to the media. Reporters are faced with the difficult task of summarizing judicial activities because of the large number of decisions, the use of technical language, lengthy opinions that are difficult to "boil down into catchy phrases and cliches," and the mundane nature of judicial issues.[55] Although highly publicized trials involving celebrities such as O. J. Simpson and those about enormously tragic events such as the Oklahoma City bombing get detailed attention, the overwhelming number of judicial decisions—significant and insignificant—go unreported in the media.

When the media do convey information about judicial policies, they serve two primary functions as part of the secondary population: first, they convey information to relevant and interested populations that might otherwise be uninformed of judicial policies or actions, and second, they convey information to the courts and to others about the reactions of various people or groups to previously announced judicial decisions. In performing each of these functions, the media have a potential impact on the implementation of judicial decisions. However, as we will see, determining the nature and degree of that impact is very difficult. (Media outlets can, of course, generate reactions to judicial policies through editorials or judgmental reporting. The conservative *National Review* is not likely to write about an abortion or affirmative action decision in the same manner as the liberal *Nation*. The media's attempts at persuasion are similar to the mobilization efforts of interest groups and will not be considered in this section.)

The Media as Conveyers of Judicial Policies

The popular media are the principal means by which both the general public and members of the implementing and consumer populations learn of court decisions. Popular media consist of a variety of outlets; but for the U.S. Supreme Court, the actual reports about decisions are done primarily by a small band of reporters working for the major wire services, for a few national newspapers such as the *New York Times* and *Washington Post,* and for the major television networks. A study by Chester Newland in the 1960s found that less than a dozen regular reporters covered the Court; they provided the news used by most newspapers and broadcast media.[56] Thirty years later, another study by Richard Davis found roughly the same number of regular reporters assigned to the Court for roughly the same media outlets.[57]

Although journalists who cover the Supreme Court try to report its decisions accurately, they are always under the pressure of a fast-approaching deadline. Davis quotes one reporter as saying: "You only have a couple of hours to tell the world in eighth grade language what the Court has done."[58] Time is especially important for radio coverage of major decisions. ABC's regular court reporter, Tim O'Brien, recalled that "when the Court upheld the constitutionality of the all-male draft [*Rostiker v. Goldberg,* 1981], when that happened at 10:02, I was on the phone by 10:02:30, and the decision was out by 10:03. That's fast."[59]

Most Supreme Court decisions get some coverage. Davis noted 389 stories by the Associated Press (the most comprehensive news service) about 138 Court decisions in the 1989 term. Television coverage is less comprehensive. A study by Ethan Katish found that "each network gives some coverage to approximately one out of five Supreme Court decisions."[60] However, both Davis and Katish noted a tendency to overemphasize First Amendment and civil rights decisions and to underreport economic ones. Television news gives very limited coverage to oral arguments or denials of certiorari.[61]

There is some debate over how accurate media reports about Court decisions are. Major cases can get in-depth coverage, but others may get only sketchy attention. The choices of what to cover can be arbitrary or affected by the importance of other events in the news. And sometimes reporters and editors do not understand the judicial process itself. For example, denials of certiorari have sometimes been reported as decisions on the merits.[62]

Few scholars have tried to track and evaluate local coverage of court cases. Research that has focused on local coverage of cases of interest indicates that the reporting is reasonably unbiased and informative. Richard Johnson, for example, found that the newspapers in the communities he studied gave accurate summaries of the *Engel v. Vitale* (1962) and *Abington School District v. Schempp* (1963) decisions on school prayers. However, headlines sometimes distorted facts. Thus, "The conscientious observer had ample opportunity to be appraised of the Court's policies and the reasoning behind them. But the more casual observer might have received a partial and somewhat distorted view of what the Court had said."[63] Richard Pride and David Woodward analyzed media coverage of local desegregation efforts involving busing in Louisville and Nashville; they found that the local media tended to be unsensational and evenhanded in their reporting of these events. By contrast, national television networks tended to emphasize opposition to desegregation efforts through stories about local opponents and a focus on the potential for violence.[64]

Media Impact on Reactions to Judicial Policies

Most communications scholars agree that the media's primary impact on the American political system involves setting the agenda for political discussion.[65] By this they mean that whatever topic the media choose to focus upon becomes a topic of discussion by the general public and by the decision makers. To some extent, the media serve the same function for judicial policies. Although the media may not set the agenda for the implementation of court decisions, they may often play a role in focusing public attention on where implementation is or is not done faithfully. This discretion can affect the reactions to judicial policies by implementors, consumers, and members of the secondary population.

Researchers trying to explain nationwide shifts in public attention have found mixed evidence of media influence. Empirical analysis of media coverage of Supreme Court cases from 1947 to 1990 by John Bohte, Roy Flemming, and Dan Wood revealed that a small number of decisions caused "short-term spikes in coverage, . . . yet these impacts often faded away" over time. The authors noted, however, that a few critical cases in the areas of desegregation, church and state relations, and freedom of expression did have "permanent effects on media attention." These results suggest that "the Court played a major role in setting the agenda for school desegregation, free speech, and church-state issues," but had a minor agenda-setting role for most others.[66] Charles Franklin and Liane Kosaki reached the same conclusion after studying attention to the Court in both the national media and the *St. Louis Post-Dispatch*. While relatively few decisions received much attention during the nineteen months of their survey, Franklin and Kosaki concluded that highly controversial decisions received enough media coverage to assure some measure of popular awareness.[67]

Some occupational groups need more systematic and thorough reporting of judicial decisions than the popular media furnish. In studying occupational needs, Larry Berkson found that many attorneys, legislators, and law enforcement officials supplemented what they learned from popular media with information from specialized publications. Even physicians, members of the clergy, and school board members said they often learned about Supreme Court decisions from specialized publications. Not surprisingly, Berkson found that those who used supplemental sources were much more likely to know the law as it affected their occupations than were those who relied almost exclusively on the popular media.[68] Neal Milner's study of the various ways by which police officers learned about the *Miranda* decision in four Wisconsin cities found that reliance on particular sources did not affect the officers' attitudes toward the decision, except that those who read the FBI's material were more likely than the others to approve of the decision.[69]

There have been very few studies of how local media have influenced the implementation of judicial decisions. Those few focused on desegregation and seemed to show a limited media impact on implementation efforts. Robert Crain's analysis of disturbances in New Orleans associated with desegregation led him to doubt that press coverage actually affected the course of desegregation in that city's schools.[70] The Woodward and Pride study of press coverage of desegregation in Louisville and Nashville found no differences attributable to how the local and national media reported the events. White flight in these two cities was more directly tied to structural differences in the cities' desegregation and busing plans than to treatments of the issue by the media.[71]

ATTENTIVE AND MASS PUBLICS

Individuals may respond to a judicial decision even though they are not involved in either its implementation or its consumption and are not public officials, interest group members, or part of the media. In other words, the public at large is a part of the secondary population. We divide the public at large into two groups: the attentive public and the mass public. Public opinion research and surveys reveal that a small segment of the population is interested in and informed about political topics.[72] This segment is called the *attentive public*. While its composition will vary somewhat depending on the issue at hand, the attentive public is generally composed of people who are relatively well educated and work in higher status occupations, especially those that touch on public affairs. Thus, we make a distinction between an informed attentive public and a largely uninformed mass public as we discuss the public at large as part of the secondary population. As we will discuss, it is likely that the attentive public has a greater influence on the impact of judicial policies.

To consider the degree to which the public at large influences the impact of judicial policies, we need to evaluate two questions. First, what do members of this subgroup know about judicial policies? And second, what influence do attentive and mass publics have on the implementation and impact of judicial policies?

Who Knows What About Judicial Policies?

Researchers can find out who knows what about judicial policies fairly easily by conducting scientific public opinion polls that ask questions to ascertain the respondents' knowledge in this area. As a general matter, the American public knows very little about the Supreme Court and its decisions. A recent analysis by Charles Franklin, Liane Kosaki, and Herbert Kritzer shows that the public thinks highly of the Supreme Court but knows very little specifically about its activities.[73] But a growing body of research suggests that the general public may be quite knowledgeable about a few controversial or personally salient decisions. Franklin and Kosaki show that immediately following *Roe v. Wade,* for example, knowledge of the controversial abortion decision was quite high—87.4 percent of the respondents in a national poll indicated that they were familiar with the decision.[74] Of course, few decisions reach this level of visibility.

Research at the local level reveals more about knowledge of salient cases among the public. Valerie J. Hoekstra and Jeffrey A. Segal examined local public responses to a church-state relations case (*Lamb's Chapel v. Center Moriches School District,* 1993) originating in the New York suburb of Center Moriches. They found that the level of public awareness was "nothing less than astounding [with] nearly 85% (84.6) of our Center Moriches sample correctly identifying how the Court had ruled."[75] Respondents in Suffolk County, which includes Center Moriches, reported similar levels of awareness of the case. Hoekstra and Segal speculate that similar levels of awareness might not be found elsewhere; a look at thirty major newspapers across the country revealed very little coverage of the *Lamb's Chapel* case. New York papers, on the other hand, gave the case a great deal of front page coverage. Other analyses by Hoekstra produced similar conclusions about levels of awareness of different cases in the communities they affected throughout the country.[76]

Members of the attentive public are generally knowledgeable about the judiciary and judicial policies. Berkson's survey of elite occupations in the mid-1970s found that 76 percent of the respondents knew that there were nine members of the Supreme Court, and nearly an equal percentage identified Warren Burger as the chief justice. A slightly smaller percentage (64 percent) could also name at least one associate justice on the Court.[77] Berkson's survey asked whether the Court had made policies in twenty-four issue areas. He found that 69 percent of the responses were correct, 9 percent were incorrect, and 22 percent were classified as unsure or no answer. Surprisingly, however, Berkson found that the elites he surveyed were not especially aware of the direction or the content of the judicial policies. For example, there were only three occupational groups from which 50 percent or more of the respondents were able to describe the direction of decisions that were relevant to them—police officers (80 percent), lawyers (58 percent), and judges (64 percent). Less than half of the members of the remaining groups correctly described the contents of relevant decisions—lawmakers (34 percent), clergy (26 percent), schoolteachers (26 percent), and school board members (25 percent). On a more general question regarding a recent Court decision that denied states the authority to set lengthy residential requirements for voting (*Dunn v. Blumstein,* 1972), only 20 percent of the total sample answered correctly.[78] Although the percentage of correct answers on these questions may seem low, they exceed the levels of knowledge found in most national public opinion surveys regarding uncontroversial court decisions.

Commenting on the low levels of public knowledge about judicial topics, Walter Murphy and Joseph Tanenhaus speculate that individuals are concerned only about judicial policies that are salient to them, such as those that "can be viewed in an intensely personal fashion: race, religion, and security of life and property."[79] More recent research would suggest that occupational relevance and geographic proximity can also increase knowledge and awareness of court decisions.

Finally, one interesting question that has received increasing attention by political scientists is whether the Supreme Court is persuasive in decisions that actually make an impression on the public. Thomas Marshall examined polls related to eighteen Supreme Court decisions spread over almost a half century. He found little evidence that public opinion moved systematically in any direction after the Court announced its decision.[80] Franklin and Kosaki, on the other hand, found that public opinion did shift more favorably toward the Court's decision in *Roe v. Wade* when respondents considered "abortions in cases of threat to the mother's health, rape, and probable birth defects." However, on the issue of discretionary abortions, the Court's decision resulted in no shift in the direction of public opinion and, in fact, resulted in greater polarization of opinions in the American public.[81] In their study of *Lamb's Chapel,* a less controversial decision, Hoekstra and Segal showed the public opinion in the immediate community was unaffected (and not polarized) after the decision, but that opinion shifted in support of the Court's decision in Suffolk County, where citizens were less involved in the case.[82] Finally, an analysis by Timothy R. Johnson and Andrew D. Martin of the Supreme Court's abortion decision in *Webster* (1989) and death penalty cases in *Furman v. Georgia* (1972) and *McCleskey v. Kemp* (1987) showed that the Supreme Court seems to affect public opinion with first-time rulings in new policy areas. Subsequent decisions, however, appear to have little or no impact on public opinion.[83]

Because attitudinal surveys are expensive and can be contaminated by extraneous events, several political scientists have approached this question experimentally. The basic experiment works like this: after an initial survey of the subjects' attitudes about certain policies, the subjects are informed that the High Court had made a (sometimes nonexistent) decision about these policies. The subjects are then asked about their support for the decision. There may be a matched control group that is not informed of the Court's "decision." The results have been mixed—in some instances support increased modestly and in others it did not.[84]

Public Opinion and the Implementation of Judicial Policies

Because public opinion about judicial policies is often vague and ill-informed, and because researchers and pollsters rarely ask questions about carrying out specific Supreme Court decisions, assessing what impact the public has on the implementation of judicial decisions is difficult. However, many scholars believe there is a positive linkage between public attitudes toward the Court (that is, legitimacy; discussed in Chapter 6) and successful implementation of its decisions.

Conversely, negative reaction to court decisions might reduce public support for the Court. Analyzing twenty-nine separate surveys published between 1966 and 1984, Gregory Caldeira found that public confidence in the Court varied or declined somewhat in reaction to its policies. While some variables extraneous to the Court (such as declining confidence in government generally) contributed to this trend, two relating specifically to the Court were also significant—the number of federal laws declared unconstitutional and the percentage of cases decided in favor of criminal defendants. Caldeira speculates that an increase in judicial activism and systematic decisions counter to prevailing views on criminal justice "accordingly exacts a cost in confidence" in the Court by the general public.[85] Caldeira does not, however, link measures of public confidence to specific decisions, nor does he attempt to link variations in public confidence to the implementation of judicial decisions.

In the small number of studies on such matters, the findings seem to suggest that public opinion has only a potential impact on the implementation of judicial decisions. Dolbeare and Hammond's research in five communities showed little evidence that the local population was concerned about school prayer. Nonetheless, school officials evaded implementation to avoid arousing community concern.[86] Bond and Johnson's research on hospital abortion policies revealed that local public sentiment about abortion had little impact on whether a hospital offered abortion services of any type.[87]

In sum, when the public is indifferent to an issue, implementors may be relatively free to act as they wish. But if the mass public is already aroused about an issue, as the South was about desegregation, implementors can ignore public sentiment only at their political peril. From the opposite perspective, the range of action available to implementors may be greater when the public has no discernible opinion on an issue.

The influence of the attentive public is hard to determine. Dolbeare and Hammond suggest that local elite concerns were important determinants of school boards' inaction with respect to school prayer.[88] In many southern communities, the attitudes of business and civic elites who believed desegregation was necessary came to prevail over those of the mass public. However, Bond and Johnson found that hospitals' abortion policies were not much influenced by community leaders.[89]

Whether the attentive public influences members of the interpreting or implementing population probably depends on several factors. First, if the mass public is unmoved by a judicial policy, then members of the attentive public may affect implementation processes to the same degree as they normally influence judges, affected agencies, or others such as Congress. Second, if the mass public is uninterested in a judicial policy, then the attentive public may have considerable difficulty in generating popular opposition to the policy because the mass public is "simply unaware of, but generally favorable toward, the Supreme Court."[90] Thus, in instances where public approval or disapproval of a policy could influence its implementation, members of the attentive public are likely to have a limited impact either on the mass public or on the implementation of the judicial policy. Finally, if the mass public is moved in one direction or another by a judicial policy, then individuals in the attentive public may have little say over its implementation, at least in the short run, except as their sentiments parallel those of the mass public.

SUMMARY

The secondary population is a residual category that we have divided into four groups: public officials, interest groups, the media, and the public at large. Members of these groups sometimes fall in the implementing and consumer populations, but our focus here is on circumstances when they are not directly affected by or involved in carrying out judicial policies.

Public officials often find it politically necessary to react to judicial decisions—especially unpopular ones. Congress and state legislatures can change the policies that involve statutory interpretation, but it is not so easy for them to do so in matters of constitutional interpretation. Legislators have two basic options in the latter situation. First, they can directly change the policy, for example, by proposing a constitutional amendment, or they can seek to restrict a policy's scope (for example, as many state legislatures have tried to limit women's access to abortion). Second, they can strike at the offending court more generally, for example, by not raising judges' salaries or by trying to alter the court's personnel. There have been many attempts to use both options throughout American history, particularly against the Supreme Court, with varying degrees of success. Some scholars hypothesize that at bottom public officials hold the courts, and most of all the Supreme Court, sacrosanct and thus are unwilling to impair their authority seriously. For its part, the Court will sometimes back away from policies that generate enduring hostility among public officials, but on occasion it will stand firm.

The president can pursue several avenues when he disagrees with a Supreme Court policy. He can use his leadership position to persuade the public and Congress to change laws or even pass a constitutional amendment; he can appoint new justices with different policy positions; and he can have the Justice Department argue for discontinuation or modification of the offensive policy.

New or changed judicial policies often lead to the creation of new interest groups or give a new dimension to existing ones. These groups sometimes help mobilize persons who are attentive but unaffected to support or oppose the implementation of a judicial policy. For instance, many young whites ventured south in the 1960s to help end segregation, and a large number of men have pressured politicians on behalf of one side or the other of the abortion question. Often interest groups will increase the number of consumers of judicial policies through publicity about potential benefits. Groups opposed to a judicial policy may offer counseling about or help establish alternatives to the offending policy.

The media perform two basic functions: informing the public about judicial policies and informing the courts and the public about reactions to these policies. Media reporting of judicial decisions is usually but not always accurate, although coverage is often sketchy. At times, the media may perform an agenda-setting function because of their selective coverage of court cases and public reactions. Little research exists to determine what effect the media coverage has either upon public knowledge about and reactions to judicial policies or upon how courts follow up initial decisions.

We consider two publics. One is the mass public, which is largely uninterested in judicial policies except for the most controversial ones like *Roe v. Wade* or ones that affect the individuals personally. Among the mass public, opinions are usually vague and poorly informed, so that its members seldom influence a policy's implementation. The other public is the attentive public, a smaller set of people who know more about law and politics and have some knowledge of judicial policies. While the evidence is mixed, members of the attentive public appear to have greater influence on a policy's implementation. Scholars have explored the Supreme Court's ability to persuade the public to support its policies, but, again, the findings are mixed.

NOTES

1. Two books with excellent descriptions of historical and contemporary interactions between Congress and the federal courts are Edward Keynes, *The Court vs. Congress* (Durham, N.C.: Duke University Press, 1989), and Robert A. Katzmann, *Court and Congress* (Washington, D.C.: Brookings Institution, 1997).

2. See, for example, *Tennessee Valley Authority v. Hill,* 437 U.S. 153, at 193–195 (1978); *McCarty v. McCarty,* 453 U.S. 210, at 236 (1981); and *Department of Defense v. Federal Labor Relations Authority,* 127 L.Ed. 2d 325, at 339, 343 (1994). See also Pablo T. Spiller and Emerson H. Tiller, "Invitations to Override: Congressional Reversals of Supreme Court Decisions," *International Review of Law and Economics* 16 (1996): 503–521.

3. William N. Eskridge, "Overriding Supreme Court Statutory Interpretations," *Yale Law Review* 101 (1991): 331–445. See also Beth M. Henschen, "Statutory Interpretations of the Supreme Court: Congressional Response," *American Politics Quarterly* 11 (1983): 441–458, and Thomas R. Marshall, "Policy-Making and the Modern Supreme Court: When Do Supreme Court Rulings Prevail?" *Western Political Quarterly* 42 (1989): 493–508.

4. For an in-depth examination of this clash, see C. Herman Pritchett, *Congress Versus the Supreme Court, 1957–1960* (Minneapolis: University of Minnesota Press, 1961), and Walter Murphy, *Congress and the Court* (Chicago: University of Chicago Press, 1962).

5. See Michael E. Solime and James L. Walker, "The Next Word: Congressional Response to Supreme Court Statutory Decisions," *Temple Law Review* 65 (1992): 425–458.

6. See William N. Eskridge, "Reneging on History? Playing the Congress/Court/President Civil Rights Game," *California Law Review* 75 (1991): 613–684.

7. The Eleventh Amendment negated *Chisholm v. Georgia* (1793), the Fourteenth negated *Scott v. Sandford* (1857), the Sixteenth negated *Pollock v. Farmers' Loan and Trust Co.* (1895), and the Twenty-sixth negated *Oregon v. Mitchell* (1970). A proposed Child Labor Amendment was passed by Congress following *Hammer v. Dagenhart* (1918), but it fell a few states short of the three-fourths required for ratification.

8. Stephen L. Wasby, *The Impact of the United States Supreme Court: Some Perspectives* (Homewood, Ill.: Dorsey Press, 1970), 207.

9. Keynes, *The Court vs. Congress,* chaps. 6–9. See also John Schmidhauser and Larry L. Berg, *The Supreme Court and Congress: Conflict and Interaction, 1945–1968* (New York: Free Press, 1972).

10. James Meernik and Joseph Ignagni, "Judicial Review and Coordinate Construction of the Constitution," *American Journal of Political Science* 41 (1997): 447–467.

11. Ibid. See also John A. Clark and Kevin T. McGuire, "Congress, the Supreme Court and the Flag," *Political Research Quarterly* 49 (1996): 771–781.

12. Cited in Dean L. Yarwood and Bradley C. Canon, "On the Supreme Court's Annual Trek to the Capitol," *Judicature* 63 (1980): 324. In *Swann v. Charlotte-Mecklenburg County Board of Education,* 402 U.S. 1 (1971), the Court approved cross-district busing as a remedy for past school segregation.

13. William W. Crosskey, *Politics and the Constitution in the History of the United States* (Chicago: University of Chicago Press, 1953), vol. 2, 1243–1246. *Hunter's Lessee* held that a treaty was superior to state laws.

14. Cited in Schmidhauser and Berg, *The Supreme Court and Congress,* 10. *Sims,* a 1964 reapportionment decision, was misspelled in the *Congressional Record.*

15. The cases are *Hepburn v. Griswold,* 8 Wall. 603 (1870), and *Knox v. Lee,* 12 Wall. 457 (1871).

16. See Jon R. Bond, "The Politics of Court Structure: The Addition of New Federal Judges, 1949–1978," *Law and Politics Quarterly* 2 (1980): 181–188.

17. Katzmann, *Courts and Congress,* 37.

18. Mark Silverstein, *Judicious Choices: The New Politics of Supreme Court Confirmation* (New York: W. W. Norton, 1994), chap. 1.

19. See "Spiking Judges for Rulings," *National Law Journal,* June 30, 1997, A-1; "The GOP's Judicial Freeze," *U.S. News and World Report,* May 26, 1997, 23; and "Senate Imperiling Judicial System, Rehnquist Says," *New York Times,* January 1, 1998, A-1.

20. "Spiking Judges for Rulings."

21. Pritchett, *Congress Versus the Supreme Court,* and Murphy, *Congress and the Court.*

22. "Spiking Judges for Rulings." See also Keynes, *The Court vs. Congress,* 201.

23. See Mark C. Miller, "Congressional Committees and the Federal Courts: A Neo-Institutional Perspective," *Western Political Quarterly* 45 (1992): 949–970.

24. Quoted in C. Herman Pritchett, *The American Constitution,* 3d ed. (New York: McGraw-Hill, 1977), 123.

25. See "Defying Courts, Lawmakers Approve School District for Hasidim," *New York Times,* August 5, 1997, A-19.

26. "Alabama Governor Says High Court Sometimes Should Be Disobeyed," *Louisville Courier-Journal,* May 6, 1998, A-14.

27. In *Donovan v. Priest,* 931 S.W.2d 119 (Ark., 1996), the Arkansas Supreme Court found such a law unconstitutional and the U.S. Supreme Court denied certiorari.

28. Lawrence A. Baum, *The Supreme Court,* 6th ed. (Washington, D.C.: CQ Press, 1998), 257.

29. Lawrence A. Baum and David Frohnmayer, *The Courts: Sharing and Separating Powers* (New Brunswick, N.J.: Eagleton Institute, 1989), 35.

30. Henry R. Glick, *The Right to Die: Policy Innovation and Its Consequences* (New York: Columbia University Press, 1992).

31. Richard Lehne, *The Quest for Justice: The Politics of School Finance Reform* (New York: Longman, 1978), focuses on New Jersey, and Mark Yudof, "School Finance Reform in Texas: The *Edgewood* Saga," *Harvard Journal of Legislation* 28 (1991): 499–505, on Texas. Also see G. Alan Tarr, *Judicial Process and Judicial Policy-Making* (St. Paul, Minn.: West, 1994), 369–377.

32. See, for example, Barbara Hinkson Craig and David M. O'Brien, *Abortion and American Politics* (Chatham, N.J.: Chatham House, 1993), 175–176.

33. Henry J. Abraham, *Justices and Presidents,* 3d ed. (New York: Oxford University Press, 1992), 266.

34. Lawrence A. Baum, *The Supreme Court,* 6th ed. (Washington, D.C.: CQ Press, 1998), 118.

35. Lee Epstein, Jeffrey A. Segal, Harold Spaeth, and Thomas C. Walker, *The Supreme Court Compendium,* 2d ed. (Washington, D.C.: CQ Press, 1996), 631.

36. See Lincoln Caplan, *The Tenth Justice* (New York: Random House, 1987), for a discussion of the relationship between the solicitor general's office and the Supreme Court.

37. Baum, *The Supreme Court,* 103–104. The case was *Knox v. U.S.* (1993).

38. Caplan, *The Solicitor General,* chaps. 2 and 3.

39. Ibid., chap. 5. The case was *Bob Jones University v. United States* (1983). The Court appointed a private attorney to argue on behalf of the United States.

40. Among the several studies of interest groups and the courts, see the following for a thorough treatment of the subject: Lee Epstein, *Conservatives in Court* (Knoxville: University of Tennessee Press, 1985); Lee Epstein, "Interest Groups and the Courts," in *The American Court: A Critical Assessment,* ed. John B. Gates and Charles A. Johnson (Washington, D.C.: CQ Press, 1991); Lee Epstein and C. K. Rowland, "Debunking the Myth of Interest Group Invincibility in the Courts," *American Political Science Review* 33 (1991): 825–841; and Stephen Wasby, *Race*

Relations Litigation in an Age of Complexity (Charlottesville: University Press of Virginia, 1995).

41. Stuart Scheingold, *The Politics of Rights: Lawyers, Public Policy and Political Change* (New Haven, Conn.: Yale University Press, 1974), 85.

42. "Abortion Foes Gain State-Level Victories," *Lexington Herald Leader,* January 18, 1998, A-12.

43. Scheingold, *The Politics of Rights,* 131.

44. Ibid., 132.

45. For example, see a Web page supported by the Students for Access and Opportunity, an organization working to overturn the *Hopwood* decision. http://www.geocities.com/CollegePark/Quad/2701/SAO.html (6/22/98).

46. Karen O'Connor, *Women's Organizations' Use of the Courts* (Lexington, Mass.: Lexington Books, 1980), 125–126.

47. Stephen Halpern, "Assessing the Litigative Role of ACLU Chapters," in *Civil Liberties,* ed. Stephen Wasby (Lexington, Mass.: Lexington Books, 1976), 165.

48. Jack Greenberg, *Crusaders in the Court: How a Dedicated Band of Lawyers Fought for the Civil Rights Revolution* (New York: Basic Books, 1994), 254–255.

49. O'Connor, *Women's Organizations' Use of the Courts,* 18–19.

50. Joel Handler, *Social Movements and the Legal System: A Theory of Law Reform and Social Change* (New York: Academic Press, 1978), 128–129.

51. Joseph Stewart Jr. and James F. Sheffield Jr., "Does Interest Group Litigation Matter? The Case of Black Political Mobilization in Mississippi," *Journal of Politics* 49 (1987): 780–798.

52. "New Hampshire Supreme Court Declares Property Tax Funding of Public Schools Unconstitutional," *New York Times,* December 21, 1997, 19.

53. Taken from several First Amendment Center Watch reports during 1997.

54. "Settlement Ends High Court Case on Preferences," *New York Times,* November 22, 1997, A1, A12.

55. Doris Graber, *Mass Media and American Politics* (Washington, D.C.: CQ Press, 1980), 217–218.

56. Chester A. Newland, "Press Coverage of the United States Supreme Court," *Western Political Quarterly* 17 (1964): 15–36.

57. Richard Davis, *Decisions and Images: The Supreme Court and the Press* (Englewood Cliffs, N.J.: Prentice Hall, 1994), 63–69.

58. Ibid., 81.

59. Ibid.

60. Ethan Katish, "The Supreme Court Beat: How Television Covers the U.S. Supreme Court," *Judicature* 67 (1983): 8.

61. Davis, *Decisions and Images,* 136. See also Elliott E. Slotnick and Jennifer A. Segal, *Television News and the Supreme Court: All the News That's Fit to Air* (New York: Cambridge University Press, 1998).

62. Elliott Slotnick and Jennifer A. Segal, "'The Supreme Court Decided Today. . . ,' or Did It?" *Judicature* (1994): 89–95. See their *Television News and the Supreme Court* also.

63. Richard Johnson, *The Dynamics of Compliance* (Evanston, Ill.: Northwestern University Press, 1967), 95.

64. Richard A. Pride and J. David Woodward, "Busing Plans, Media Agenda, and White Flight: Nashville and Louisville" (Paper presented at the Annual Meeting of the Southwestern Political Science Association, Houston, 1978).

65. See Maxwell E. McCombs, "The Agenda Setting Approach," in *Handbook of Political Communication,* ed. Dan Nimmo and Keith Sanders (Beverly Hills, Calif.: Sage, 1981), 121–140, and Shanto Iyengar and Donald R. Kinder, *News That Matters* (Chicago: University of Chicago Press, 1987).

66. John Bohte, Roy Flemming, and B. Dan Wood, "The Supreme Court, the Media, and Legal Change: A Reassessment of Rosenberg's *Hollow Hope*" (Paper presented at the Annual Meeting of the American Political Science Association, Chicago, 1995), 24. A revised version of this paper is published as: Roy Flemming, B. Dan Wood, and John Bohte, "The Public and the Supreme Court: Individual Justice Responsiveness to American Policy Moods," *American Journal of Political Science* 41 (1997): 468–498.

67. Charles H. Franklin and Liane C. Kosaki, "Media, Knowledge, and Public Evaluations of the Supreme Court," in *Contemplating Courts,* ed. Lee Epstein (Washington, D.C.: CQ Press, 1995), 352–375.

68. Larry Berkson, *The Supreme Court and Its Publics* (Lexington, Mass.: Lexington Books, 1978), 64ff.

69. Neal Milner, *The Court and Local Law Enforcement* (Beverly Hills, Calif.: Sage, 1971), 201ff.

70. Robert Crain, *The Politics of School Desegregation* (Chicago: Aldine Press, 1968), 284–287.

71. Pride and Woodward, "Busing Plans, Media Agenda, and White Flight," 17.

72. Our conception of attentive publics is drawn from Donald Devine, *The Attentive Public* (Chicago: Rand McNally, 1970). For a recent treatment of elite/mass opinion, see John Zaller, *The Nature and Origins of Mass Opinion* (New York: Cambridge University Press, 1992).

73. Charles Franklin, Liane C. Kosaki, and Herbert Kritzer, "The Salience of United States Supreme Court Decisions" (Paper presented at the Annual Meeting of the American Political Science Association, Washington, D.C., 1993). See also Kenneth Dolbeare and Phillip Hammond, "The Political Party Basis of Attitudes Toward the Supreme Court," *Public Opinion Quarterly* 32 (1968): 16–30.

74. Charles H. Franklin and Liane C. Kosaki, "Republican Schoolmaster: The U.S. Supreme Court, Public Opinion, and Abortion," *American Politial Science Review* 83 (1989): 762.

75. Valerie J. Hoekstra and Jeffrey A. Segal, "The Shepherding of Local Public

Opinion: The Supreme Court and *Lamb's Chapel," Journal of Politics* 58 (1996): 1088–1090.

76. See, for example, Valerie J. Hoekstra, "The Supreme Court and Public Opinion: The Impact of Economic Decisions on Local Public Opinion" (Paper presented at the Annual Meeting of the American Political Science Association, Chicago, 1995).

77. Berkson, *The Supreme Court and Its Publics,* 16.

78. Ibid., 18, 79, 86.

79. Walter Murphy and Joseph Tanenhaus, "Public Opinion and the Supreme Court: Mapping Some Prerequisites for Court Legitimation of Regime Changes," in *Frontiers of Judicial Research,* ed. Joel Grossman and Joseph Tanenhaus (New York: Wiley, 1969), 278–279.

80. Thomas Marshall, *Public Opinion and the Supreme Court* (Boston: Unwin Hyman, 1989).

81. Franklin and Kosaki, "Republican Schoolmaster: The U.S. Supreme Court, Public Opinion, and Abortion," 759.

82. Hoekstra and Segal, "The Shepherding of Local Public Opinion," 1093–1094.

83. Timothy R. Johnson and Andrew D. Martin, "The Public's Conditional Response to Supreme Court Decisions," *American Political Science Review* 92 (1998): 299–309.

84. Larry Baas and Dan Thomas, "The Supreme Court and Policy Legitimation: Experimental Tests," *American Politics Quarterly* 12 (1984): 335–360; Jeffrey Mondak, "Perceived Legitimacy of Supreme Court Decisions: Three Functions of Source Credibility," *Political Behavior* 12 (1990): 363–384; and Valerie Hoekstra, "The Supreme Court and Opinion Change: An Experimental Study of the Court's Ability to Change Opinion," *American Politics Quarterly* 23 (1995): 109–129.

85. Gregory Calderia, "Neither the Purse nor the Sword: Dynamics of Public Confidence in the Supreme Court," *American Political Science Review* 80 (1986): 1222. See also Robert H. Durr and Christina Wolbrecht, "Public Opinion and the U.S. Supreme Court" (Paper presented at the Annual Meeting of the American Political Science Association, Chicago, 1995).

86. Kenneth M. Dolbeare and Phillip E. Hammond, *The School Prayer Decisions: From Court Policy to Local Practice* (Chicago: University of Chicago Press, 1971), chap. 6.

87. Jon Bond and Charles A. Johnson, "Implementing a Permissive Policy: Hospital Abortion Services after *Roe v. Wade," American Journal of Political Science* 26 (1982): 385–405.

88. Dolbeare and Hammond, *The School Prayer Decisions,* 23.

89. Bond and Johnson, "Hospital Abortion Services after *Roe v. Wade.*"

90. Kenneth Dolbeare, "The Public Views the Supreme Court," in *Law, Politics, and the Federal Courts,* ed. Herbert Jacob (Boston: Little, Brown, 1967), 210.

CHAPTER SIX

Judicial Impact Theory

We have discussed in Chapters 2 through 5 the responses of different populations to judicial policies, and we have offered explanations for these responses culled from the research on judicial policies and their impact. These explanations do not fit into any simple framework: some are drawn from investigations of particular settings or circumstances; others are speculation about results that were unanticipated by the researchers; still others appear to confirm specific theories that guided research. In this chapter we hope to bring order to these diverse explanations by reviewing several theories of judicial impact, then discussing applications of the theories.

The main benefit to understanding such theories is that they provide an *explanation* for variations in responses to judicial policies. Social science research seeks to explain systematically human behavior under a variety of circumstances; policy makers and implementors sometimes make use of such explanations as they shape or carry out public policies. For example, if we observe police officers abiding by Supreme Court criminal justice decisions in spite of opposition within their ranks, then we might conduct research to see if, say, legitimacy theory explains the compliant behavior under conditions where noncompliance might be expected. Further, if we see that some police officers follow the Court's policy and others do not, we could gather data on the officers' views of the Court's legitimacy to test whether this theory is an appropriate explanation for the difference in compliance.

Although social scientists in general are committed to organized and cumulative research, theory has played only a modest role in judicial impact research. Judicial impact research began in the 1950s and 1960s with a descriptive focus. The findings of widespread noncompliance with Supreme Court decisions by early researchers such as Gordon Patric, Frank Sorauf, and Walter Murphy were rather startling and seemed to demand explanation.[1] By the late 1960s some scholars were developing or applying theories to explain noncompliance and other variations in responses. Some theories were relatively comprehensive and offered explanations for patterns of behavior in a wide variety of situations. Others were quite narrow, offering simple explanations of how one variable affected another in particular circumstances. Since then much judicial impact research has been guided by relevant theories. Unfortunately, some research is still descriptive and is loosely speculative.

We will discuss a number of theories that have been advanced to explain the impact of judicial policies. Some are derived from psychology, some from economics, some from the study of communications, some from the study of organizational behavior, and some from political science and sociology. For the sake of an orderly discussion, we have divided them by these focuses. Remember that the theories are not mutually exclusive. They are interactive—they may reinforce each other in some situations and be at odds in others. All are probably operative to some degree. However, there is little research on the interactions of two or more theories. For this reason, our review concentrates on simple statements of the theories, rather than on their interaction.

PSYCHOLOGICAL THEORIES OF JUDICIAL IMPACT

Researchers contend that people's responses to a new policy are shaped by their preexisting attitudes toward the policy or toward things symbolized by or associated with the policy or the agency making the policy. Such attitudes may be acquired from a variety of sources, such as parents, peers, churches, community norms, magazines, and television shows. These attitudes may be based upon facts or upon misinformation; they may stem from accurate or from erroneous versions of history. Attitudes may or may not be logically connected with the policy at issue. Regardless, they become embedded in everyone's outlook on life and politics, and are difficult—though by no means impossible—to change. They color reactions to judicial decisions as well as to other political events. Nonetheless, we all have what might be termed a *zone of indifference* in relation to some policies. That is, for some policies either we have no preexisting opinions or we hold them so weakly that they do not significantly affect our acceptance and response decisions. Whether a policy falls inside or outside the zone depends upon some nonattitudinal factors, such as external pressures and how the policy affects daily life. But there are also some general attitudinal patterns that researchers have noted. These patterns are explained by what we call psychological theories of judicial impact.

Legitimacy Theory

We have introduced the concept of legitimacy in several of the earlier chapters of this book. In Chapter 2 we identified legitimacy as one of the variables that affect a lower court judge's willingness to accept a higher court decision, and in Chapter 3 we noted that implementors are more likely to accept a judicial policy that they consider legitimate. In Chapter 5 we noted the arguments about what role Congress's perception of the Supreme Court's legitimacy had in its consideration of bills to punish the Court or alter its authority.

Legitimacy theory has several facets. These facets can relate to either of two things: the *institution* making the policy (the court) or the *substance* of the policy. In this section, we discuss three related but distinguishable facets. Our focus is primarily on how they relate to the courts themselves, but sometimes institutional legitimacy is intertwined with the legitimacy of specific policies.

Generally speaking, people are more likely to respond positively to commands from those who they believe have the right to issue such commands. The legitimacy they accord to the source of the command affects the nature of their response. The success of political institutions and even of governments themselves depends in large part on whether citizens believe that the institutions are behaving legitimately. Legitimacy is not synonymous with approval or even with correctness. Rather, a law, an administrative policy, or a court decision is legitimate in an individual's eyes if he or she concedes that the institution's proper function in society is to make such a decision and that the decision itself is not grossly biased or totally absurd.

Legitimacy theory—explaining individuals' acceptance of and response to institutional policies as a function of their attitudes toward the institution's authority and role in the governance of society—is a familiar one in political science through the works of such scholars as David Easton.[2] In very general terms, judicial scholars such as Alexander Bickel, Charles Black, and Michael Petrick have used legitimacy theory to explain why a court, particularly the Supreme Court, is able to secure the psychological acceptance of and appropriate behavioral responses to its decisions.[3] Legitimacy theory is quite comprehensive in the sense that it can be applied to the behavior of persons in the interpreting, implementing, consumer, and secondary populations. Legitimacy theory, however, does not purport to explain acceptance or, more particularly, behavioral responses completely. Legitimacy is a background factor that interacts with more immediate factors in any given situation.

LEGITIMACY AS SOCIAL DISTANCE. Courts engage in various activities that by design or coincidence enhance the perceived legitimacy of their decision-making role by maintaining a social distance from the other participants in the political system. Drama and ritual enhance this distance. Judges wear robes, everyone rises when they enter the courtroom, and they are addressed as "Your Honor." The distance is augmented by the absence of lobbyists in the courts, by the rule that judges cannot talk with anyone about a pending case, and by the norm that judges cannot even appear to be involved in partisan politics.

The Supreme Court's legitimacy is reinforced not only by this social distance, but as Richard Johnson observes, by the fact that it is *the* Supreme Court. As the highest court in the land, there is no judicial appeal of its decisions. In particular, "It is perceived as having a legal and constitutional right to do what it does." Johnson argues that the maintenance of a visible social distance from other political actors is particularly important for the Court because it is "in a position to enunciate broad social principles and in turn take the brunt of the criticism when those nearer the scene of battle implement the principles."[4] Of course, not everyone accepts the Court's legitimacy uncritically. Some people may accept the Court's authority in general, but feel that particular Court decisions are illegitimate because they violate some cherished principle such as majority rule, federalism, or separation of powers.

LEGITIMACY AS FINDING THE LAW. Another facet of legitimacy involves people's perceptions of how courts function. Many people believe that courts do not make policy, that they simply serve as vehicles by which the law is determined and applied. This belief is sometimes referred to as the "myth of the courts." Jerome Frank, a prominent legal scholar and federal judge in the 1930s and 1940s, was the leading analyst of this myth.[5] Frank argued that even adults who are engaged in politics and legal disputes have a psychological need for a father figure. In other places or times, priests, kings, or the leaders of totalitarian parties have fulfilled this need. In modern, secular America, where the ideal is a government of laws and not of men, we turn to impartial judges to fulfill this need—we impute to them wisdom, concern, and capabilities beyond those possessed by other political actors. As one judicial scholar puts it, this myth "transforms courts from instruments of naked power to legitimate authorities capable of proclaiming and implementing policies without the use of force."[6]

To the extent that such myths permeate our thinking, they shelter the courts from public scrutiny and induce members of the various populations to accept and respond positively to judicial policies. The uncritical acceptance of this myth is not so widespread today, especially among the political elite.[7] As the power of the myth declines, so may the legitimacy of the courts, a decline that in turn could jeopardize the acceptance of judicial policies. Nonetheless, the myths retain a considerable influence on the American public.

LEGITIMACY AS FAIRNESS AND REALISM.   Stephen Wasby offers a slightly different perspective on the legitimacy of the courts, especially that of the Supreme Court. He notes that if the Court is perceived as "not ruling fairly on a subject or on the basis of adequate knowledge," then the reception given the decision may be negative.[8] In the same vein, if people perceive that a court's past policies have been unfair, were made without proper procedure, or seem unrelated to the real world, they will not accept the court's legitimacy. In other words, legitimacy is a product not only of how people view the court's function in society, but also of how well they think a court is fulfilling its function. A court can undermine its legitimacy by making seemingly unfair or unrealistic decisions. Conversely, a court that is perceived as having a strong record of impartiality, accompanied by an understanding of life's realities, may win acceptance of an unpopular decision.

These three facets of legitimacy—as social distance, as finding the law, and as fairness—are closely connected. A court that loses one facet of legitimacy may well lose the other two. For instance, in the wake of numerous anti-labor decisions in the years from 1890 to 1935, organized labor and its sympathizers came to believe that the Supreme Court was not keeping its distance from the political system, that the Court's policies were not derived from the Constitution, and that the justices were deliberately hostile to the workers' interests. All three perspectives on legitimacy are based on the underlying hypothesis that the greater the perceived legitimacy of the Court, the greater the probability that its policies will be accepted and faithfully implemented.

COMPARATIVE LEGITIMACY. Legitimacy theory may also be used in comparing the efficacy of courts with that of other institutions. That is, people may perceive the courts as more legitimate or less legitimate than other institutions, such as Congress and the presidency. When the policies of two branches clash, individuals will presumably accept the policy of the institution they consider more legitimate and reject the other. As we saw in Chapter 5, for instance, the Supreme Court had sufficient legitimacy in the public mind to withstand President Franklin Roosevelt's 1937 attempt to pack it—although it gave ground in the political dispute during the process. On the other hand, on issues involving foreign policy and military security, the public is probably less likely to view decisions of the Court as legitimate if that body is in conflict with the president.

RESEARCH ON LEGITIMACY THEORY. Walter Murphy and Joseph Tanenhaus were among the first of many political scientists to directly assess the public's evaluation of the Supreme Court's legitimacy. Roughly 40 percent of the respondents in their 1966 survey described the Court's work in terms of constitutional adjudication, and 26 percent mentioned the Court's work in terms of policy making or litigation. Slightly more than one-third of the respondents indicated that they felt the Court could carry out its responsibilities in an "impartial and competent fashion."[9] Gregory Casey concluded from a later study that large segments of the public continue to hold what he describes as mythical views about the Supreme Court's function.[10] There have been other public opinion surveys conducted about the Court, but most measure knowledge of or attitudes toward the Court's specific policies instead of how the respondents regard the Court per se. Most of these have found that the public knows little about the Court's decisions.[11]

Several researchers have demonstrated that the Court does have an impact on public opinion (see Chapter 5). Their studies suggest that the Court influences public opinion in some circumstances (for example, when a decision affects a local agency or when a local agency is involved in the Court's decision), but they do not speak directly to the question of whether the perceived legitimacy of the Court was a factor in changing public opinions.[12]

A more direct analysis of the influence of perceived legitimacy can be found in a series of experimental studies conducted by Jeffery J. Mondak and by Valerie J. Hoekstra. Mondak's studies test a "political capital" hypothesis: "If institutional approval can be used to confer policy legitimacy, and if in conferring policy legitimacy institutional support is expended, then institutional legitimacy functions as a political currency; public support allows the 'purchase' of some increment of policy approval."[13] Mondak devised experiments to evaluate whether respondents approved more of policies when they were attributed to the Court than when the same policies were attributed to other institutions, such as Congress, the U.S. Army, state governments, and bureaucrats. He found that the Supreme Court was, in fact, the most respected institution among his respondents. Moreover, associating a policy with the Supreme Court "produced a positive effect for policy legitimacy" across eight policy areas, as well as "strong evidence that a credible institution can enhance the legitimacy of unpopular actions."[14] Finally, Mondak also discovered that associating an unpopular decision with the Court can increase its acceptability to a degree, but when the Court makes too many unpopular decisions, its legitimacy diminishes.[15]

Hoekstra also used an experimental design to assess the perceived legitimacy of the Court and its influence on the public's acceptance of Supreme Court decisions. She found that decisions attributed to Congress hardly persuaded anyone, but those attributed to the Court were modestly influential. The most acceptable or influential source, however, was a hypothetical "nonpartisan think tank." When she considered attitudes toward the Court, the data supported the widely presumed link between positive views of the Court and acceptance of the decisions.[16]

Timothy R. Johnson and Andrew D. Martin offer a slightly different theory about the influence of perceived legitimacy of the Supreme Court. Their analysis of public opinion suggests that after major Court decisions the Court's legitimacy prompts citizens to pay attention to and discuss those decisions. Legitimacy does not, however, lead to an uncritical shift in public opinion toward the policy announced by the Court.[17]

A separate question is the extent to which political elites accord the Court greater legitimacy. Elites are crucial to the effectiveness of judicial policies because they make up the entire interpreting population, much of the implementing population, and the key elements of the secondary population insofar as feedback is concerned. While there is evidence that elites support civil liberties to a greater extent than the public at large,[18] there are also data showing that elites are less likely to see the Supreme Court as a font of legitimacy than is the general public.[19] Indeed, most of the examples in this book of defiance, evasion, and avoidance of judicial policies involve political elites.

Cognitive Dissonance Theory

Cognitive dissonance theory is based on the widely accepted psychological tenet that an individual's opinions on a particular subject need to be internally consistent with his or her behavior. When inconsistencies occur, tensions arise within the individual, who then takes conscious or unconscious steps to reduce the tension. The debate on affirmative action illustrates this tension. Most government and university administrators subscribe to the principle that persons should be hired or promoted on their own merits and not because of their race or ethnic background. Yet many also believe that most African Americans and Hispanics are disadvantaged in the job market for various reasons associated with their background. They set up affirmative action programs to help rectify this disadvantage. When the courts proclaim the "merit only" principle (as the Supreme Court did in *Adarand Constructors v. Pena,* 1995), these administrators find themselves under internal cross-pressures.

Two of the most informative early studies of judicial impact employed cognitive dissonance theory to understand better how and why school personnel reacted as they did to the Supreme Court's decision banning prayers in public schools (*Abington School District v. Schempp,* 1963). Both Richard Johnson and William Muir have suggested that a decision such as this would be likely to fall outside many persons' zone of indifference and thus would motivate them to respond in some manner.[20] Johnson argues that a directive from a court that a person respects ordering that person to cease practices to which he or she is committed is likely to create a cognitive imbalance and generate tensions to return to some form of cognitive consistency.

Several means may be employed to achieve cognitive consistency after a judicial decision. Cognitive dissonance theory is concerned with these means, by which an individual either increases the desirability of the chosen alternative or decreases the desirability of the rejected alternative. The theory does not predict which alternative an individual will choose, just that some change in attitude or behavior will occur. Muir's list of possible ways individuals may handle dissonance includes the following:

1. Denying the existence of the judicial decision
2. Depreciating the decision by interpreting it to be inapplicable
3. Disassociating himself or herself from the field covered by the decision

4. Becoming indecisive
5. Keeping the original attitude and exaggerating the coercive effects of the law
6. Accentuating the original attitude and derogating the law
7. Converting to the legal attitude
8. Diminishing the importance of or eliminating an originally equivocal attitude

The first five of these responses Muir labels the *nullist* reaction, and the remaining three patterns he terms *backlash, conversion,* and *liberating,* respectively.[21]

Muir found that school personnel used some of these patterns of behavior to work out any dissonance they experienced after deciding how to react to the Court's school prayer decision. Muir (and Johnson, with a slightly different list of reactions) explained individual responses by idiosyncratic variables, but their research does little to satisfy our search for a systematic explanation of the circumstances that cause individuals to reduce cognitive dissonance in a particular manner.

Attitudes Toward Judicial Policies

Throughout this book we have noted the importance of a person's attitude toward a particular judicial policy. Regardless of how an individual feels about the Supreme Court as a policy maker, the nature of the policy itself is likely to have a substantial effect on his or her reaction to the judicial decision. For example, a person may not like the fact that the Supreme Court made policy in *Roe v. Wade* (1973) because he or she believes that abortion policy should be made by legislative bodies. Nevertheless, that person may agree with the policy itself and therefore may react positively to it. Substantive policy likes and dislikes are what the zone of indifference concept is all about.

The most straightforward hypothesis employing personal attitudes suggests that individual policy preferences influence reactions; that is, individuals with positive attitudes toward a judicial policy will be more likely to respond positively to the policy than individuals with negative attitudes toward the policy. While this hypothesis may seem trite because it should be obvious, there have been few tests of it, and those that have been made do not always support it. Neal Milner reports a 78.9 percent opposition to the Supreme Court's *Miranda v. Arizona* (1966) decision among police officers in four Wisconsin cities; yet the officers' behavioral reactions were for the most part positive, that is, compliant. Thus, even though the officers held negative attitudes toward *Miranda,* their reactions were contrary to the attitudes hypothesis, which predicts that compliance would be minimal.[22]

Of course, as we have noted in earlier chapters, personal policy preferences often do make a difference. Racial attitudes have no doubt influenced people's reactions to desegregation rulings and to some extent now affect responses to affirmative action decisions. People's attitudes about the sanctity of life help affect their responses to abortion, "right to die" rulings, and death penalty decisions. The basic attitudes of members of Congress and state legislatures help produce these bodies' responses to Supreme Court rulings.

Thus, the challenge is to explain the differences between occasions when attitudes are influential and occasions when they are not. At times attitude is modified by pressures external to the individual, and these pressures in turn can overwhelm a person's internal pressures to react consistently with his or her attitudes. Police officers may dislike court decisions such as *Miranda,* but if they do not comply with the decisions, the charges against those they arrest are likely to be dropped. School officials may wish to comply with the Court's decisions regarding prayers, but they may fear strong adverse community reactions. Where response is solely a product of an individual's attitudes, his or her policy preferences will be likely to be influential. Where the reaction is affected by external factors, individual attitudes become only one factor influencing reactions to judicial policies.

UTILITY THEORY:
A PSYCHOLOGICAL/ECONOMIC APPROACH

Cost-Benefit Analysis

Utility theory, in which a cost-benefit analysis of alternatives explains responses to judicial policies, was advanced in the 1970s by Robert Stover and Don Brown theoretically and by Harrell Rodgers and Charles Bullock in their studies of southern school desegregation.[23] Basically, utility theory is borrowed from the work of the eighteenth-century British philosopher Jeremy Bentham[24] and from the rational choice theories of modern economists. Bentham's central assumption is that individuals seek to maximize pleasure and minimize pain; the economists' main assumption is that people seek to maximize financial gain and minimize financial loss. Each approach postulates that individuals make rational decisions that they believe will best achieve these goals. For Bentham, psychological well-being was essential, while economists concentrate on monetary profits or losses. Judicial scholars, especially Stover and Brown, fit these emphases into a single theory, and we will do so in our discussion of utility theory.

Stover and Brown describe the concept of utility as it applies to judicial policies as follows:

> Utility refers to the net benefit or loss which the individual *expects* to result from reactions to a particular law. The utility in this situation is a product of a person's values and his/her expectations of eventual outcomes. Their values refer to their attitudes toward relevant objects such as the court, the policy, or significant others affected by the policy. The expectations refers to perceived probabilities that taking a particular course of action will actually result in a benefit or a cost to oneself.[25]

Although complete information is not often available to (or even sought by) the decision makers, rationality is assumed insofar as individuals are expected to make choices maximizing pleasure or profit instead of pain or loss based on the information they do have. Thus, Stover and Brown offer the basic postulate of this theory: "A person with the capacity to either comply or not comply with a given law will not comply when the utility of noncompliance is greater than the utility of compliance."[26]

Rodgers and Bullock note that the range of factors considered in the utility calculation can be expressed in the inequality:

$$B_n + C_n <?> B_c + C_c$$

where:

B_n = benefits of noncompliance
C_n = costs of noncompliance
B_c = benefits of compliance
C_c = costs of compliance

Noncompliance is expected if the net value of $B_n + C_n$ is greater than the net value of $B_c + C_c$. Compliance is expected if the reverse is true. Explaining these elements in more substantive terms, Rodgers and Bullock suggest that the benefits of noncompliance (B_n) could include "financial gain, expected power and prestige, or simply convenience." The costs of noncompliance (C_n) could include the certainty and severity of "formal or informal sanctions." The benefits of compliance (B_c) may involve "maintaining personal esteem, financial gains, or . . . the esteem of others." And finally, the costs of compliance (C_c) may include "inconvenience, ostracism, or increased responsibilities."[27]

Utility Theory and Law-Abidingness

Utility theory particularly complements legitimacy theory. Legitimacy theory largely explains a person's decision whether or not to accept a judicial policy. This acceptance decision in turn influences the behavioral response. Utility theory, by contrast, looks at a person's behavioral response rather than the acceptance decision. A person may feel that a policy is legitimate but that his or her own interests are best served by noncompliance. For instance, some persons cheat on their income tax even though they would not argue that the tax is unconstitutional or even unfair. They cheat because it maximizes their financial gain and they feel that the probabilities of getting caught are sufficiently low to take the risk of underpaying their taxes. (The converse is also true. Some persons may consider the income tax illegitimate but carefully pay every penny due in order to avoid the negative utility of going to prison or paying a large fine if they are audited.)

Rodgers and Bullock nicely highlight the opposite perspectives of the two theories. Studies exploring the concept of legitimacy, they note, indicate that most citizens tend to be law-abiding, that respect for the law and obedience to it are characteristic of most individuals from early childhood on. But they also note that in some areas (such as speed limits) noncompliance or disobedience is widespread and widely accepted. Thus, they conclude, "Individual attitudes about law and law-abidingness do not provide a very accurate guide to behavior where specific laws are concerned."[28] Instead of following their inclinations to be law-abiding, most individuals engage in some type of cost-benefit calculus before reacting to a decision—at least when their own preferences are important.

Rodgers and Bullock emphasize an individual's commitment to law-abidingness as a factor that is frequently included in the calculations of the cost-benefit inequality we set out earlier. Individual commitments to law-abidingness may vary, of course, but when an individual is considering disobeying a judicial decision, these authors maintain that "the psychic costs of violating the commitment [to law-abidingness] could be a highly constraining factor."[29] A positive attitude about law-abidingness could be so strong that the costs of noncompliance with a judicial policy would exceed the benefits of noncompliance, thus pushing the individual toward compliance. But these pressures may be overcome under some circumstances. If the individual can rationalize the noncompliance, then psychic costs of noncompliance may be reduced and the pressures for law-abidingness neutralized. In such an instance, through a process much like the balancing notion used in cognitive dissonance theory, noncompliance is rationalized, commitments to law-abidingness neutralized, and equilibrium restored for the individual.

Rodgers and Bullock hypothesize that the norm of law-abidingness is least constraining when the individual "(1) disagrees with a law; (2) believes that he would benefit from breaking the law; (3) doubts that he would be punished for breaking the law; and (4) perceives that he would suffer little public sanction for breaking the law and might even be esteemed by important peers for doing so."[30] This combination of factors, the authors contend, was what came about in the South during efforts to desegregate public schools. School officials frequently openly resisted the Supreme Court's *Brown v. Board of Education* (1954) decision. They were reasonably certain that little would happen to them if they did so, and they actually were applauded for opposing the law by local citizens. Under these circumstances, individuals normally committed to law-abidingness were able to ignore a judicial policy and still maintain a sense of mental balance.

Applicability of Utility Theory

Utility theory is most easily tested when the costs and benefits are economic. It is difficult to obtain reliable information on psychological benefits; even if we could, it would be nearly impossible to make interpersonal comparisons of such benefits. Thus, most utility theory research about judicial policies and their impact has followed an economic approach. At the macro-theory level, the most visible proponent is federal appeals judge Richard Posner. He argues that the development of both common and constitutional law was and is largely shaped by economic considerations. His work is impressive, although perhaps more persuasive when he has focused on tort, contract, and property law than when he has considered civil liberties issues.[31] In recent years, many political scientists have borrowed utility (also called rational or public choice) theories from economics and applied them to political phenomena, including the study of judicial decision making.[32]

Surprisingly, there has been very little work applying utility theory to the implementation and consumption of judicial policies in recent times. In the 1970s, Rodgers and Bullock found, in brief, that as the financial costs—especially the loss of federal funds—of maintaining segregated schools increased, resistance declined.[33] Similarly, as we noted in Chapter 4, Micheal Giles and Douglas Gatlin's 1980 study found that financial considerations were the most determinative of whether white consumers of court-ordered busing actually avoided sending their children to desegregated schools.[34] These studies suggest the importance of economic factors over psychological factors in utility calculations, when the two clash. They also illustrate the value of using utility theory because it taps a major and universal human motivation: money. When people respond to judicial policies as the economic focus of utility theory predicts, it explains their behavior; when they respond differently, it signals us to search for an alternate motivation that outweighs financial well-being.

It can be very difficult to test whether individuals engage in a series of cost-benefit calculations after a judicial decision, but Stover and Brown propose another hypothesis which is both important and testable. They observe that focusing on the cost-benefit inequality forces us to consider the range of factors that may influence compliance and that may be manipulated to achieve behavioral change. According to these researchers, as an institution's ability to manipulate terms in the inequality increases, its influence over reactions will also increase. The authors suggest (and we have noted in Chapters 2 and 3) that courts have little control over the costs of noncompliance with their own general policies. Nor do courts have the same ability to dispense benefits to or limit the costs of those who do comply. In a general sense, then, courts are less likely than other branches to achieve changes in behavior, especially if they limit themselves to issuing orders and perform little or no follow-up.[35]

COMMUNICATIONS THEORY

The communication of judicial decisions is a haphazard, multistage process which often inadequately informs others in the political system about the decisions of the courts. Research shows that police officers, for example, learn about judicial decisions from a variety of sources—sometimes from friends or the general media, and sometimes through training sessions and bulletins from law enforcement agencies.[36] Similarly, most members of the implementing, consumer, and secondary populations get their information from a variety of sources.

In fact, the term *theory* as applied to the communications that link judicial decisions with their consequences is something of a misnomer. There is no overarching or well-recognized theory. Rather, we have a number of separate propositions about the relationship between the nature of the communication of a judicial policy and the responses to that policy. Nonetheless, researchers have given considerable attention to various aspects of the communication of judicial decisions, and it is reasonable to assume that the communicative process has particular effects on the chain of events following a judicial decision.

Existing research establishes that sources and levels of information vary from population to population, and from group to group within the respective populations. We have noted some of these variations in earlier chapters. However, it is less clear whether levels or sources of information are related to variations in responses to judicial policies.

There are two features of the communications process that affect responses to judicial decisions.[37] First, the context of the decision itself can be important, since some responses may be affected not only by what the decision is but also by how it is "packaged." Second, the channels through which the decision is communicated will affect how people perceive the message. Each of these features of the process lends itself to hypotheses, which we discuss in the following sections.

Context of the Decision

How a court chooses to announce a policy can be very important to the reception of the policy by affected groups. Speaking primarily of compliance with Supreme Court decisions, G. Alan Tarr suggests that responses may be "a function of the perceived finality of the standards enunciated by the Supreme Court, the clarity of those standards, and the persuasiveness of the Court's justification of its decisions."[38] This perspective, shared by many legal scholars, holds that responses to a Supreme Court decision are affected positively by the persuasiveness of the opinion announcing the decision. What constitutes a final, clear, and persuasive policy is not, however, easily determined.

Tarr suggests that the perception of finality of a policy is governed by three factors. First, the level of support for the policy on the court may be important. If the policy is announced with only minimal support, a five-to-four vote on the Supreme Court, for example, then changes or modifications in policy could occur with changes in personnel or even changes in the policy preferences of one justice. If support for a policy is marginal, its finality is open to question and its implementation may be ineffective. The Court's affirmative action decisions, most of them decided by close votes, are a good example (see Chapter 2). Its latest decision rejected affirmative action by a 5–4 vote (*Adarand Constructors v. Pena,* 1995). But another appointment to the Court by President Clinton could change the balance to 5–4 in favor of affirmative action. Thus, although *Adarand* was written in very definitive terms, some regard it as just another battle in an ongoing war. By contrast, *Brown v. Board* (1954) was decided unanimously, and the Court made it a point to decide all desegregation cases unanimously for the next two decades.

Second, finality may be evident from the degree to which the policy has been applied by a court in the past or is later subject to attack. Longstanding policies and those to which a court has expressed a firm commitment will be seen as more permanent than will novel policies or older ones that have been questioned or surrounded with exceptions. For instance, in *Oregon Employment Division v. Smith* (1990), the Court overturned the "compelling state interest" test for determining whether religious practices that violated general laws could be prosecuted and adopted the less protective "valid secular policy" test instead. *Smith* has been subject to considerable attack by lower court judges, members of Congress and state legislatures, and law review articles, as well as in concurring or dissenting opinions in later Court decisions. The Court reiterated its adherence to the valid secular policy standard in 1997 (*City of Boerne v. Flores*), but the controversy is unlikely to diminish.

Third, the perception of finality may be affected by whether a decision is subsequently used by a court to support other decisions. Continued use of a particular decision or standard by the court would demonstrate a commitment to the policy involved, thus indicating a sense of closure regarding that policy. Conversely, failure to mention the decision again leaves its finality uncertain. For example, since the 1960s the Court has found one reason or another not to apply to cases before it its famous doctrine that "fighting words" are not protected by the freedom of speech clause (*Chaplinsky v. New Hampshire,* 1942), and the doctrine's viability is now uncertain.

The clarity of a decision is determined by whether interpreters and implementors readily understand what they must do. Clear decisions minimize the choices of the interpreting and implementing populations, so that it is more difficult for someone, especially a judge, to argue that the decision means something the court did not intend. Clarity also provides a basis for "sanctions such as strongly critical [judicial] opinions" against noncompliant judges.[39] Although clear opinions are not necessarily more likely to be accepted or to evoke a positive response, they do set forth the expectations for affected groups. Unless those expectations are clearly articulated, implementors will not know what behavior is called for and interpreters will not know how to evaluate responses that are made. James F. Spriggs II demonstrates that federal agencies' reactions are strongly affected by the specificity of policy change in Supreme Court decisions. Spriggs's analysis shows that when opinions were "totally lacking specificity then only 3.4% of agency [follow up] decisions exhibit major policy change, whereas 95.5% of agency implementations conclude with major policy change if the Court is very explicit."[40]

Clear decisions not only minimize leeway, they also minimize distortion in the communication of the decision to relevant groups. Richard Johnson points out, for example, that "behavior congruent with the message depends in large measure upon whether the ruling is received in a relatively undistorted state by those who are affected."[41] Thus, for those who are largely indifferent to a court's policy, a clear statement of expectations is more likely to be met with acceptance and positive responses than is an ambiguous one. And for those who are not inclined to obey a court policy, a clear policy statement provides a standard against which nonacceptance or noncompliance can be evaluated and perhaps sanctioned.

The persuasiveness of a judicial opinion refers both to the quality of the arguments and to other devices that may be included to induce acceptance. Presumably a persuasive argument is logically sound, abides by the canons of judicial construction, is supported by demonstrable historical or social facts, is buttressed by precedent, shows proper deference to constitutional principles, and is felicitously written. In short, it should make "construction of contrary legal arguments more difficult and render those arguments less likely to gain other adherents."[42] Even within these parameters, a persuasive decision is not always easily identified.

In addition to constructing quality arguments, a majority opinion can communicate incentives and disincentives that affect acceptance and compliance, that is, references to individual or societal rewards to be gained by compliance or speculation about the unpleasant consequences that may result from noncompliance.[43] At times, such incentives can affect behavior to a far greater extent than logic. Criminal justice decisions such as *Mapp v. Ohio* (1961) or *Miranda v. Arizona* (1966) are classic examples. Although the police may not be persuaded of the rightness of these decisions, they stand in danger of having a court disallow evidence, thus losing convictions when they violate the Court's commands.

While it is reasonable to hypothesize that final, clear, and persuasive decisions receive greater compliance than those lacking such qualities, scattered research indicates that this relationship is not always supported. Studying state court reactions to a series of religion decisions by the Supreme Court, Tarr found no such relationship. He speculates that few judges actually read an entire Court opinion, much less pay attention to the details that could indicate some measure of finality, clarity, or persuasiveness.[44] Likewise, Charles Johnson's research into the way that lower courts treated over 300 Supreme Court decisions indicates little relationship between compliance and Court finality, clarity, or persuasiveness. His analysis related positive and negative treatments by these lower courts to such attributes as size of the majority, number of dissenting opinions, and whether the chief justice authored the majority opinion. Less than 5 percent of the variance in lower court reactions was accounted for by any of these indicators.[45] Thus, it may be that as a determinant of reactions the substance of the decision is more important than the way it is phrased, especially beyond the interpreting population.

Channel of the Communication

In reviewing legitimacy theory, we have already seen how people's reactions can depend upon the perceived legitimacy of the court making the policy. However, except for judges and attorneys, most people do not obtain their information directly from the originating court. Its policy, rather, is mediated through some channel—perhaps a lower court, perhaps a newspaper article or television news report, or perhaps by word of mouth from a lawyer, friend, or employer.

In considering the effects of the communications process, our basic concerns are: Who transmitted the message? What were the biases, conscious or unconscious, of the transmitter? Was the message received by the affected groups in a relatively unaltered state, or were parts deleted, distorted, or misinterpreted? Clearly, some of the features we discussed earlier affect these concerns. It is, of course, easier to relay accurately a clear, unambiguous policy statement than one characterized by poor writing or multiple opinions. However, even the same decision may receive different treatments from different sources. Although few have proposed systematic theories on this matter, many scholars believe that different responses are likely to follow when different channels are used because distortions are introduced, producing variation in the message at the end of the process.

News reports, an essential source of information in the United States, can be misleading. By their nature the media—especially television—tend to simplify things, and their reporting of court decisions is no exception. Reports often concentrate on who won or lost the decision and ignore the court's rationale, which is essential to guiding acceptance and behavioral responses to a decision. At best, a lengthy opinion will be condensed into a few sentences, often under a very tight deadline. Beyond this, there is often a tendency on the part of the media to exaggerate the potential consequences of decisions. Contrariwise, the media may virtually ignore important Supreme Court decisions announced—along with so many others—at the end of the Court's term in June, or when a major crisis is dominating the news.[46]

Oral communication is subject to even greater distortion. Lawyers are perhaps the main word-of-mouth communicators. Being busy, they often read decisions hastily and only with a view of a particular client's interests in mind. Thus, the client (or others to whom the attorney talks) may receive a quick or narrow perspective on the decision. Recipients of attorneys' versions of a decision may, in turn, spread it around, perhaps distorting it further in the process.

Distortion is most likely to occur when the channel has a particular bias. Interest groups are particularly likely to exaggerate or minimize the potential consequences of decisions in informing their members about them. For example, African American or Hispanic groups may exaggerate the consequences of decisions constraining affirmative action programs. Groups can both exaggerate and minimize simultaneously. Organizations on the so-called religious right often interpret schoolhouse religion cases very narrowly while at the same time warning against dangerous intrusions by the "Godless" Supreme Court. Existing research has not yet clearly identified the relationship between these sources and the individuals' eventual reactions.

An additional factor in the relationship between sources and responses is attentiveness to the media. For example, Richard Johnson reports that while the headlines reporting the *Schempp* decision were largely negative, "the conscientious observer had ample opportunity to be appraised of the

Court's policies and the reasoning behind them." But "the more casual observer might have received a partial and somewhat distorted view of what the Court had said [and if he] had a commitment on the issue, . . . he could selectively expose himself to materials which would tend to reinforce his commitment."[47]

ORGANIZATIONAL THEORIES

Theories based on organizational concepts have been used by a variety of scholars to explain the behavior of lower courts, administrative agencies, and corporations. These theories are based on the idea that although it is individuals who make acceptance and compliance decisions, they often do so in the context of organizational goals and policies. Martin Shapiro argued years ago that a court is just another government agency trying to implement its preferred policy, that it must compete with other agencies, which often prefer different policies. In practice, this means that agencies are not likely to accord judicial policies any special consideration unless the courts can bring special pressures to bear.[48] Similarly, Lawrence Baum argues that the implementation of court decisions is a variant of how all public policies are carried out. Thus, we should not expect judicial policies to result in 100 percent compliance because other forces will influence their implementation.[49]

In this section we examine two sets of theories that help explain how organizations implement judicial policies: *policy tensions* and *organizational inertia*. Features of these two theories are found in current treatments of organizational relationships described by principal-agent theories, which we discuss at the end of this section.

Policy Tensions

If an organization realizes that it is not serving its constituents or customers satisfactorily and that this shortcoming is costing it support or profits, then the organization faces a "performance gap" and it will look for ways to improve services.[50] However, Charles Johnson has pointed out that when an external actor, such as a court, decides that the agency is performing inadequately (for example, contrary to the law), change in the organization does not follow the expected pattern. When an agency is committed to its defined goals or preferences and those differ from the judicial policy, *and* when it is legally bound to follow a court decision, the agency is caught between two opposing forces. The tension between these two forces substantially affects the agency's responses. These forces are "a commitment to agency programs and [the] threat of sanctions or loss of resources if changes are not made in those programs." Under such circumstances, "the agency is expected to preserve existing programs to the extent that this is possible." [51] An intervening factor that may affect agency responses is whether the agency has the resources to resist orders to change, pay for the required changes, or influence the court to the extent that the court moderates or relinquishes its demand for change.

Johnson provides an illustration of this explanation of responses to judicial decisions (see Figure 6-1), which "represents a continuum of alternative programs constituting a single dimension of policy." [52] In this figure, point A represents the present program of the agency that has been overruled by a judicial decision; point B represents the programs the court may wish the agency to adopt; and points C_1, C_2, and C_3 represent alternatives the agency might consider and adopt. Under certain circumstances, the agency may choose to remain with its original program (point A)— for example, if the agency is highly committed to the program, if it believes the risks of enforcement or sanctions are reasonably low, or if it believes it has sufficient resources to resist court efforts to require change. Another reason for remaining at point A may be that the agency cannot afford the costs of changing its policies or practices. On the other hand, if the agency is not highly committed to the program; if the court's policy is not perceived as endangering the program significantly; if risks or sanctions are too great for the agency; or if resources are insufficient to resist change but sufficient to support it, then movement to alternatives near point B (the court's policy) would be likely.

The most likely outcome of the circumstances anticipated by this theory is that the agency will not try to retain the status quo, nor will it change completely to the court's policy preference. The compromise is likely to be at a point C_i, the particular location of which is a function of the three factors mentioned above: commitment, perception of threat from the court, and resources for resistance. If commitment is high, external pressures and threat are low, and resources for resistance are low, then the agency may respond by moving only slightly, to C_1. If the reverse is true, then its response may go as far as C_3.

Martin Shapiro's study of a long-running policy clash between the Patent Office and the Supreme Court illustrates this process well. [53] Put

Figure 6-1   Organizational Policy Choices That Lead to Policy Tensions

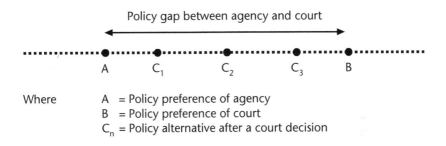

Policy gap between agency and court

A C_1 C_2 C_3 B

Where   A = Policy preference of agency
         B = Policy preference of court
         C_n = Policy alternative after a court decision

briefly, the Court believed the Patent Office's standards for what constituted an invention were too lenient—that many patents were granted for items that lacked an innovative idea or were based on ideas already in the common domain. Over the years the Court invalidated many patents that it believed were too loosely granted, but it lacked the ability and resources to get the Patent Office to change its general policy. After all, the Court did not itself make initial judgments about patent applications, nor did the situation permit it to give precise, detailed commands about the standards by which the applications should be judged. Shapiro tells us:

> The Patent Office had clearly won the war since it continued its operational policies unchanged in the face of Supreme Court opposition. . . .
> [It makes little] difference that the highest court would invalidate when it hardly ever sees a patent so long as it cannot get the Patent Office to invalidate at the point where the mass of patent policy decisions are made, the point of application.[54]

In short, the situation gave the agency the resources for resistance and denied the Court the ability to put much pressure on the recalcitrant organization.

Inertia in Organizations

The idea that organizations develop inertial forces supporting their policies and practices is not a new one. Since inertia plays an important role in most organizational theories, it deserves a closer look. The sources of inertia in organizations are several, and judicial impact scholars have focused on two broad categories: sources that are system based and sources that relate to individuals who occupy various positions within the organization. We discuss them in turn, but note that it is difficult to separate them analytically because they often produce the same behavior.

SYSTEM-BASED INERTIA. Most organizations are structured to carry out a particular mission or to attain a defined set of goals. Police departments, for example, are devoted to the maintenance of law and order; school systems try to transfer cognitive skills and cultural values from one generation to another. Normally, organization officials accept and defend the mission or goal of the organization and behave accordingly. The commitment of officials to organizational goals may be substantial when agencies are considering responses to judicial decisions. One commentator notes, "In an organization that has successfully instilled a sense of mission, those who believe in the bureaucracy's mission are likely to resist judicial efforts to alter it."[55] Such beliefs are inertial—that is, they are difficult to overcome, even when support from clientele groups or other government agencies is weak and an adverse judicial policy has been handed down.

The negative impact that organizational goals and missions can have on the implementation of judicial decisions is perhaps best shown in the area of criminal justice. Research into police resistance to court decisions expanding suspects' rights is reported in Chapter 3; there is considerable conflict between a police officer's role as a protector of law and order and the officer's role as a protector of the rights of defendants. Often these two roles are not compatible. But the former role is primary and habitual while the latter one, even if accepted by the police, is secondary and intermittent. So officers' first and strongest response is to the law and order role; observance of suspects' rights can get lost in the shuffle.

There is more to inertia than commitment to organizational policies. Organizations also develop subsidiary goals, such as saving money, protecting their clientele, maintaining their prestige, avoiding excessive work, and more generally continuing their existence without a fundamental change in function or activities. Judicial decisions that threaten the status quo run up against a reluctance to change—in other words, inertia. For example, in the 1970s the Supreme Court held that public schools could not suspend students and welfare agencies could not terminate benefits without a hearing (*Goss v. Lopez,* 1975; *Goldberg v. Kelly,* 1970). Full-blown hearings can be quite time consuming. Accordingly, school systems and welfare agencies developed mechanisms for holding "quickie" or pro forma hearings.

INERTIA FROM INDIVIDUAL COMMITMENTS. Another source of inertia arises from the individual commitments and preferences of organizational personnel. Baum highlights some of these preferences. He hypothesizes that "the more subordinates' interests are favored by faithful implementation of appellate decisions, the more faithful their implementation will be," and offers two reasons for such a relationship. First, there are "psychic and material costs of policy change" for individuals—inconvenience—and resistance is likely to be a function of the degree to which agency personnel find current policies rewarding or efficient. Second, when no detailed agency policy exists in an area, subordinates will "tend to adopt policies which maximize their interests." However, when a court comes along and requires that they abandon "the interest-maximizing policies, then the court is likely to be resisted."[56]

The explanatory power of the concept of inertia extends beyond organizational behavior. As we discussed in Chapter 4, despite *Bates v. State Bar of Arizona* (1977) and other Supreme Court decisions allowing attorneys to advertise, fewer than a third have done so over the last twenty years. Inertia (as well as other considerations) has kept many lawyers from running ads. In short, even when the courts legitimize some activity, change does not necessarily follow.[57]

While inertia in organizations may be a powerful force, it is not insurmountable. Inertia maintains behavior patterns through habit, convenience, efficiency, or status—not passion. Southern resistance to desegregation was not primarily inertial. Passion can induce lengthy and unreasoning resistance. But inertia can be overcome in a couple of ways. One relates to the legitimacy of a court decision as perceived by the organization, and to the sense of law-abidingness of agency leaders and subordinates, as we have mentioned. The more legitimate the decision and the greater the sense of law-abidingness in the agency, the easier it is to overcome inertia. As Baum writes, "Subordinates' interests and preferences often incline them against obedience to higher officials, but the authority which they attach to those officials' decisions tends to counteract these centrifugal tendencies and to provide an important motivation for faithful implementation."[58]

Inertia can also be overcome by judicial sanctions. Most courts have an array of tools they may employ to enforce their actions. As we noted in Chapter 3, contempt citations and fines are not always efficient, and judges are sometimes reluctant to impose extreme penalties; sanctions are "far from overwhelming."[59] But because inertial forces are not motivated by impassioned resistance, organizations are usually willing to cease resistance when threatened with sanctions. In sum, sanctions are generally sufficient to overcome inertial forces when they are weak or localized and a plaintiff is willing to pursue the matter vigorously, but they are less successful when inertia is widespread and the plaintiff or court is not willing or able to press for fundamental changes.

PRINCIPAL–AGENT MODELS OF IMPLEMENTATION. Principal-agent models of the interactions between organizations have been discussed widely in recent social science literature. These models examine what often happens when a hierarchically and authoritatively superior officer or agency—a principal—seeks to direct the behavior of individuals or departments reporting to them—an agent. Although the principal has authority over the agent, the dynamics of their interactions may give an agent considerable latitude to pursue different policies or goals. Factors such as limited ability to monitor agents' behavior, the greater control of information by agents, and the sheer cost of enforcing compliance by the principal give the agent much leeway in the actual implementation of a principal's policy.[60]

Donald Songer, Jeffrey Segal, and Charles Cameron studied the reactions of U.S. Courts of Appeals to Supreme Court search and seizure decisions using principal-agent theory to guide their analysis. The authors reasoned that this theory might illuminate relationships between the Supreme Court as a principal and lower federal courts as its agents because their relationship matches the expectations of the theory, especially as it relates to the difficulties of monitoring agents' behavior and agents' alternate policy preferences.[61]

Analyzing decisions from 1961 through 1990, these authors found a "high degree of appeals court congruence with Supreme Court search and seizure doctrine."[62] Moreover, the agents tended to follow shifts in the principal's search and seizure policy, even when the prevailing ideology of the appeals court judges was taken into account. Nevertheless, the data also showed that the ideology of the responding court of appeals judges did have a substantial independent impact on their decisions. The authors noted, for example, that "a search that had a 50% chance of being upheld by the most liberal panel in our sample has an estimated chance of 87% of being upheld if the case is heard instead by the most conservative panel."[63] While these data seem to show some independence of the lower court judges as agents, Songer and his co-authors concluded that court of appeals judges were "relatively faithful agents of their principal, the Supreme Court."[64]

The finding of general congruence between the Supreme Court and lower federal courts was replicated by John Kilwein and Richard A. Brisbin in a study of state supreme court responses to Supreme Court directives. Though less clearly a principal-agent relationship because state courts are not always agents of the Supreme Court, such courts are nevertheless obligated to recognize the authority of relevant Supreme Court precedents. Unlike federal courts, however, state courts can rely on state constitutions if their decisions are not contrary to provisions of the U.S. Constitution. Recognizing this latitude, Kilwein and Brisbin show that state supreme court policies and U.S. Supreme Court policies generally converged as principal-agent theory predicted, but that these courts were also swayed by local political concerns when there was leeway for discretion.[65]

Positive Policy, Judicial Capabilities, and Organizational Theory

Traditionally, many court decisions are negative in the sense that they tell an agency that it cannot carry out some policy it has developed. Other court decisions may be positive in the procedural sense, for example, they specify that an agency has to hold hearings or consider certain evidence before it acts. But courts have seldom dictated in any positive manner the substantive policies that an agency has to carry out.

Over the last three decades, however, courts have sometimes required implementing organizations to carry out positive, substantive policies—sometimes spelled out in considerable detail. *Miranda* is a good early example, although as we discussed in Chapters 3 and 4, its burden on police resources and functioning was minimal. But following *Swann v. Charlotte-Mecklenburg County Board of Education* (1971), federal district courts began issuing detailed orders regarding crosstown busing, racial ratios among teachers and pupils, curriculum offerings, and other features of the school system thought necessary to achieve desegregation. Federal district courts also began issuing detailed orders to end discrimination in public employment and housing. In the 1970s the federal courts began requiring states and localities to improve conditions in penitentiaries (see Chapter 3, Box 3-2), mental hospitals, halfway houses, and other institutions. In addressing prison conditions, for instance, courts would prescribe such things as the minimum number of square feet of cell space to which an inmate was entitled, the minimum dietary and exercise requirements, and the details of vocational rehabilitation programs. Many states actually reduced their prison population in order to meet the judicially imposed requirements.

Others dramatically increased appropriations to build new prisons or renovate old ones. State courts also joined in the trend to making positive, substantive policy by reforming tax assessment policies or the financing of public schools.

Much of the discussion over positive, substantive judicial policy making focuses on the proper role of the courts—the merits of judicial activism versus judicial restraint—and is beyond the scope of this book. Some criticism, however, is practical, holding that courts cannot successfully engage in such policy making. The leading proponents of this position are perhaps Donald Horowitz, Nathan Glazer, and Gerald Rosenberg.[66] They argue that courts by their nature lack the capacity to supervise agencies closely enough to ensure compliance in spirit as well as in letter. Moreover, they argue, the substitution of policies made by courts for those made by legislators or agency professionals has serious unintended consequences for society generally and an agency's clientele in particular. For example, Horowitz points out that the District of Columbia school board complied with a court order to equalize expenditures on a teacher-per-pupil basis at each school by transferring the teachers who were most easily moved, regardless of the schools' subject area needs. And when Alabama had to increase its expenditures on mental hospitals, much of the money came from funds that would have been spent on prisons and welfare.

While Rosenberg advances some hypotheses about Supreme Court capabilities that we will consider in Chapter 7, little real theory has been tested concerning the limits or consequences of lower courts' ability to make major positive and substantive policy. Arguments that such courts are exceeding their capabilities are largely drawn from case studies or particular experiences or based upon speculation. But Glazer offered some hypotheses that are open to empirical testing. He believes that positive judicial policy making, among other things, will: (1) lead agencies to give greater weight to theoretical considerations than to practical ones; (2) give greater weight to abstract speculations and social science theory in the formulation of policy; and (3) increase the power of the legal profession in the formulation of policy.[67]

ENVIRONMENTAL THEORIES

As is the case with communications theories, environmental explanations are not connected to an overarching theory. Rather, they involve a number of hypotheses that explain actors' acceptance and behavioral decisions in terms of common beliefs or norms prevailing in their community. (Although the term community usually refers to a city or town, it can also apply to racial, ethnic, or religious communities, or to occupational communities.) Throughout this book, we have pointed to the importance of forces or influences surrounding those who must respond to judicial policies. These include general community opinion, the opinion of community elites, and the prevailing traditions in the community. All of these factors are external to the respondents; that is, they exist in the social, economic, or political environment of the actors affected by the judicial policy. For example, we have repeatedly noted the strong influence of local segregationist sentiment on the progress of desegregation in the South; less visible, perhaps, is the norm in some professional communities (such as medicine and law) that relegates those who advertise for clients to the margins of professional status.

The underlying assumption of many researchers is that environmental pressures shape or influence reactions to judicial policies. In some situations, this appears obvious. Southern school boards opposed desegregation because the southern culture opposed it; obscene publications or videos are more likely to be sold in culturally tolerant New York City or Las Vegas than in small homogeneous towns in the so-called Bible Belt. But environmental pressures are not always so obvious or so easily linked to actors' responses to judicial policies. Unfortunately, we have no well-developed theories to predict either when less visible environmental factors will be important or what particular environmental factors will have the greatest force in accounting for reactions.

One proto-theory can be found in the discussion of "triggering" factors in Dolbeare and Hammond's study of the impact of *Abington School District v. Schempp* (1963) on five Indiana towns. After finding that none of the school systems had actually ceased religious activities, the authors argued that compliance "requires some decisive trigger." In this case, the trigger could have been "clear cues from state enforcement authorities, strong determination on the part of key local actors, . . . or thick-skinned commitment on the part of local citizens."[68] Positive responses by any of these actors, they believe, could have had an effect on the local systems; but since no actions were taken, nothing was done by any of the local school systems. Likewise, police departments seemed readier to resist *Mapp v. Ohio* (1961), Bradley C. Canon found, if they were supported by a "law and order" mayor and city council.[69]

Viewed from the trigger perspective, the basic thesis is that groups responding to a judicial decision are directly affected by the direction and nature of environmental pressures, often pre-existing but also prompted by the decision. While the most attention has been focused on the interpreting and implementing populations, triggers also affect decisions in the consumer and secondary populations. Indeed, in Chapter 5 we saw that Congress's responses to Supreme Court decisions were often triggered by constituent reactions.[70]

At least two major assumptions underpin an environmental trigger theory of judicial impact. The first is that if environmental pressures are influential, they must first be perceived by the responding population. That is, a judge, school administrator, student, or other actor must first be aware of environmental pressures before responding to them in reacting to a Court decision. Evidence regarding the degree to which individuals are aware of environmental pressures concerning judicial policies is limited and mixed. In some policy areas, environmental pressures stemming from public or even elite opinion are quite obvious to the judges, implementors, and consumers of a judicial policy. For example, resistance to desegregation dominated southern culture in the years following *Brown*. Communities are not always of one mind, even on controversial matters. Attitudes toward school prayers or abortion may be more varied, especially in heterogeneous communities, and triggering may depend upon which group makes the most noise or whom responding actors look to for guidance. Public officials in liberal communities who are good Catholics, for example, can be subject to two sets of environmental pressures regarding abortion, 180 degrees apart. For policies with low visibility, there may be no triggering at all.

The second assumption is that responding groups and populations are relatively open to and potentially influenced by these forces. Obviously, environmental pressures do influence responses to judicial policies. In many situations, however, we try to insulate actors from environmental pressures. Judges, for example, are supposed to decide matters before them only on the basis of the relevant facts and law. We noted in Chapter 2 that for some judges environmental pressures are influential, but often judges are unwilling to be moved by extrajudicial pressures. Similarly, we bind implementors with rules and regulations to reduce the influence of popular pressures. Indeed, as organizations become more national in scope, distant control of local factories and offices can insulate their managers from community pressures. Finally, some organizations have been successful in insulating themselves from environmental pressures. Jon R. Bond and

Charles A. Johnson found that few hospitals included community representatives in discussions about their abortion policy following *Roe v. Wade*.[71] By design or by accident, some responding groups that could be affected by environmental pressures are not so affected because those pressures either are unnoticed or are effectively blocked.

SUMMARY

The development and testing of theories are essential parts of social science research, for only with theories can scholars explain what they have observed and decide where to proceed with further research. In this chapter we have reviewed nine major theoretical perspectives that we believe can be tested empirically in regard to judicial impact. Table 6-1 summarizes aspects of these theories: to what extent the theory as been applied (or might be applied) to a population and whether the theory has been supported by research.

The entries in Table 6-1 are rough and somewhat subjective, but they provide a basic summary of the status of the theories relative to the various populations. Except for principal-agent theory, no new theories have emerged in recent years, but some older theories have been tested empirically. The implementing population remains the most closely examined population for theory-testing purposes, although the interpreting and secondary populations have received increased scholarly attention since the mid-1980s. Research on the consumer population that tests hypotheses derived from one or more of these theories remains limited; we think the area deserves more attention from judicial impact researchers.

Table 6-1 also demonstrates that many of the theoretical perspectives discussed in this chapter have met with some measure of empirical support, though a few theories have mixed findings for particular populations. Thus, it appears that judges serving as interpreters can be influenced by their attitudes, factors associated with the communication of a higher court's decision, commitments to past policies (inertia), and pressures coming from the political or social environment. Similar observations can be made for other populations where different combinations of positive findings point to the potential influence of many factors in accounting for responses to judicial policies.

Because responses to judicial policies can be potentially influenced by several factors, the next generation of theoretically driven scholarship will

TABLE 6-1

Status of Theories of Judicial Impact

Theories	Populations			
	Interpreting	Implementing	Consumer	Secondary
Psychological				
Legitimacy		★	★	+a
Cognitive dissonance		+b		
Attitudinal	+c	+d/_e	+f	+g
Utility				
Psychological/				
economic		+h	+i	
Communications				
Context	_j	+k	★	
Channels	+l	+m/_n	★	+o
Organizational				
Tension	★	+p	NA	NA
Inertia	+q	+r	+s	NA
Principal-agent	_t	_u	NA	NA
Environmental				
Environmental trigger	+v	+w/_x	★	+y

★	Theory discussed in the literature as relevant to the particular population, but no hypotheses specifically tested.
+	Theory supported by tests of hypotheses for specific populations.
-	Theory not supported in tests of hypotheses for specific populations.
-/+	Theory received mixed support in tests of hypotheses for specific populations.
No entry:	Theory not discussed in the literature as relevant to specific populations.
NA:	Not applicable.

[a] Mondak, see note 11, and Hoekstra, see note 12. [b]Muir, see note 21. [c]Songer and Haire, see note 72. [d]R. Johnson, see note 20. [e]Milner, see note 22. [f]Giles and Gatlin, see note 34, and Bowen, see note 57. [g]Clark and McGuire, see note 70. [h]Rodgers and Bullock, see note 29. [i]Giles and Gatlin, see note 34. [j]Tarr, see note 38. [k]Spriggs, see note 40. [l]Bradley C. Canon and Kenneth Kolson, "Compliance with *Gault* in Rural America: The Case of Kentucky," *Journal of Family Law* 10 (1971): 300–326. [m]Dolbeare and Hammond, see note 68. [n]Milner, see note 22. [o]Valerie Hoekstra and Jeffrey Segal, "The Shepherding of Local Public Opinion: The Supreme Court and *Lamb's Chapel*," *Journal of Politics* 58 (1996): 1079–1102. [p]Charles A. Johnson, "Judicial Decisions and Organizational Change: Some Theoretical and Empirical Notes on State Court Decisions and State Administrative Agencies," *Law and Society Review* 14 (1979): 27–56. [q]Songer et al., see note 61, and Kilwein and Brisbin, see note 65. [r]Ben Crouch and James W. Marquart, *An Appeal to Justice: Litigated Reform of Texas Prisons* (Austin: University of Texas Press, 1989). [s]Bowen, see note 57. [t]Songer et al., see note 61. [u]Spriggs, see note 40. [v]Micheal Giles and Thomas Walker, "Judicial Policy-Making and Southern School Segregation," *Journal of Politics* 37 (1975): 917–989. [w]Dolbeare and Hammond, see note 68. [x]Bond and Johnson, see note 71. [y]Clark and McGuire, see note 70.

likely focus on comparing the relative strengths of differing theoretical explanations. Some researchers have begun to do so for the interpreting population. Donald Songer and Susan Haire, for example, test the relative influence of attitudes and communications factors in their analysis of lower court decisions in the area of obscenity.[72] Similarly, Kilwein and Brisbin develop a multivariate model examining the influence of communications factors, attitudes, and commitments to past policies.[73] And Charles Johnson's research on lower court responses examines the relative impact of attitudes and communications factors in explaining responses to Supreme Court decisions.[74] Research of this nature will be important in comparing the relative strengths and weaknesses of the theories discussed in this chapter. It will also help researchers focus on the circumstances in which particular theories best explain the impact of judicial policies.

NOTES

1. Gordon Patric, "The Impact of Court Decisions: Aftermath of the *McCullom* Case," *Journal of Public Law* 6 (Fall 1957): 455–464; Frank Sorauf, "*Zorach v. Clauson:* The Impact of a Supreme Court Decision," *American Political Science Review* 53 (1959): 777–791; and Walter Murphy, "Lower Court Checks on Supreme Court Power," *American Political Science Review* 53 (1959): 1017–1031.

2. David Easton, *A Systems Analysis of Political Life* (New York: Wiley, 1965); see also Seymour M. Lipset, *Political Man* (New York: Doubleday, 1960).

3. Alexander Bickel, *The Least Dangerous Branch* (Indianapolis: Bobbs-Merrill, 1962); Charles L. Black, *The People and the Court* (New York: Macmillan, 1960); and Michael Petrick, "The Supreme Court and Authority Acceptance," *Western Political Quarterly* 31 (1968): 5–19.

4. Richard Johnson, *The Dynamics of Compliance* (Evanston, Ill.: Northwestern University Press, 1967), 27, 41.

5. Jerome Frank, *Law and the Modern Mind* (New York: Brentano, 1930). See also Max Lerner, "Constitution and Court as Symbols," *Yale Law Review* 46 (1937): 1290–1319.

6. Gregory Casey, "The Supreme Court and Myth: An Empirical Investigation," *Law and Society Review* 8 (1974): 386.

7. See Jeffrey A. Segal and Harold Spaeth, *The Supreme Court and the Attitudinal Model* (New York: Cambridge University Press, 1993), chap. 2, for a discussion of the myth's acceptance in modern times.

8. Stephen Wasby, *The Supreme Court in the Federal Judicial System* (New York: Holt, Rinehart and Winston, 1978), 234.

9. Walter Murphy and Joseph Tanenhaus, "Public Opinion and the United States Supreme Court," *Law and Society Review* 2 (1968): 357–384.

10. Casey, "The Supreme Court and Myth."

11. Kenneth Dolbeare, "The Public Views the Supreme Court," in *Law, Politics, and the Federal Courts,* ed. Herbert Jacob (Boston: Little, Brown, 1967), 194–212; John Kessel, "Public Perceptions of the Supreme Court," *Midwest Journal of Political Science* 10 (1966): 167; and Liane Kosaki, "Public Awareness of Supreme Court Decisions" (Paper presented at the Annual Meeting of the American Political Science Association, Washington, D.C., 1991).

12. See, for example, Charles Franklin and Liane Kosaki, "Republican Schoolmaster: The U.S. Supreme Court, Public Opinion and Abortion," *American Political Science Review* 83 (1989): 751–771, and Valerie J. Hoekstra, "The Supreme Court and Opinion Change: An Experimental Study of the Court's Ability to Change Opinion," *American Politics Quarterly* 23 (1995): 109–129.

13. Jeffery J. Mondak, "Institutional Legitimacy, Policy Legitimacy, and the Supreme Court," *American Political Quarterly* 20 (1992): 458. See also Jeffery J. Mondak, "Policy Legitimacy and the Supreme Court: The Sources and Contexts of Legitimation," *Political Research Quarterly* 47 (1994): 675–692.

14. Mondak, "Institutional Legitimacy," 473.

15. Ibid.

16. Hoekstra, "The Supreme Court and Opinion Change," 119, 121.

17. Timothy R. Johnson and Andrew D. Martin, "The Public's Conditional Response to Supreme Court Decisions," *American Political Science Review* 92 (1998): 299–309.

18. David G. Lawrence, "Procedural Norms and Tolerance: A Reassessment," *American Political Science Review* 70 (1976): 80–100; see also Michael Corbett, *Political Tolerance in America* (New York: Longman, 1982), chap. 7.

19. Gregory A. Caldeira and James Gibson, "The Etiology of Public Support for the Supreme Court," *American Journal of Political Science* (1992): 635–664.

20. R. Johnson, *The Dynamics of Compliance,* and William K. Muir, *Prayer in Public Schools: Law and Attitude Change* (Chicago: University of Chicago Press, 1967).

21. Muir, *Prayer in the Public Schools,* 10.

22. Neal Milner, *The Court and Local Law Enforcement* (Beverly Hills, Calif.: Sage, 1971).

23. Robert Stover and Don Brown, "Understanding Compliance and Noncompliance with the Law: The Contributions of Utility Theory," *Social Science Quarterly* 56 (1975): 363–375, and Harrell R. Rodgers Jr. and Charles S. Bullock III, *Law and Social Change: Civil Rights Laws and Their Consequences* (New York: McGraw-Hill, 1972).

24. Jeremy Bentham, *An Introduction to the Principles of Morals and Legislation* (New York: Hafner, 1948).

25. Stover and Brown, "Understanding Compliance," 369.

26. Ibid., 369–370.

27. Rodgers and Bullock, *Law and Social Change,* 4.

28. Ibid., 183–184.

29. Harrell R. Rodgers Jr. and Charles Bullock III, *Coercion to Compliance* (Lexington, Mass.: Lexington Books, 1976), 69.

30. Ibid., 70.

31. Richard Posner, *Economic Analysis of Law,* 4th ed. (Boston: Little, Brown, 1992). See also Maxwell L. Stearns, *Public Law and Public Choice* (Cincinnati: Anderson, 1997).

32. See, especially, Lee Epstein and Jack Knight, *The Choices Judges Make* (Washington: CQ Press, 1998), and Lawrence Baum, *The Puzzle of Judicial Behavior* (Ann Arbor: University of Michigan Press, 1997). For specific uses of this approach, see Forest Maltzman and Paul Wahlback, "Strategic Policy Considerations and Voting Fluidity on the Burger Court," *American Political Science Review* 90 (1996): 581–592, or Saul Brenner and Harold Spaeth, "Marginal Opinion Assignments and the Maintenance of the Original Coalition on the Warren Court," *American Journal of Political Science* 32 (1988): 72–81.

33. Harrell R. Rodgers Jr. and Charles S. Bullock III, "School Desegregation: A Multivariate Test of the Role of Law in Effectuating Social Change," *American Politics Quarterly* 4 (1976): 153–175.

34. Micheal Giles and Douglas Gatlin, "Mass Level Compliance with Public Policy: The Case of School Desegregation," *Journal of Politics* 42 (1980): 722–746.

35. Stover and Brown, "Understanding Compliance," 371–372. This is also a major theme in Gerald N. Rosenberg, *The Hollow Hope: Can Courts Bring About Social Change?* (Chicago: University of Chicago Press, 1991).

36. Stephen Wasby, "The Communication of the Supreme Court's Criminal Procedures Decisions: A Preliminary Mapping," *Villanova Law Review* 18 (1973): 1086–1118.

37. R. Johnson, *The Dynamics of Compliance,* 26.

38. G. Alan Tarr, *Judicial Impact and State Supreme Courts* (Lexington, Mass.: Lexington Books, 1977), 89–90.

39. Ibid., 91.

40. James F. Spriggs II, "The Supreme Court and Federal Administrative Agencies: A Resource-Based Theory and Analysis of Judicial Impact," *American Journal of Political Science* 40 (1996): 1138.

41. R. Johnson, *The Dynamics of Compliance,* 60.

42. Tarr, *Judicial Impact and State Supreme Courts,* 92.

43. R. Johnson, *The Dynamics of Compliance,* 42.

44. Tarr, *Judicial Impact and State Supreme Courts,* 102.

45. Charles A. Johnson, "Lower Court Reactions to Supreme Court Decisions: A Quantitative Examination," *American Journal of Political Science* 23 (1979): 792–804; see Charles Johnson, "Law, Politics, and Judicial Decision Making: Lower Federal Court Uses of Supreme Court Decisions," *Law and Society Review* 21 (1987): 325–340.

46. Chester Newland, "Press Coverage of the United States Supreme Court," *Western Political Quarterly* 17 (1964): 15–36; David Grey, *The Supreme Court and the News Media* (Evanston, Ill.: Northwestern University Press, 1968); Richard Davis, *Decisions and Images: The Supreme Court and the Press* (Englewood Cliffs, N.J.: Prentice Hall, 1994); and Elliot Slotnick and Jennifer Segal, *Television News and the Supreme Court: All the News That Is Fit to Air* (New York: Cambridge University Press, 1998).

47. R. Johnson, *The Dynamics of Compliance,* 95.

48. Martin Shapiro, *Law and Politics in the Supreme Court* (New York: Free Press, 1964).

49. Lawrence Baum, "Implementation of Judicial Decisions: An Organizational Analysis," *American Politics Quarterly* 4 (1976): 86–114.

50. James March and Herbert Simon, *Organizations* (New York: Wiley, 1958), and Anthony Downs, *Inside Bureaucracy* (Boston: Little, Brown, 1968).

51. Charles A. Johnson, "Judicial Decisions and Organizational Change," *Administration and Society* 11 (1979): 31–32.

52. Ibid.

53. Martin Shapiro, *The Supreme Court and Administrative Agencies* (New York: Macmillan, 1968), 143–226.

54. Ibid., 200.

55. Note, "Judicial Intervention and Organization Theory: Changing Bureaucratic Behavior and Policy," *Yale Law Journal* 89 (1980): 513–537.

56. Baum, "Implementation of Judicial Decisions," 97, 98.

57. See Lauren Bowen, "Attorney Advertising in the Wake of *Bates v. State Bar of Arizona* (1977): A Study of Judicial Impact," *American Politics Quarterly* 23 (1995): 461–484, and Carroll Seron, *The Business of Practicing Law: The Work Lives of Solo and Small Firm Attorneys* (Philadelphia: Temple University Press, 1996).

58. Baum, "Implementation of Judicial Decisions," 101.

59. Ibid., 105.

60. Terry Moe, "The New Economics of Organization," *American Journal of Economics* 28 (1984) 739–777.

61. Donald R. Songer, Jeffrey A. Segal, and Charles M. Cameron, "The Hierarchy of Justice: Testing a Principal–Agent Model of Supreme Court–Circuit Court Interactions," *American Journal of Political Science* 38 (1994): 673–696.

62. Ibid., 684–685.

63. Ibid., 688.

64. Ibid., 690.

65. John C. Kilwein and Richard A. Brisbin Jr., "Policy Convergence in the Federal Judicial System: The Application of Intensified Scrutiny Doctrines by State Supreme Courts," *American Journal of Political Science* 41 (1997): 122–148.

66. Donald Horowitz, *The Courts and Social Policy* (Washington: Brookings Institution, 1977); Nathan Glazer, "Should Judges Administer Social Services?" *The Public Interest* 50 (1978): 64–80; and Rosenberg, *The Hollow Hope.*

67. Glazer, "Should Judges Administer Social Services?" 80.

68. Kenneth M. Dolbeare and Phillip E. Hammond, *The School Prayer Decisions: From Court Policy to Local Practice* (Chicago: University of Chicago Press, 1971), 139.

69. Bradley C. Canon, "Testing the Effectiveness of Civil Liberties Policies at the State and Federal Levels: The Case of the Exclusionary Rule," *American Politics Quarterly* 5 (1977): 57–82.

70. See John A. Clark and Kevin T. McGuire, "Congress, the Supreme Court, and the Flag," *Political Research Quarterly* 49 (1996): 771–781.

71. Jon R. Bond and Charles A. Johnson, "Implementing a Permissive Policy: Hospital Abortion Services after *Roe v. Wade,*" *American Journal of Political Science* (1982): 1–24.

72. Donald Songer and Susan Haire, "Integrating Alternative Approaches to the Study of Judicial Voting: Obscenity Cases in the U.S. Courts of Appeals," *American Journal of Political Science* 36 (1992) 963–982.

73. Kilwein and Brisbin, "Policy Convergence in a Federal Judicial System."

74. Charles A. Johnson, "Law, Politics, and Judicial Decision Making."

CHAPTER SEVEN

The Impact of Judicial Decision
as Public Policy

In the preceding chapters, we have reviewed the research on the impact of court decisions on the four populations and we have also explored the scholarly theories advanced to explain variations in judicial impact. But we have for the most part looked at the impact of particular decisions. We have not examined judicial impact as an overall phenomenon and asked: Just how much do the courts affect American life?

We generally assume that judicial decisions have an important impact on the political, the economic, and to some extent the social structures of the nation. Scholars have written numerous books and articles focusing on the implications of various decisions and policies of the U.S. Supreme Court. Politically active citizens, too, see the Supreme Court as having a powerful impact. Their belief is manifest in the campaigns against such Court actions as the desegregation decisions, the school prayer decisions, and the abortion decision—as well as in the efforts of these and other groups that bring cases to the Court with the hope of establishing new policies. Many such campaigns have been at least as broad and enduring as those relating to any congressional or presidential decision, and they certainly are evidence of the belief in the Court's impact.

It is not easy to measure this presumed impact. As we saw in Chapter 4, much of the Court's influence occurs through permission and suggestion rather than through command. More important, the Court's decisions and policies interact with those of other government agencies. If legislative bodies pass laws reinforcing a judicial policy, to whom is the impact attributable? Similarly, who gets the credit or the blame when Court decisions complement those of Congress, state legislatures, or the president?

Nonetheless, some scholars have tried to measure the Supreme Court's impact on American life. Their findings have been contradictory. Some claim that the courts at best have only a marginal influence on public policy, while others attribute considerable influence to the courts. Thus scholarship has not made clear how much influence the courts, especially the Supreme Court, have on political, economic, and social policies and behavior in America. Claims of extensive influence are quite controversial. In this chapter we look at these findings and the controversy surrounding them.

We will explore three strands of research. The first focuses on clashes between the Supreme Court and other branches of government, particularly Congress. Who wins and who loses when they push different policy preferences? The second looks at other courts as policy makers: What impact do they have on society? The third focuses on the ability of the courts through their decisions to mobilize the public to political action— that is, to inspire citizens to demand policy change from legislators and executive agencies or to exercise rights that were heretofore unrealized or unused. In addition, we will analyze Gerald Rosenberg's controversial book, *The Hollow Hope: Can Courts Bring About Social Change?*[1] Although *The Hollow Hope* contributes to the research on both the clash between branches and the mobilization of the public, it is a major work in itself. In a nutshell, Rosenberg answers his title question with a resounding no, an answer disputed by others.

SUPREME COURT CLASHES WITH OTHER BRANCHES

We feel that the degree to which the Supreme Court prevails when in opposition to other political institutions is a strong test of how much impact it has in determining public policy. Such a focus cannot tell the whole story of the Court's impact, but it has the advantages of being reasonably measurable and giving the Court sole credit when it prevails.

Declaring Acts of Congress Unconstitutional

Throughout its history the Supreme Court has been viewed as a champion of political minorities. For much of its history, the Court was seen as a bulwark for the propertied interests against populist majorities. In the last half century, the Court has been portrayed as the shield of the oppressed groups in society, championing their rights and liberties against invasion by overweening majorities. However, not everyone believes that the Supreme Court is primarily a protector of minorities. Some argue that it changes positions with major shifts in the political winds. As humorist Peter Finley Dunne's barroom philosopher, Mr. Dooley, remarked a century ago, "The Supreme Court follows the election returns."[2]

DAHL'S THESIS. The first empirical challenge to the presumption that the Supreme Court is a check on the other branches of government was advanced by political scientist Robert Dahl in 1957.[3] The Court is not a protector of minorities of any type, he argued, but rather it is an integral part of the political majority and often assists in imposing the majority's will upon minorities.[4]

Dahl argued that there is a dominant "national law making majority" that remains in power for two or three decades. It is a stable coalition of interests sufficiently large to elect the president and a majority of Congress and thus make national policy. One example is the New Deal coalition forged by President Franklin D. Roosevelt. It consisted of such interests as the labor movement, big city political machines, ethnic and racial minorities, and the South. Similar successful coalitions were developed by presidents Jefferson, Jackson, and Lincoln and by the Republicans when William McKinley was president. After commanding national politics for a generation, a coalition eventually breaks up in the face of a crisis, like the Civil War or the Great Depression, and a new national law-making majority emerges after a short transitional period.

Dahl argued that the Supreme Court is normally in harmony with the law-making majority because its members are appointed by the president, who usually appoints justices with similar political views to his own. On the average, a Supreme Court vacancy occurs every twenty-two months. Although a law-making majority just coming to power may face a potentially hostile Court, it should have a sympathetic one within a decade. Thus Dahl hypothesizes that "the policy views dominant on the Court are never for long out of line with the policy views among the law-making majorities in the United States."[5]

Dahl tests this proposition by looking at Court decisions that declared an important act of Congress unconstitutional and then determining whose policy ultimately prevailed, the Court's or the law-making majority's. He looked only at laws voided within four years of enactment, arguing that major congressional policies would be challenged within that time. Also, he felt that Congress might be less interested in pursuing older policies. Further, he included only laws that had policy implications for the law-making majority's program. For the Supreme Court to strike down routine legislation concerning such matters as river navigation or Indian reservations would hardly be a challenge to the powers that be. Dahl found twenty-three instances in which the Supreme Court struck down an act of Congress important to the law-making majority within the four-year period. He also found that Congress ultimately prevailed in seventeen of these instances—or 74 percent of the time. In another four cases, it was unclear who had prevailed. In only two cases during 168 years (1790–1957) had the Court successfully blocked the enactment of policies desired by the law-making majority—both involving Reconstruction laws penalizing Confederate officers.

Perhaps four additional major cases decided between 1957 and 1996 can be put on Dahl's list:[6] (1) *Oregon v. Mitchell* (1970), which struck down a federal law lowering the voting age to eighteen in state elections, was reversed by the 1971 adoption of the Twenty-sixth Amendment to the Constitution; (2) *National League of Cities v. Usery* (1976), which nullified a law extending the federal minimum wage to state employees, was overruled by the Court in 1985 (*Garcia v. San Antonio Metropolitan Transit Authority*); (3) *Bowsher v. Synar* (1986), which struck down a law allowing the comptroller general to execute budgetary laws, has not been subsequently challenged; and (4) *U.S. v. Eichmann* (1990), which voided the Flag Protection Act of 1989 passed by Congress in response to the Court's striking down Texas's flag protection law the previous year (*Texas v. Johnson*), has been attacked but not overcome. Following *Eichmann,* the House of Representatives approved a constitutional amendment penalizing destruction of the flag, but it failed in the Senate. Thus, the issue remains controversial.

These cases raise to twenty-seven the number of the Supreme Court's major declarations of unconstitutionality within four years of enactment, with nineteen being reversed, four prevailing, and four unclear. Activity since his work appeared has not seriously altered the data underlying Dahl's conclusion about the Court's relationship to the law-making majority.

How was it possible for Congress's policy making to prevail over the seemingly final power of judicial review? The answer usually involved time. At some later date after the Court had nullified a law, Congress passed essentially the same legislation and the Court upheld it. In some instances minor differences between the laws allowed the Court to save face, but usually the real explanation for the Court's approval of the second law was a change of justices on the high bench. Indeed, at times the Court did not even bother with the face-saving charade; it overruled its earlier decision directly or by implication. Only twice was a constitutional amendment necessary to enforce the will of Congress: the Twenty-sixth as noted above, and the Sixteenth authorizing a national income tax after the Court held an earlier such tax unconstitutional (*Pollock v. Farmers' Loan & Trust Co.,* 1895).

Many of the nineteen cases in which Congress prevailed related to major pieces of legislation that were controversial in their time, such as workmen's compensation laws, child labor laws, and New Deal agricultural and economic programs. Both sides felt strongly about both the substance and the philosophy of these policies. Thus Congress's 70 percent success rate is an impressive indicator of the Court's inability to stand against the firm desires of a law-making majority. The crisis between the Court and the Roosevelt administration over the constitutionality of the New Deal is illustrative. Unluckily for Roosevelt, no Supreme Court seats became vacant during his first term (1933–1937), and a Court dominated by appointees of the old coalition struck down eight important New Deal laws. In Roosevelt's second term, however, the law of averages caught up with him and he appointed five justices. By 1941 the eight anti–New Deal decisions, as well as the constitutional philosophy underlying them, were unceremoniously swept under the rug.

Dahl concluded that "by itself the Court is almost powerless to affect the course" of fundamental national policy.[7] It does make many secondary policies that complement the majority coalition's enactments. The Court is not a mere rubber stamp for the dominant coalition, but is, in Dahl's words, "an essential part of the political leadership." Thus the Court can often be important in determining the scope and effectiveness of policy, especially when the elements of the coalition are not united in their enthusiasm for a particular policy.[8]

CRITIQUES OF DAHL'S THESIS. Dahl's hypothesis is open to several objections. Jonathan Casper argued that it is misleading to ignore the cases in which the Court declared federal legislation unconstitutional more than four years after enactment.[9] These constitute around 70 percent of all declarations of unconstitutionality. Many are controversial decisions with important policy implications, and it cannot be concluded without investigation that the law-making majority was no longer interested in maintaining the policies found in such laws. Moreover, for various reasons, challenges to newly enacted laws may not occur right away or may take more than four years to get to the Supreme Court. For example, in an important and still controversial 1976 decision, the Court declared parts of the Federal Election Campaign Act of 1971 unconstitutional (*Buckley v. Valeo*). More recently, *U.S. v. Lopez* (1995) struck down a 1990 act of Congress making it a crime to take guns into school zones. This decision angered President Clinton and many in Congress, so a similar provision was reenacted the following year; the issue has not yet come back to the Court. By eliminating the more-than-four-year-old cases from the analysis, Dahl excludes much of the evidence bearing on the Court's effectiveness in striking down federal laws.

Second, the statistics supporting Dahl's argument come disproportionately from just one short time period—the Court's epic struggle against the New Deal in the mid-1930s. Eight strike-downs (within four years of enactment) occurred then, and Congress soon prevailed in seven.[10] Subtracting these from the twenty-seven total strike-downs leaves only nineteen Court-Congress face-offs over a 200 year history, about one per decade, with Congress winning in twelve. The lesson may be that the Court is a loser in intense clashes, but that it has some chance of winning in normal times.

Also, any current application of Dahl's thesis rests on the assumption that majority law-making coalitions still dominate American government. But this is a dubious premise in the last half of the twentieth century.[11] For thirty of the fifty years between 1946 and 1996, control of Congress and the presidency has been divided between Democrats and Republicans. Among the citizenry sectional and class differences have declined. Thus it is hard to argue that there has been a dominant national law-making majority in recent decades. Moreover, many of the Court's important decisions nowadays are in the civil liberties and rights areas, not economic policy, so there is less pressure from business, labor, and the professions to overcome them. As noted, only two of the four Court decisions we added to Dahl's list were eventually rejected (with *Usery*'s demise being largely the Court's own doing). Moreover, a good number of the Court's nullifications of important laws over four years old have prevailed. Other examples besides *Buckley* and *Lopez,* noted above, are *Kinsella v. Singleton,* (1960)

BOX 7-1
Does Public Opinion Influence the Supreme Court?

Is the Supreme Court guided by public opinion when it makes policy? Recently some scholars have argued that the justices discern how the public (not Congress or the president) feels about issues and decide accordingly. Thus, it is claimed, the Court will strike down laws that are not supported by public opinion, or severely modify its earlier rulings when they become unpopular.[a] For example, when the Court changed its stand on the death penalty's constitutionality, it cited changes in public opinion, as revealed in national poll data among other places, to justify its shift (*Gregg v. Georgia,* 1976).

Using national poll data on 130 issues that the Supreme Court decided (shortly before or after the poll) from the late 1930s until the late 1980s, Thomas Marshall showed that the Court's holding coincided with majority opinion 63 percent of the time. This is modest but not overwhelming evidence for claiming the Court follows public opinion. By chance, Court decisions and public opinion should coincide about 50 percent of the time. Marshall's data indicate that public sentiment influences the Court only in one of every four cases where the Court might otherwise decide in a contrary manner.[b]

Recently James Stimson developed a "domestic policy mood index" as a measure of public opinion.[c] This index is a composite, aggregate measure of the public's views about the role of government since 1956, placed on a liberal to conservative continuum. Using it, changes in the public's domestic policy mood can be compared with changes in the liberalism/conservatism of Supreme Court decisions. The drawback is that a policy mood is not the same thing as public opinion on a particular issue the Court decides, so the comparisons between public opinion and Court decisions are less precise than are Marshall's. The Court may make some liberal decisions in the face of a conservative public mood (or vice-versa) because it does not perceive the public as conservative on the issue at bar. Several researchers have compared changes in the index to trends in Supreme Court liberalism and conservatism and concluded that Court decisions become more liberal or conservative following such changes in the public policy mood.[d]

Although new appointees have some effect on such changes, the researchers also see the justices' perceptions of public mood as causative.[e] Roy Flemming and B. Dan Wood, and William Mishler and Reginald Sheehan separately explored this linkage further by examining changes in individual justices' votes in response to public policy mood changes.[f] Flemming and Wood found that most, but not all, justices' voting patterns shifted in the same direction in response to public mood changes. Votes in civil rights and civil liberties cases were more susceptible to these shifts than those in criminal justice and economic regulatory cases. Mishler and Sheehan found that public mood affected the moderate justices (for example, O'Connor and White) to a much greater extent than the strongly ideological justices (for example, Brennan or Rehnquist). Notably, however, both sets of researchers found the justices' attitudes toward an issue were a better predictor of their votes than were changes in policy moods.

At this point, we cannot fully answer the question about the extent to which public opinion influences the Court's policies. But the evidence indicates it has some effect, perhaps more so on the ideologically moderate justices and on issues having continuing national salience. Even so, the Court makes numerous rulings at odds with public opinion.

[a] Thomas R. Marshall, *Public Opinion and the Supreme Court* (Boston: Unwin Hyman, 1989), 84ff, and David G. Barnum, "The Supreme Court and Public Opinion: Judicial Decision-Making in the Post–New Deal Period," *Journal of Politics* 47 (1985): 652–666.

[b] Marshall, *Public Opinion and the Supreme Court,* 78–90.

[c] James A. Stimson, *Public Opinion in America: Moods, Cycles and Swings* (Boulder, Colo.: Westview, 1991).

[d] William Mishler and Reginald S. Sheehan, "The Supreme Court as a Countermajoritarian Institution? The Impact of Public Opinion on Supreme Court Decisions," *American Political Science Review* 87 (1993): 87–101; James A. Stimson, Michael B. MacKuen, and Robert S. Erikson, "Dynamic Representation," *American Political Science Review* 89 (1995): 543–565; and Michael W. Link, "Tracking Public Mood in the Supreme Court: Cross-Time Analysis of Criminal Procedure and Civil Rights Cases," *Political Research Quarterly* 48 (1995): 61–78.

[e] One exception is Helmut Norpoth and Jeffrey A. Segal, who analyzed the Stimson data and Supreme Court decisions and concluded that there is no direct link between public mood and Court policies. See their "Popular Influence on Supreme Court Decisions," *American Political Science Review* 88 (1994): 711–716.

[f] Roy B. Flemming and B. Dan Wood, "The Public and the Supreme Court: Individual Justice Responsiveness to American Policy Moods," *American Journal of Political Science* 41 (1997): 468–498; William Mishler and Reginald S. Sheehan, "Public Opinion, the Attitudinal Model, and Supreme Court Decision Making: A Micro-Analytic Perspective," *Journal of Politics* 58 (1996): 169–200.

striking down a law subjecting civilian employees or dependents of the armed forces abroad to trial by court-martial, and *Sable Communications v. FCC* (1989), voiding a law prohibiting "indecent" broadcasts or telephone conversations. Thus it can be argued that Dahl's conclusions are more applicable to the nation's past than to modern times.

Finally, it should be noted that although Congress has often reversed the Supreme Court when federal laws have been struck down, sometimes the Court's policy prevailed for many years. For instance, the Court successfully prevented the adoption of a national law prohibiting child labor for twenty-three years and, more spectacularly, frustrated a national civil rights law for over eighty years.[12] Few policies last forever. Surely, the Court must be given some credit for having an impact on society in those cases where its preferences prevailed for a generation or longer.

Statutory Interpretation

A mainstay of judicial business is the interpretation of statutes. Courts inevitably make some policy as they do this; in interpreting major but broadly written laws (in areas such as antitrust, environmental protection, and civil rights), courts can sometimes make very important policy. Legislative bodies can usually rewrite a law if they do not like the interpretation, but as we noted in Chapter 5 popular pressures and divisions within its ranks have kept Congress from acting on many judicial interpretations. No scholar has advanced or tested a broad hypothesis bearing on the impact of statutory interpretation, so it is difficult to draw detailed conclusions here. We do know that the Court can make lasting policy interpretations more easily when the policy preferences of members of Congress or citizens are sharply divided.

Declaring State Laws Unconstitutional

Another major area of the Court's work is judicial review of state constitutions, laws, and local ordinances. Nearly 1,200 have been struck down since 1800, and 10 to 20 nullifications a year have been the norm in recent years.[13] The national law-making majority often has no clear preferences about local issues or policies. But some state or local laws are common throughout the nation; striking them down can have a widespread impact and may be far more controversial than an exercise of judicial review at the federal level. This has been especially true during the last half century.

Certainly the Court's decisions on desegregation, school prayer, legislative reapportionment, defendants' rights, and abortion have generated more political heat than any recent decision finding an act of Congress unconstitutional. As we noted in Chapter 5, proposed constitutional amendments to reverse or modify decisions in four of these areas have received serious consideration in Congress. The Court's decisions in these areas have also been both attacked and defended in presidential campaigns.

It may be that the Supreme Court is simply acting as a part of the national law-making majority when it nullifies many state and local policies—that is, it is making national policy in line with the wishes of Congress and the president, but which they cannot make directly. John Gates investigated this thesis and concluded that "Supreme Court policy making, as gauged by judicial review of state policies, is clearly connected to the forces of realignment."[14] In particular, the Court used judicial review to minimize state and local laws inimical to national economic policies during the Republican coalition era in the first part of the twentieth century, for example, the classic case of *Lochner v. New York* (1905), striking down a state law establishing maximum working hours. Later, New Deal economic policies received Court protection, such as *Thornhill v. Alabama* (1940), nullifying a law prohibiting picketing during a strike. But Gates goes on to argue that Court decisions helped precipitate the demise of national law-making coalitions by making such rigid policies (such as *Dred Scott* in 1857 or *Lochner* in 1905) that they drove major interests out of the majority coalition.

Moreover, as we noted earlier in this chapter, the concept of a national law-making majority seems less applicable to recent American politics. There seems to be little consensus among Congress, the president, and party leaders about how to handle busing, affirmative action, abortion, defendants' rights, and other current issues. Thus the Court is making fundamental national policy by striking down state laws on these topics; it is not doing so on behalf of any majority coalition. Indeed, the Court's exercise of judicial review of state and local laws is its most important and most often used policy-making tool in modern times.

OTHER COURTS AS POLICY MAKERS

Other courts are somewhat constrained as policy makers because their policy decisions can be appealed to higher courts; but they, too, sometimes make important policy.

State Supreme Courts

Beyond the U.S. Supreme Court, state supreme courts are the foremost policy makers in our judicial system. As we noted in Chapter 2 (Box 2-1), they sometimes expand individual rights beyond those the U.S. Supreme Court establishes. In addition, they have final authority to rule on legal issues involving state policy when no federal question is present and on common law issues such as torts, property, and contracts. Common law decisions, particularly in torts, can have important policy implications. In Box 7-2 we list some examples of recent important state supreme court policy decisions. Over the last 100 years, innovative tort decisions have largely favored consumers and created greater liability for manufacturers, financial institutions, health care providers, and others. Innovations by one state supreme court are often adopted by other state courts.[15] Indeed, some recent state decisions have so bothered Congress that in 1996 it passed a bill imposing liability ceilings for some defective products and services, but President Clinton vetoed the bill.

In the 1980s state supreme courts found state laws unconstitutional 2.4 times per court, per year.[16] This figure is similar to the average number of times the U.S. Supreme Court finds federal laws unconstitutional each year. Nonetheless, our strong impression is that no state supreme court has a policy impact in its state comparable to that the U.S. Supreme Court has in the nation. Herbert Jacob called state courts "the least visible branch" of state government.[17] In fact, no one has studied the general policy impact of state supreme courts, and only a few scholars have focused on a particular court.[18] Nor has anyone followed in Dahl's footsteps and determined who prevailed in conflicts between state supreme courts and legislatures or governors.

Most likely, the policy impact of the fifty state high courts varies considerably. Craig Emmert found a range of 3 percent to 46 percent in state supreme courts' willingness to nullify laws challenged on constitutional grounds.[19] Frequent voidings do not necessarily imply a major impact, however, and some courts at the top of Emmert's list, such as South Carolina's and Maryland's, do not have national reputations for policy activism. Sometimes policy impact can best be gauged by local observers. Legislators in Massachusetts, for example, report that their supreme court is "an extremely passive actor in state politics"; they seldom know what it is doing. Ohio legislators, by contrast, say that their court sometimes acts "like a second legislature."[20]

Box 7-2
Some Recent State Supreme Court Policy Decisions

State supreme courts make important policies. The following are examples of policies state supreme courts adopted in 1997.

- South Carolina's supreme court ruled that fetuses existed in their own right and could sue for injuries.
- New York's highest court created the new tort of repetitive stress injury.
- The Missouri Supreme Court held that people have no privacy right in their photographs when they leave film for developing.
- California's supreme court allowed patients to sue health maintenance organizations (HMOs) for fraud despite a contractual requirement that disputes be settled by binding arbitration.
- The Florida Supreme Court rejected an argument that grandparents should have visitation rights for their grandchildren.
- The Tennessee Supreme Court held that the state's right of privacy law did not prevent employers from firing employees who failed random drug tests.

Sources: Articles about the decisions can be found in the *National Law Journal* for 1997 as follows: (S.C.) November 17, B-14; (N.Y.) December 8, B-2; (Mo.) October 20, B-15; (Calif.) July 14, B-1; (Fla.) January 13, B-24; (Tenn.) June 9, B-22.

The California Supreme Court has a reputation for being the leading policy maker among state high courts, particularly in developing consumer protection doctrines in tort law. It was also the only such court to declare the death penalty unconstitutional (*People v. Anderson,* 1972), an action that was soon reversed by an amendment to the state constitution. That court's anti–death penalty decisions (even after the amendment), along with several other unpopular decisions, generated a political counterattack that resulted in the voters' removal of Chief Justice Rose Bird and two other justices in the 1986 retention election (see Box 2-1). Subsequently, California's high court has been less activist, although in 1997 it became the first state supreme court to nullify a law requiring parental consent prior to a minor's obtaining an abortion (*American Academy of Pediatricians v. Lundgren*). High courts in a few other states, most notably Florida, Hawaii, Michigan, New Jersey, New York, and Oregon, have a reputation for engaging in considerable policy making. In most states, however, the supreme court appears to have only a modest impact, and a few courts, such as those in Idaho and Virginia, seem virtually dedicated to the status quo.

Nearly every state supreme court has been asked since the mid-1970s to find that the state's system of financing public schools through property taxes violates the state constitution. Plaintiffs claim that this funding method gives wealthy districts better schools than poor ones, contrary to state constitutional provisions requiring equal protection of the laws, an efficient educational system, or some similar language. Over fifteen high courts have ordered reforms, with a few like Kentucky's promoting structural or curricular changes as well (*Rose v. Council for a Better Education,* 1989). In most of these states, the decisions have produced a significant redistribution of funds across school districts and, in some, have led to a statewide tax increase—an impact comparable to almost any U.S. Supreme Court decision outside the desegregation or abortion areas.[21] But around twenty state high courts rejected the reformers' position, arguing either that the state constitution's language did not warrant a reform decision or that school finance reform was best left to the political branches.[22]

State Trial Courts

Political scientist Herbert Jacob argued that trial courts have a *norm enforcement* function, while appellate courts have a *policy-making* function.[23] Although he recognized that trial judges have discretion in situations such as divorce and criminal sentencing, Jacob felt that because they largely followed pre-established legislative or appellate court policies they did not engage in policy making. "Only when a norm is itself challenged can courts engage in policy-making," Jacob said, and only infrequently do trial courts side with such challenges.[24] For example, a New Jersey trial court ruled that Atlantic City casinos could be held responsible for customers' gambling losses when the casinos had plied them with free liquor.[25] However, Henry R. Glick argues that trial courts can make cumulative policy by being consistent in their exercise of discretion.[26] For example, we sometimes hear stories to the effect that the judge in county A sends all drunk drivers to jail for thirty days while the judge in county B just fines them $200. This would be a policy difference, and it might affect the behavior of those who would drink and drive in the two counties. Social scientists have studied such differences with some frequency, especially through looking at prosecutor-judge-defense attorney "work groups" in criminal cases.[27] But their focus is more on explaining the politics or sociology of the differences than in examining to what extent they affect behavior of people in different jurisdictions. Trial courts can and do make policy in some situations, but unfortunately the impact of such policies is not well researched.[28]

There is one comprehensive study of the impact of local courts— Kenneth Dolbeare's examination of suburban Nassau County, New York. Using interviews and newspaper articles, he identified the most important policy disputes that occurred there between 1949 and 1964; then he looked at the local courts' decisions concerning these policies. Several disputes such as those concerning highway construction and mass transit were never litigated. The courts' greatest impact came in zoning policy, but courts also affected local taxes and defined and sometimes limited the regulatory powers of local government agencies. Local courts also served as a safety valve in some community disputes, especially those involving the schools, by allowing the losing side to have its day in court. But Dolbeare concluded that the local courts' main impact was economic, favoring businesses and property owners in zoning and regulatory disputes. Moreover, the courts' economic impact was largely negative—vetoing or delaying public improvements and other economic change in favor of the status quo. The trial courts did not initiate much policy.[29]

LOWER FEDERAL COURTS

Although scholars have paid considerable attention to both the federal courts of appeals and the district courts, no impact study comparable to Dolbeare's has been undertaken about them.[30] Even so, the literature permits a few observations about the general impact of these courts. As is true for state trial courts, much of the activity in federal district courts involves norm enforcement.[31] The courts' independent policy making can be more dramatic than that of state courts in complex local situations where the Supreme Court (or statutory provisions) has given lower federal courts a good deal of discretion in fashioning remedies. The power of lower federal courts has been particularly evident in school desegregation cases (see Chapter 4), but the courts' policy making also occurs in environmental and occupational safety cases as well as those involving housing and employment discrimination. The district courts have much less impact where the law or Supreme Court policy is reasonably clear and the policy does not need to be tailored to fit local situations. District courts can develop innovative and sometimes attention-grabbing policies involving questions not yet decided by higher courts (see, for example, *American Federation of State, County and Municipal Employees v. Washington*, 1983, discussed in Chapter 2), but ultimately these are almost always decided by a court of appeals and sometimes by the Supreme Court.

In the 1970s and 1980s, some district judges took to developing unprecedented and detailed policies affecting state institutions in their districts, most often prisons (see Box 3-2 in Chapter 3) or mental health hospitals. Responding to claims that these institutions violated constitutional standards through overcrowding, the imposition of harsh punishments, the unnecessary drugging of patients, or the like, the judges issued orders limiting inmate populations, types of punishment, or the administration of drugs or certain therapies. Although the Supreme Court eventually imposed boundaries on district judges' discretion in such cases, the judges retain considerable flexibility in finding violations and fashioning remedies. It is fair to say that much of the responsibility for reforms in the nation's prisons and mental institutions (and markedly increased state funding for them) comes from pioneering policy activism by district judges such as Frank M. Johnson Jr. of Alabama, William Wayne Justice of Texas, and others who followed their lead. However, some district judges were unsympathetic to serious reform and ordered relatively minimal changes.

Much of the activity of the U.S. courts of appeals involves norm enforcement. But they make policy more frequently than district courts do, and they sometimes decide important policy questions that the Supreme Court declines to settle or puts off for years. Such decisions are known as *the law of the circuit;* they bind district court judges throughout the circuit and often influence other courts of appeals, federal district courts, and state courts. Occasionally the policy in one circuit is diametrically opposed to that in another circuit. For example, in the 1960s and 1970s the law of the circuit for five courts of appeals was that public schools could regulate students' hair length, while in five other circuits the "law" was that such regulations were unconstitutional.[32] During the 1980s, in some circuits, public universities could give money from mandatory student fees to "cause" groups such as student environmental or civil liberties organizations, while other courts of appeals held that such involuntary giving violated the First Amendment's freedom of speech and association guarantees.[33]

JUDICIAL MOBILIZATION OF POLITICAL ACTION

In Chapter 5, we discussed research indicating that some court decisions have a positive impact on public opinion. Beyond changing public opinion, however, researchers have asked: Can court decisions mobilize people to engage in social or political actions that they would otherwise not take? In other words, can decisions place a policy issue on the nation's political agenda?[34]

A number of scholars answer yes, arguing that certain decisions can mobilize the public or interested elites to action. A court decision may cause people to realize that they have "rights" or common interests that they were virtually unaware of (or that did not exist) beforehand. As law professor Marc Galanter puts it, court decisions often "work through the transmission and reception of information rather than by strict imposition of controls."[35] Leaders, particularly in self-conscious identity groups such as African Americans, women, or the disabled, will mobilize members of their community to vindicate these rights. Group mobilization is often necessary because officeholders or other leaders may be indifferent or may resist changing the status quo, as happened in the South following *Brown v. Board* (1954). Groups mobilize their members to pressure Congress, the president, state officials, or other agencies, demanding the adoption of policies that will facilitate rights rather than discourage their use. Mobilization may include public demonstrations, strikes and the like. Indeed, mobilization may soon extend to goals beyond vindication of a court-established right. Demands arise that Congress, city councils, and other policy makers develop new policies or rights that benefit the group (an example is affirmative action). A decision can also produce legal mobilization, that is it encourages interest groups or lawyers to undertake vindicative litigation or to seek expansion of judicial policies beyond the original court decision.[36]

However, some researchers, most notably Stuart Scheingold in his book *The Politics of Rights,* and Gerald Rosenberg more recently in *The Hollow Hope,* say no, that judicial mobilization seldom occurs and is not very successful.[37] (We will consider Rosenberg's book more generally in the next section of this chapter.)

Studying judicially generated mobilization is not easy. A court decision and subsequent political pressures in the same area can be highly visible, but the linkage between them is not. Alternate causes are possible; perhaps some other government action led to the mobilization or perhaps people's interest and willingness to act were rising independently of the court decision. Exploring the details of causality is time consuming, and the process is unusually difficult if the research is focused on events that took place decades earlier. Consider *Brown* in this context. Certainly it was a highly visible Court decision, a judicial attempt to generate one of the greatest social reforms in American history. And certainly in the years that followed, African Americans and their allies brought considerable pressures on other governmental bodies to desegregate the schools. Indeed, the pressures soon went far beyond schools to demand integration of all aspects of American life. African Americans mobilized not only in legislative halls but in the streets; the 1960s were full of "sit-ins" and other demonstrations demanding an end to racial discrimination; even today such demonstrations occur from time to time. But the question remains: Was *Brown* a major cause of this mobilization?

Rosenberg empirically examined the causal linkage between *Brown* and civil rights mobilization. He looked at periodical coverage of civil rights from 1940 to 1965 and found that while attention was up briefly in 1954, it reverted to pre-1954 levels in the 1955–1960 period before rising markedly during the sit-ins of the 1960s. He also noted that public opinion polls reported little change in attitudes toward racial integration prior to the 1960s. Rosenberg also found that civil rights demonstrations did not increase significantly in the late 1950s, nor did the membership and income of various civil rights groups. He thus concluded, "I have found no evidence that [*Brown's*] influence was widespread or of much importance to the battle for civil rights."[38] Mobilization for battle, he argues, occurred largely independently of the Court's decision.

Other scholars of the civil rights movement have attributed much greater influence to *Brown* in the mobilization process.[39] Moreover, Rosenberg's data and analysis have been subjected to criticism. He did not search under the key heading "Desegregation" when he gathered periodical data, so he undercounted the number of articles about *Brown*.[40] Nearly all of the periodicals Rosenberg examined were aimed at white audiences, although blacks were the primary group to mobilize after the decision. Nor would public opinion polls reveal respondents' changing perspectives—their willingness to act on behalf of a cause—as opposed to their attitudes, which may not have changed much. It is also argued that Rosenberg misinterpreted the data on membership and contributions to black organizations and that in fact they did increase their strength after *Brown*.[41]

Beyond these criticisms, we argue that Rosenberg's conception of causality is too time-bound. History teaches that perspectives are not changed overnight; a decade or even a generation may pass before a major impact occurs. The young, with their more flexible mindsets and social niches, are often more inspired than the middle aged or the elderly. Thus, although those who participated in the sit-ins of the early 1960s may have been in junior high school when *Brown* came down, and perhaps some could not cite the case by name, *Brown* may well have been the vital symbolic beginning of the inspirational linkage producing their behavior.

Another major study of mobilization, Michael McCann's *Rights at Work,* looks at a wider but less visible range of post-decision activity.[42] McCann conducted in-depth studies of a dozen state and local mobilizations in favor of equal pay following the Supreme Court's decision in *County of Washington v. Gunther* (1981). He came to a rather different conclusion about the inspirational impact of Court decisions than had Rosenberg. *Gunther* ruled that women guards at a county jail who received significantly less pay than male guards could sue under the gender discrimination provisions (Title VII) of the 1964 Civil Rights Act. *Gunther* was not nearly as prominent as *Brown* and it was, moreover, not expanded or even reinforced by subsequent Supreme Court decisions.[43]

Nevertheless, McCann found that *Gunther* inspired "movement building" among women's groups and "progressive" lawyers. Their use of legal tactics based upon *Gunther* usually compelled formal policy concessions from employers. The movement invoked "the clout that judicial intervention might provide, but [avoided] the uncertainty, financial cost and loss of control that exclusive reliance on litigation might bring."[44] McCann also noted that the movement established a legacy of increased consciousness of rights, which became very useful in moral and public relations discourse as well as in legal negotiation. Thus McCann more generally concludes that court decisions often play an important (but not exclusive) role in developing discussion frameworks and visions of opportunity within which citizens act.

Some segments of society are less amenable to mobilization. Vulnerable groups such as tenants and marginal employees, for example, are less likely to make waves than are more secure middle-class groups such as environmentalists or groups whose situation evokes sympathy such as the disabled or mental patients.[45]

Court decisions can also lead to counter-mobilization when other groups feel threatened. Indeed, a decision can produce a new sense of self-identity. For example, over fifteen states had eased or repealed their abortion laws before *Roe v. Wade* (1973) without causing major nationwide controversy. *Roe,* however, was such a nationally visible symbol that it soon generated the formation of nationally active right-to-life groups. As noted in Chapter 1, these groups vigorously lobbied state legislatures and Congress against abortion and backed sometimes successful litigation to limit *Roe's* scope (such as *Planned Parenthood v. Casey,* 1992). It is arguable, although by no means certain, that had the Supreme Court not ruled on abortion and let the issue be battled out in every state legislature, the opposition to abortion would not be so well organized. Other examples include the rise of "white citizens' councils" in the South in the 1950s to fight racial integration and the efforts of religious groups to keep prayer in the public schools. It is plausible, as Rosenberg suggests, that major Court decisions are better at mobilizing the public to opposition than they are at mobilizing demand for implementation and expansion.[46]

THE COURTS AND SOCIAL CHANGE

Our final inquiry in this chapter is: What role do the courts have in achieving social change and reform in the United States? American society has constantly changed, particularly in the twentieth century. Most of the change does not originate in government. But governmental actions often facilitate social change. History identifies Jacksonian leadership as ushering in policies favoring "the common man" and free enterprise. Lincoln and the Reconstruction Congresses destroyed slavery. And Franklin Roosevelt's New Deal gave the federal government primary responsibility for regulating the national economy.

These examples feature the president and Congress as the main forgers of social change. This portrayal comports with the idea that in a democracy the people's elected representatives should precipitate change. Moreover, courts are supposed to make decisions based upon law and not on what changes the judges think might be good for society. Nonetheless, as we have seen throughout this book, courts do make policy, and sometimes their policies facilitate or require major social change. So an inquiry into what role the courts have in achieving social and political reform is relevant.

What the courts' role should be is a controversial question in public debate. Many conservatives, who are usually opposed to reform, argue that "activist" courts are imposing social change on the country against the public's will and urge rejection of judicial nominees who are perceived as activists. On their side, liberals praise justices such as Earl Warren or William Brennan whose decisions produced social reforms and urge rejection of nominees seen as unsympathetic to such change. Indeed, liberals sometimes file lawsuits in the specific hope of reforming some aspect of American society. Such behavior clearly implies a belief that the courts do influence social change and reform in the U.S.

The Hollow Hope

Going beyond the arguments about the proper role of the courts, social scientists have studied how effective courts are as instruments of social change. This is a matter of some controversy. Debate centers on Gerald Rosenberg's 1991 book, *The Hollow Hope: Can Courts Bring About Social Change?*, which we have discussed in the context of desegregation in the preceding section. (Despite the title, the focus is exclusively on the impact of the Supreme Court.) Simply put, Rosenberg argues that the Supreme Court cannot produce significant social reform, that is, "policy change with a nationwide impact." [47] The Court may make some marginal changes, but, acting alone, it "can *almost never* be [an] effective producer of social reform" (emphasis in original). [48] He compares reformers who pin their hopes on court decisions to flies attracted to flypaper.

Rosenberg offers three reasons, or Constraints as he terms them, why the Supreme Court cannot generate significant policy reform:

> *Constraint I*—The bounded nature of constitutional rights prevents courts from hearing or effectively acting on many significant social reform claims, and lessens the chances of popular mobilization.

> *Constraint II*—The judiciary lacks the necessary independence from other branches of the government to produce significant social reform.

> *Constraint III*—Courts lack the tools to readily develop appropriate policies and implement decisions ordering significant social reform. [49]

Constraint I may keep the Court from considering reforms that are too far removed from constitutional text or understandings (for example, a right to welfare payments), but, as experience shows, the Constitution's more open-ended provisions give the Court much room for considering reforms. This constraint is not relevant to examining those policy reforms the Court has made. We will focus more on Constraints II and III in our discussion of *The Hollow Hope.*

Rosenberg then offers four Conditions under which the Court "may effectively produce significant social reform" (that is, overcome the constraints), all but one of which (Condition III) seem to require the assistance of other governmental actors:

Condition I—when other actors offer positive incentives to induce compliance.

Condition II—when other actors impose costs to induce compliance.

Condition III—when judicial decisions can be implemented by the market.

Condition IV—by providing leverage, or a shield, cover, or excuse for persons crucial to implementation who are *willing to act.*(Emphasis in original.)[50]

The Hollow Hope then tests what might be termed the *judicial impotence* hypothesis by examining several recent social reforms in which the Supreme Court was involved. We have already discussed *Brown v. Board,* the case to which Rosenberg gives the most attention. We have argued that the 1964 Civil Rights Act and other legislation to achieve desegregation resulted from mobilization generated by *Brown* and did not occur independently of *Brown.*

The other reforms Rosenberg looked at are criminal justice, reapportionment, and abortion. (Surprisingly, he also focused on women's rights and the environment, but it was the other branches, not the Supreme Court, that initiated major policy changes in these areas.) In the rest of this section, we will briefly assess his conclusions about the impact of the Court's policies in these three areas and we will also discuss three Court-generated reforms that *The Hollow Hope* fails to examine: greater availability of sexually oriented material, diminished schoolhouse religion, and the rise of advertising by professionals.[51]

As we do this, we need to make a distinction between judicial reforms that require government implementation and those that consumers can take advantage of without any government action. Changes in criminal justice procedures, legislative apportionment, and religion in the public schools require that government actors—the implementing population—change their policies. By contrast, current Court doctrines allow the consumer population to obtain abortions, buy sexually oriented publications and films, and be exposed to advertising by professionals without the need for any government implementation. Indeed, the essence of these reforms is to ensure that the government not prohibit consumers' access.

Rosenberg's Constraint II holds that Court-generated reforms fail when they do not receive support from the other branches. If this is true, then when other branches do not endorse certain Court reforms, we would expect the reforms that require implementation to be unsuccessful. However, Constraint II does not apply to consumer choice reforms, so we would not particularly expect such reforms to be unsuccessful. Their success depends largely upon the existence of consumer demand and economic incentives to those who would provide the requisite materials or services. We will discuss first reforms requiring implementation and then those that give consumers a choice.

Reforms Requiring Implementation

CRIMINAL JUSTICE. Calling it "The Revolution That Wasn't," Rosenberg argued that the Court's efforts to reform the criminal justice system through decisions imposing the exclusionary rule in search and seizure (*Mapp v. Ohio,* 1961), *Miranda* warnings (*Miranda v. Arizona,* 1966), and other protections for defendants were largely a failure. They failed because of legislative and presidential resistance (even President Clinton, a Democrat, has pushed tough anticrime proposals) that reflected the public's fear of crime and because of police and trial court behavior that minimized the decisions' impact (that is, warnings have become ritualized, police may lie, judges may be willing to admit questionably obtained evidence). The Court's decisions curbed some of the worst abuses of the criminal justice system and routinized the administration of defendants' rights. Nonetheless, as research discussed in Chapters 3 and 4 indicates, these decisions have not produced major changes in how the criminal justice system operates.[52] Crime control is such an essential function to American society and defendants are so numerous that it is difficult for the implementing population to act on much more than an assembly-line basis. *The Hollow Hope's* analysis of this reform may well be reasonably accurate.

REAPPORTIONMENT. Rosenberg acknowledges that state legislatures and the U.S. House of Representatives are now apportioned on a "one person, one vote" principle, but he calls the Court's reapportionment decisions a failed reform because the reapportioned bodies did not pass more legislation favoring cities (see Chapter 4). His critics note, however, that there is no evidence that the justices were motivated by urban-oriented policy preferences in *Baker v. Carr* (1962) and its follow-up decisions. Reforms center on principle, they argue, and the Court adopted the "one person, one vote" principle and made it stick, despite opposition by Congress and state legislatures (Constraint II), a largely indifferent public, limited enforcement tools (Constraint III), and the absence of any conditions Rosenberg believed necessary to overcome the constraints.

SCHOOLHOUSE RELIGION. *The Hollow Hope* does not address decisions removing religious exercises from public schools. Some might argue that the Court's decisions declaring prayer and Bible reading in the public schools unconstitutional are not a significant reform because they are more symbolic than real. No doubt great symbolism is associated with these activities, but they were highly valued by large numbers of people. Local implementation of these decisions was required, albeit the minimal one of ceasing religious activities. As we saw in Chapter 3, however, both active opposition and inertia could perpetuate prayers and Bible readings.

Congress, state legislatures, and governors did nothing to assist in implementing these decisions and often bitterly opposed them. Over the years, one house or the other of Congress has approved a constitutional amendment to allow prayers in public schools. This course of action gained new life in the late 1990s when the Republicans gained control of Congress; in June 1998 such an amendment won a majority but not the necessary two-thirds vote in the House of Representatives. Despite the long-term opposition from Congress and other governmental actors, the Court has not only stuck to its initial rulings, but it has expanded them to bar activities such as posting the Ten Commandments in schools (*Stone v. Graham,* 1980) and offering nondenominational prayers at graduation ceremonies (*Lee v. Weisman,* 1992). Moreover, the removal of prayers and Bible reading has been successfully implemented. Occasional exceptions attract attention because they are exceptions, and such activities are usually terminated when revealed. Thus the Supreme Court has effectuated an important social reform here despite Constraints II (noncooperation by other branches) and III (lack of enforcement tools).

Consumer Choice Reforms

Consumer choice reforms require no implementation by government agencies. As we noted in Chapter 4, consumer choice policies often have both direct (private providers) and indirect consumers (users). A reform will be successful if demand for the reform exists and if providers find it economically feasible to meet the demand. At most, the government can only discourage consumption of the reform, so Rosenberg's Constraint II is only marginally relevant to success. Likewise, Constraint III is not very meaningful because sophisticated judicial enforcement tools are largely unnecessary. Thus Conditions I, II, and IV, which relate to overcoming these constraints, are not very important. Condition III, however, is important to the reforms discussed here because providers will not operate on a widespread scale without an economic incentive.

ABORTION. As we noted in Chapter 1, abortions increased greatly in the years following *Roe v. Wade* (1973), exceeding 1,500,000 in the U.S. in 1980 and remaining around that number well into the 1990s. These figures contrast with the roughly 500,000 abortions performed in 1972.[53] Reminiscent of his argument that mobilization to end segregation was rapidly jelling independently of *Brown v. Board* (1954), Rosenberg argues that the rapid rise in abortions was taking place before *Roe*. He notes that legal abortions had risen from virtually zero in 1966 to 500,000 in 1972, and continued rising at the same rate before leveling off at 1,600,000 around 1979. (See Chapter 1.) This is what Matthew Wettstein calls "the abortion rate paradox"—a huge rise in abortions during the 1970s but without *Roe* having any statistically significant relationship to it.[54] *Roe* did dramatically redistribute the location of abortions: in 1972, 84 percent occurred in the five jurisdictions that had repealed their abortion laws, but by 1976 only 35 percent took place in these states.[55] The decision also enabled lower-middle-class and working women to obtain abortions more easily.[56] The thrust of Rosenberg's argument is that the Court "was reflecting social change rather than legislating it,"[57] although he concedes that without *Roe* few additional states might have allowed abortions (and some might have reinstated their restrictions). It is certainly likely that if abortion were limited to five states (including remote Alaska and Hawaii), the rate would not have increased by 1,000,000 over the 1970s. Despite the paradox, the Court's decision went far beyond a marginal role in securing abortion rights.

More important, as we noted at the beginning of this section, social reforms seldom originate in government agencies. But some official approval (here the Supreme Court's) is often necessary to legitimate and secure the changes—especially when strenuous opposition exists, as is certainly the case with abortion. As we discussed in some detail in Chapter 1, both Congress and many state legislatures have continuously passed laws discouraging women from obtaining abortions (see Table 1-1). While the Supreme Court has upheld some of the less intrusive laws, it has steadfastly stuck to *Roe*'s basic holding—that women have a right to get abortions (see Appendix, Table A-1).

Clearly, the Court's policy has prevailed despite great hostility and non-cooperation from other branches and intense opposition from a large segment of the public. The profit motive offers some explanation for the rapid rise of abortion clinics after *Roe,* but obviously the demand is there: for varying reasons large numbers of women are willing to obtain abortions. Without the Court's decisions in *Roe* and subsequent cases, this demand would have been accommodated only tenuously and fitfully.

SEXUALLY ORIENTED MATERIAL. *Roth v. U.S.* (1957) was the breakthrough ruling in which the Supreme Court held that sexually oriented material was protected by the First Amendment unless the dominant theme of the work, taken as a whole, appealed to prurient interests and lacked redeeming social value. Although the topic is not discussed in *The Hollow Hope,* we believe it is important to note that society's sexual mores underwent a dramatic change between the 1950s and the 1960s. Nudity, sex, and obscene language were never shown in 1950s Hollywood movies; even married couples slept in separate beds. By contrast, the 1960s was the decade of the "sexual revolution" as books and films focusing on sex, nudity, and obscene language abounded, not just in art houses or seedy downtown buildings but in suburban malls and small town theaters. While the Court's *Miller v. California* (1973) decision put some boundaries on what was permissible, it was hardly a call for returning to our Puritan heritage. Indeed, *Miller* might be considered a "peace treaty" ratifying all but the excesses of the 1960s.

Again it might be argued that the Court was just reflecting changing social mores. Large numbers of Americans had turned away from Victorian moral codes. Nonetheless there was no visible public pressure for changing obscenity laws. No president or governor ever urged greater availability of sexually oriented material, and neither Congress nor the state legislatures enacted any laws expanding access. In fact, most public officials looked askance at such a policy. The Supreme Court was the only government body that initiated or pursued this reform. Only *Roth* and some follow-up cases enabled this major social reform to take place on a pervasive basis (see Box 5-2). The Court accomplished this reform quite rapidly without help from the other branches. The loosened legal restraints and rising public interest in sexually oriented material ensured that providers would find a market.

ADVERTISING BY PROFESSIONALS. Prior to the mid-1970s, the First Amendment provided no protection for advertising (or "commercial speech" as it is called in legal parlance). Because advertising is an essential part of modern commerce, government did not regulate it to any great extent. But advertising by those in the licensed professions (such as physicians and attorneys) was usually prohibited. The Supreme Court ended this prohibition on First Amendment grounds in the 1976 case of *Virginia Board of Pharmacy v. Virginia Consumers Council*. The case involved pharmacists, but a year later the Court extended its logic to attorneys (*Bates v. Arizona Bar Association*) and by implication to all professionals.

Here, too, the Court received virtually no assistance from other government agencies. While some consumer organizations and economically hungry professionals favored such advertising, the general public gave it little thought, and it was largely opposed by state and national professional organizations such as the American Bar Association, groups from which legislators and regulators normally take their signals. Yet the Court adopted this reform and went on to expand the scope of permissible advertising in later cases.

Certainly *Virginia Pharmacy* and its progeny have had an impact. We hear pitches for lawyers, accountants, dentists, and other professionals on radio from time to time and occasionally see them on television. Telephone books are replete with professionals' box ads, and we sometimes receive direct mail solicitations from them. Nonetheless, the impact has been limited—the floodgates have not opened. As we noted in Chapter 4, recent surveys of the legal profession show that only a third of attorneys whose practice depends upon high turnover of clients resort to advertising.[58] In sum, the Court has initiated a major reform here despite governmental and public opposition or indifference. But its impact on the indirect consumer (the potential users of professionals' services) has been more modest than has been the case with abortion or sexually oriented material because many professionals have decided that the costs of advertising were not worth the benefits.

Evaluation

The Hollow Hope portrays a Supreme Court that is almost powerless—a government appendage acting in minor ways or occasionally being of assistance in securing major policy change, but having little independent capacity to produce significant change. By contrast, our review of six major reforms initiated by the Supreme Court (plus desegregation) in the last half of the twentieth century shows the Court as an independent generator of notable policy change. The justices were successful in establishing at least four and probably five of the reforms without much assistance from other government agencies and often in the face of their considerable opposition. In reforming criminal justice procedures, it is arguable that the implementing agencies muffled the reforms' effects. It is also arguable that too few professionals engage in advertising to conclude that *Virginia Pharmacy* led to widespread change. And certainly desegregation received considerable implementation assistance from the other branches of the federal government even though *Brown v. Board* largely mobilized the demand for ending segregation. The other four Court-generated reforms have succeeded quite well.

Rosenberg is correct in arguing that Constraint III (lack of tools to control bureaucratic behavior closely) limits the courts' capacity to achieve reform independently. We saw this in the analysis of desegregation and criminal justice. But as we have also seen, the Court's consumer choice reforms do not involve government agencies, and some of the reforms that require implementation (such as removing schoolhouse religion) do not need sophisticated enforcement. At bottom, Constraint II (lack of independence from other branches) is pretty similar to Constraint III, that is, the courts' dependence on the other branches is only important when the other branches must help the court implement a reform. Clearly, this is not always the case.

Certainly "American courts are not all powerful institutions" as Rosenberg reminds us.[59] But they, and particularly the Supreme Court, have had a primary role in achieving social reforms during the last half century. We must reject the *judicial impotence* hypothesis.

SUMMARY

This last chapter has focused on the overall impact of judicial decisions. Just how much impact courts have on public policy is a matter of some controversy among both scholars and the public. We first explored the question: Who prevails when the Supreme Court clashes with Congress and/or the president? Based upon his research, Dahl argued that historically the Court is part of the national law-making majority and thus has seldom opposed the other branches on major policy issues. When there were direct clashes, the Court usually lost. However, a singular national law-making majority has been a less relevant concept in the last half century, and there is some evidence that the Court has fared better in recent times. Moreover, the Court has had a clear policy impact when it has struck down important and widespread state laws, such as segregation and abortion.

Other courts also make policy, although there is much less research into their impact. State supreme courts are important policy makers in several states and have had a particularly telling impact on school financing policies in about fifteen states. The impact of state trial courts is largely unexplored, but Dolbeare's research revealed that they often favored business or property interests in zoning or regulatory disputes. Lower federal courts sometimes create innovative policies, placing them on the national agenda and sometimes getting them accepted by the Supreme Court. Their decisions also affect the administration of state institutions such as prisons. Federal courts of appeals often make *law of the circuit* policies that go unreviewed by the Supreme Court.

Occasionally court decisions will mobilize people, especially those in self-identified groups, to engage in political or legal action that they otherwise would not pursue. These decisions generate an awareness of rights heretofore unrealized, and perhaps inspire people to seek goals beyond the immediate decision. Lawsuits and political action to vindicate rights follow. But just how capable courts are at political mobilization is disputed among scholars, with much debate centering on reaction to *Brown v. Board* (1954).

In his 1991 book *The Hollow Hope,* Rosenberg advances the *judicial impotence* hypothesis, arguing that the Supreme Court cannot independently produce significant social reform. The Court, he says, is "a hollow hope" for reformers. This conclusion has been subjected to considerable criticism. We conclude that Rosenberg is probably right regarding the Court's criminal justice policies, has overstated the case in desegregation, is wrong about abortion and reapportionment, and has ignored the Court's major policy impacts in such areas as schoolhouse religion and the availability of sexually oriented material.

NOTES

1. Gerald N. Rosenberg, *The Hollow Hope: Can Courts Bring About Social Change?* (Chicago: University of Chicago Press, 1991).

2. Peter Finley Dunne, *Mr. Dooley at His Best* (New York: Archon, 1949), 77.

3. Robert Dahl, "Decision-Making in a Democracy: The Supreme Court as a National Policy-Maker," *Journal of Public Law* 6 (1957): 279–295.

4. See Girardeau Spann, "Pure Politics," *Michigan Law Review* 88 (1990): 1971–2033 for a similar argument as it relates to racial majorities and minorities.

5. Dahl, "Decision-Making in a Democracy."

6. In 1997 the Court struck down three such laws, *City of Boerne v. Flores*, 138 L.Ed 2d 624, *U.S. v. Printz*, 138 L.Ed 2d 914, and *Reno v. ACLU*, 138 L.Ed 2d 874. They were decided less than a year before this book was completed, too recently for us to assess the success of any reactions or challenges, so they are not included in this discussion.

7. Dahl, "Decision-Making in a Democracy," 293.

8. Ibid., 293, 294.

9. Jonathan Casper, "The Supreme Court and National Policy-Making," *American Political Science Review* 70 (1976): 50–63.

10. Dahl, in "Decision-Making in a Democracy," recognized the New Deal's disproportionate impact on his findings. See also Bradley C. Canon and S. Sidney Ulmer, "The Supreme Court and Critical Elections: A Dissent," *American Political Science Review* 70 (1976): 1215–1218.

11. See Byron E. Schaefer, ed., *The End of Realignment* (Madison: University of Wisconsin Press, 1991) for arguments about the decline of national majority political coalitions and its consequences.

12. Child labor: *Hammer v. Dagenhart,* 247 U.S. 251 (1918), overruled by *U.S. v. Darby Lumber Co.,* 312 U.S. 100 (1941); civil rights: *The Civil Rights Cases,* 109 U.S. 3 (1883), effectively overruled by *Heart of Atlanta Motel v. U.S.,* 379 U.S. 241 (1964).

13. See Lee Epstein et al., *The Supreme Court Compendium* (Washington, D.C.: CQ Press, 1994), 100–127.

14. John B. Gates, *The Supreme Court and Partisan Realignment* (Boulder, Colo.: Westview, 1992), 171.

15. Bradley C. Canon and Lawrence Baum, "Patterns of Adoption of Tort Law Innovations: An Application of Diffusion Theory to Judicial Doctrines," *American Political Science Review* 75 (1981): 975–987, and Lawrence Baum and Bradley C. Canon, "State Supreme Courts as Activists: New Doctrines in the Law of Torts," in *State Supreme Courts: Policy-Makers in the Federal System,* ed. Mary Cornelia Porter and G. Alan Tarr (Westport, Conn.: Greenwood Press, 1982), 83–108.

16. Henry R. Glick, "Policy Making and State Supreme Courts," in *The American Courts: A Critical Assessment,* ed. John B. Gates and Charles A. Johnson, (Washington, D.C.: CQ Press, 1991), 102.

17. Herbert Jacob, "Courts: The Least Visible Branch," in *Politics in the American States: A Comparative Analysis,* 6th ed., ed. Virginia Gray and Herbert Jacob (Washington, D.C.: CQ Press, 1996), 253.

18. G. Alan Tarr and Mary Cornelia Porter explore the roles of the Alabama, New Jersey, and Ohio supreme courts in their book, *State Supreme Courts in State and Nation* (New Haven, Conn.: Yale University Press, 1988), but do not focus

directly on their impact. See Richard Lehne, *The Quest for Justice: The Politics of School Finance Reform* (New York: Longman, 1978), for the most thorough investigation of the impact of a state supreme court school finance reform decision, *Robinson v. Cahill,* 351 A.2d 713 (N.J., 1975).

19. Emmert's data are reported in Glick, "Policy Making in State Supreme Courts," Table 4-2, p. 100. See James P. Wenzel, Shaun Bowler, and David LaNoue, "Legislating from the State Bench: A Comparative Analysis of Judicial Activism," *American Politics Quarterly* 25 (1997): 363–379, for a discussion of some correlates of state supreme court policy making.

20. Mark C. Miller, "Lawmaker Attitudes Toward Court Reform in Massachusetts," *Judicature* 77 (1993): 37, and John D. Felice and John C. Kilwein, "High Court–Legislative Relations: The View from the Ohio Courthouse," *Judicature* 77 (1993): 45.

21. See Margaret Louise Carter, "Neither Force Nor Will: The Limits of Judicial Activism in Education Finance" (Honors Thesis, Department of Government, Harvard College, 1996).

22. Allen W. Hubsch, "The Emerging Right to Education Under State Constitutional Law," *Temple Law Review* 65 (1992): 1325–1358.

23. Herbert Jacob, *Justice in America* (Boston: Little, Brown, 1965).

24. Ibid., 26. Jacob maintained this position in three later editions of *Justice in America.*

25. See Henry R. Glick, *Courts, Politics and Justice,* 3d ed. (New York: McGraw-Hill, 1993), 356.

26. Ibid., 278. For a longer discussion of the extent to which trial courts make policy, see Lynn Mather, "Policy Making in State Trial Courts," in *The American Courts: A Critical Assessment,* ed. Gates and Johnson, 119–156.

27. Two major studies of such work groups are Martin Levin, *Urban Politics and the Criminal Courts* (Chicago: University of Chicago Press, 1977), and James Eisenstein, Roy B. Flemming, and Peter F. Nardulli, *The Contours of Justice: Communities and their Courts* (Boston: Little, Brown, 1988).

28. Levin, *Urban Politics and the Criminal Courts,* discusses the impacts in political terms.

29. Kenneth Dolbeare, *Trial Courts in Urban Politics: State Court Policy Impact and Functions in a Local Political System* (New York: Wiley, 1967).

30. The most comprehensive works on federal district courts are C. K. Rowland and Robert A. Carp, *Politics and Judgment in Federal District Courts* (Lawrence: University of Kansas Press, 1996) and Robert A. Carp and Ronald Stidham, *The Federal Courts,* 2d ed. (Washington, D.C.: CQ Press, 1991).

31. Rowland and Carp, *Politics and Judgment in Federal District Courts,* 117, report that over 90 percent of the federal district court opinions go unpublished because they are relatively uncontroversial.

32. Note, "A Dilemma in the Public Schools: School Board Authority vs. the Constitutional Right of Students to Wear Long Hair," *Louisiana Law Review* 33 (1973): 697–707.

33. See "Conservative Legal Group Takes Aim at Mandatory Student Fees," *Chronicle of Higher Education,* March 6, 1998, A-32, and Thomas M. Bevilacqua, "Public Universities' Mandatory Student Activity Fees and the First Amendment," *Journal of Law and Education* 24 (1995): 1–32.

34. See Roy B. Flemming, John Bohte, and B. Dan Wood, "One Voice Among Many: The Supreme Court's Influence to Attentiveness to Issues in the United States, 1947–92," *American Journal of Political Science* 41 (1997): 1224–1250.

35. Marc Galanter, "The Radiating Effects of Courts," in *Empirical Theories of Courts,* ed. Keith Boyum and Lynn Mather (New York: Longman, 1983), 126.

36. See, for example, Michael McCann, *Rights at Work: Pay Equity Reform and the Politics of Legal Mobilization* (Chicago: University of Chicago Press, 1994), and Mark Kessler, "Legal Mobilization for Social Reform: Power and the Politics of Agenda Setting," *Law and Society Review* 24 (1990): 121–143.

37. Stuart Scheingold, *The Politics of Rights* (New Haven, Conn.: Yale University Press, 1974), and Rosenberg, *The Hollow Hope,* chap. 4. See also Richard Posner, *The Federal Courts: Challenge and Reform* (Cambridge, Mass.: Harvard University Press, 1996), 325–327. Posner is a federal court of appeals judge.

38. Rosenberg, *The Hollow Hope,* 156.

39. See, for example, Doug McAdam, *Political Process and the Development of Black Insurgency* (Chicago: University of Chicago Press, 1982), chaps. 5 and 6, and Aldon Morris, *The Origins of the Civil Rights Movement* (New York: Free Press, 1984).

40. Flemming, Bohte, and Wood, "One Voice Among Many," 1229–1230.

41. See Michael McCann, "Reform Litigation on Trial: Review of *The Hollow Hope,*" *Law and Social Inquiry* 17 (1992): 715–743, and Bradley C. Canon, "The Supreme Court and Policy Reform: *The Hollow Hope* Revisited," in *Leveraging the Law: Using the Courts to Achieve Social Change,* ed. David Schultz (New York: Peter Lang, 1998), 215–250.

42. McCann, *Rights at Work.*

43. See the discussion in Chapter 2 about a court decision expanding *Gunther* to include the comparable worth idea. Ultimately the courts rejected this idea.

44. McCann, *Rights at Work,* 280.

45. See, for example, Susan M. Olson, *Clients and Lawyers: Securing Rights to Disabled Persons* (Westport, Conn.: Greenwood Press, 1984), and Neal Milner, "The Dilemmas of Legal Mobilization: Ideologies and Strategies of Mental Patient Liberation," *Law and Policy* 8 (1986): 105–129.

46. Rosenberg, *The Hollow Hope,* 341–342.

47. Ibid, 4.

48. Ibid., 338.

49. Ibid., 13, 15, and 21, respectively.

50. Ibid., 33–35.

51. The critics we rely on in evaluating *The Hollow Hope* are: Canon, "The Supreme Court and Policy Reform"; McCann, "Reform Litigation on Trial"; Malcolm Feeley, "Hollow Hopes, Flypaper and Metaphors: Review of *The Hollow Hope*," *Law and Social Inquiry* 17 (1992): 745–760; and David Schultz and Stephen E. Gottleib, "Legal Functionalism and Social Change: A Reassessment of Rosenberg's *The Hollow Hope*," in *Leveraging the Law*, ed. Schultz, 169–214. Rosenberg responds to his critics in "Hollow Hopes and Other Aspirations: A Reply to Feeley and McCann," *Law and Social Inquiry* 17 (1992): 761–778, and in "Knowledge and Desire: Thinking About Courts and Social Change," in *Leveraging the Law*, ed. Schultz.

52. See, for example, Craig Bradley, *The Failure of the Criminal Procedure Revolution* (Philadelphia: University of Pennsylvania Press, 1993), chaps. 3 and 4.

53. Rosenberg, *The Hollow Hope*, 178–180. See also Gerald Rosenberg, "The Real World of Constitutional Rights: The Supreme Court and the Implementation of Abortion Rights," in *Contemplating Courts*, ed. Epstein (Washington, D.C.: CQ Press, 1995), 394.

54. Matthew E. Wettstein, "The Abortion Rate Paradox: The Impact of National Policy Rate Change on Abortion Rates," *Social Science Quarterly* 76 (1995): 607–618.

55. Susan Hansen, "State Implementation of Supreme Court Decisions: Abortion Since *Roe v. Wade*," *Journal of Politics* 42 (1980): 372–392. The five jurisdictions were Washington, Alaska, Hawaii, New York, and the District of Columbia.

56. Mark Graber, *Rethinking Abortion* (Princeton: Princeton University Press, 1996).

57. The quote comes from Hansen, "State Implementation of Supreme Court Decisions," 375.

58. Lauren Bowen, "Do Court Decisions Matter?" in *Contemplating Courts*, ed. Epstein, 376–389.

59. Rosenberg, *The Hollow Hope*, 343.

Appendix

TABLE A-1
Supreme Court Decisions Dealing with Abortion Issues

Case, Date, Vote, and Author of Opinion	Issue	Holding
Roe v. Wade 1/22/72 7–2 Blackmun	Whether the penumbral right to privacy encompasses a woman's right to terminate her pregnancy.	Recognized that such a right exists but distinguished the state's interest on a trimester basis.
Bigelow v. Virginia 6/16/75 7–2 Blackmun	Whether the 1st Amendment protects the right of a newspaper editor to publish advertisements for legal abortions in other states.	Held that the 1st Amendment offers rights that are not abrogated solely because they are commercial, as the information conveyed is of diverse interest and value. Further, a state cannot use its police power to control dissemination of advertisements for legal activities in other states.
Planned Parenthood of Central Missouri v. Danforth 7/1/76 7–2 and 6–3 Blackmun	Whether Missouri could validly prescribe several requirements into its abortion law, including spousal and parental consent.	Court's major differences centered on the spousal and parental consent issues, with a majority holding both to be unconstitutional.
Beal v. Doe 6/20/77 6–3 Powell	Whether a state's limitation of Medicaid assistance to abortions that are certified as medically necessary violates the equal protection clause of the 14th Amendment.	Held that a state participating in the Medicaid program is not required to fund nontherapeutic abortions although it is free to do so. Nothing in the Medicaid program requires a state to fund all procedures.

Case	Issue	Holding
Maher v. Roe 6/20/77 6–3 Powell	Companion case to *Beal v. Doe* raising very similar issues on Medicaid funding and raising equal protection issues.	Held that indigent pregnant women do not constitute a suspect class and that a state has a legitimate interest in encouraging and subsidizing normal childbirth.
Poelker v. Doe 6/20/77 6–3 Per curiam	Companion case to *Beal v. Doe* and *Maher v. Roe* that raised issue of whether a publicly financed city hospital's provision of services for childbirth but not for elective abortions violates the equal protection clause of the 14th Amendment.	Consistent with its prior opinions, the Court held that nothing in the Constitution requires the city to provide services for both childbirth and nontherapeutic abortion.
Bellotti v. Baird 7/2/79 8–1 Plurality delivered by Powell	Whether a state can require parental consent if it provides an alternative decision process if that consent is withheld, in this case a district court.	Held that if such a decision process is offered, it must be one in which the minor can receive a fair judicial interpretation of the minor's maturity or best interests—which the statute here did not provide.
Harris v. McRae 6/30/80 5–4 Stewart	Whether the state was obligated to pay for abortions which the Hyde Amendment to the Medicaid program had funding for and whether the Hyde Amendment itself constituted impermissible establishment of religion or violated the equal protection clause.	Held that states have no obligation to independently fund abortions and that failure to fund, while it falls unequally on the indigent, does not violate due process, nor does the fact that the funding preference for life coincides with the tenets of the Roman Catholic Church constitute an establishment of religion.
H.L. v. Matheson 3/23/81 6–3 Burger	Whether a state can require a doctor to notify a minor's parents prior to performing an abortion.	Since the statute did not provide the parents an absolute veto power and served state interests, the statute is constitutional.

(table continues)

TABLE A-1
Continued

Case, Date, Vote, and Author of Opinion	Issue	Holding
City of Akron v. Akron Center for Reproductive Health, Inc. 6/15/83 6–3 Powell	Whether a state can (1) require second trimester abortions to be performed in a hospital, (2) require parental consent for all minors under the age of 15, (3) require specific information to be imparted to the patient, and (4) require a 24-hour waiting period.	Held all aspects of the statute to be unconstitutional because (1) the hospital requirement creates an undue and unnecessary burden, (2) there cannot be a blanket consent requirement, (3) the state can require informed consent but cannot specify the contents, and (4) there is no legitimate state interest in imposing a waiting period.
Simopoulos v. Virginia 6/15/83 8–1 Powell	Companion case to *Akron Center for Reproductive Health*. Issue is whether state can require that abortions be performed at licensed clinics during second trimester.	Statute held constitutional as furthering the state's compelling interest in the safety of the woman.
Planned Parenthood Assoc. of Kansas City, Mo., Inc. v. Ashcroft 6/15/83 6–3 Plurality authored by Powell	Companion case to *Akron Center for Reproductive Health* and *Simopoulos* containing issues of second trimester hospitalization, parental or judicial consent, pathology reports, and second physician requirements.	Hospitalization requirements struck down for reasons enunciated in *Akron*. Remainder held to be constitutional, as the parental or judicial consent allowed a juvenile court to find a minor mature enough to make a decision and the remainder of the requirements were insubstantial.

Thornburgh v. American College of Obstetricians and Gynecologists 6/11/86 5–4 Blackmun	Whether the state can (1) require printed materials to be given to women seeking abortions informing them of alternatives and facts about gestation, (2) create public records requirements for those seeking abortions, and (3) require the presence of two physicians at abortions.	Statute declared unconstitutional in that (1) the state cannot control content of informed consent and advocate its own position, (2) the state cannot discourage abortions by publicly exposing those who seek them, and (3) the state cannot arbitrarily require the presence of a second doctor.
Bowen v. Kendrick 6/29/88 5–4 Rehnquist	Whether Congress, in enacting the Adolescent Family Life Act—which provided grants to public and private organizations to provide care for pregnant adolescents and adolescent parents and forbade grants to advocates of abortion—constitutes a violation of the First Amendment prohibition of establishment of religion.	Held the act constitutional as having a valid secular purpose, not advancing religion as its primary purpose and not excessively entangling church and state.
Webster v. Reproductive Health Services 7/3/89 5–4 Rehnquist	Whether the state could pass a statute stating that life begins at conception, preclude the use of public facilities for the practice of abortions, and preclude the use of public funds to encourage abortions.	Found that the state could validly preclude the use of its facilities for a given purpose, just as it could control funding. The Court found the statement as to when life begins to have no effect, and the remaining issue was ruled to be moot as it did not adversely affect the plaintiffs.

(table continues)

Case, Date, Vote, and Author of Opinion	Issue	Holding
Hodgson v. Minnesota 6/25/90 Court divided on several issues Plurality authored by Stevens	Whether the state could require a 48-hour waiting period after a minor's physician or agent gave notice to both parents except under exceptional circumstances, but with a proviso that a judge could enjoin the enforcement of the statute if he or she found the child to be mature and capable of giving informed consent and that such abortion was determined to be in the best interest of the minor child.	Found that the state could not validly require two-parent notification but that the judicial bypass provision rendered the statute constitutional. Further, the state had a legitimate interest in requiring a 48-hour waiting period to ensure that the minor's decision was informed and intelligent.
Rust v. Sullivan 5/23/91 5–4 Rehnquist	Whether the Secretary of Health and Human Services can impose conditions on recipients of grants of funds for family planning projects stating that such recipients may not encourage abortion as a means of family planning, not provide counseling regarding abortion, nor refer patients for abortion nor engage in activities to promote abortion, and that recipients be completely separated physically and financially from entities carrying on prohibited abortion activities.	Held that the restrictions were permissible under the statute, did not impose impermissible discriminatory conditions on recipients, and therefore did not violate the 1st Amendment. The conditions were narrowly tailored to advance Congress's goals and did not impose on a woman's ability to secure an abortion in a facility that did not receive the funds.

Planned Parenthood of Southeastern Pennsylvania v. Casey 6/29/92 Court divided on several issues Plurality authored by O'Connor, Kennedy, and Souter

Whether the state can (1) ensure that the woman gives informed consent and is provided information on abortion twenty-four hours before the abortion, (2) require a minor to obtain informed consent of one parent but provide a judicial bypass, (3) require a married woman to sign a statement that she has informed her husband, and (4) subject abortion facilities to reporting requirements that do not disclose the identity of the woman.

In a plurality opinion, the Court upheld all aspects but those related to spousal notification and reporting of failure to notify. The Court voted to retain and reaffirm the essential holding of *Roe v. Wade* but rejected the trimester structure in recognizing advances in neonatal care. In doing so the Court affirmed the right of the state to provide information to the woman as long as the information was not meant to persuade the woman against abortion.

TABLE A-2
Sample Lower Court Decisions Concerning Abortion Rights

Case	Issue	Holding
Coe v. Melahn 958 F.2d 223 (8th Cir. 1992)	Whether the state could require that insurance for abortion services be placed under a separate rider with a separate premium.	Court held that the statute did not impose an undue burden on a woman's right to seek an abortion, as such coverage had not been shown to be unobtainable or excessively expensive. Court further held that the state had a legitimate interest in keeping the rates for insurance low for its citizens and ensuring that those residents not favoring abortions were not required to subsidize them.
Lifchez v. Hartigan 735 F. Supp. 1361 (N.D. Ill. 1990)	Whether the state could prohibit experimentation on human embryos except for therapeutic purposes if it would prevent fertility work by reproductive endocrinologists.	District court held that the statute was unconstitutionally vague in not adequately defining "experimentation" and "therapeutic," particularly in light of advancing technologies that would leave doctors not knowing if they were violating the statute. The court further held that a woman's zone of privacy covered procedures to enhance as well as terminate pregnancies.

Case	Facts	Holding
Valenzuela v. Aquino I, II & III 763 S.W.2d 43 (Tex. App. Corpus Christi 1988), 800 S.W.2d 301 (Tex. App. Corpus Christi 1990), and 853 S.W.2d 512 (Tex. 1993)	Abortion protesters began picketing doctor's residence in addition to clinic where he performed abortions. Doctor sued for temporary injunction, permanent injunction, and money damages.	In *Aquino I*, the court of appeals dissolved a temporary injunction prohibiting protest within one mile of the residence as being overly broad. In *Aquino II*, the court of appeals sustained a permanent injunction from picketing within 400 feet of the center of the residence as being narrowly tailored and content-neutral in language. However, the Court reversed an $810,000 jury verdict in favor of the doctor as being chilling on the protesters' 1st Amendment rights. On appeal, the Texas Supreme Court affirmed the injunction but remanded the damages issue to determine if the protesters had violated the doctor's right to privacy.
Ex Parte State 531 So.2d 901 (Ala. 1988)	Whether the state could validly leave only a judicial decision as an alternative for a minor to obtain an abortion when her legal guardian was the state department of human services, which could not consent because it received federal funds.	The Supreme Court of Alabama held the statute constitutional under the U.S. Supreme Court rulings that merely require parental *or* judicial alternatives. However, the court determined that the trial court had erred in finding that the abortion was not in the best interest of a 12-year-old child with no family to help her support the baby.

Case Index

Abington School District v. Schempp, 374 U.S. 203 (1963), 21, 35, 56, 63, 69, 97, 140, 161, 172, 181

Adarand Constructors v. Pena, 515 U.S. 200 (1995), 48, 51, 66, 129, 138, 161, 169

Adkins v. Childrens Hospital, 261 U.S. 525 (1923), 106

American Academy of Pediatricians v. Lundgren, 940 P. 2d 797 (Cal., 1997), 201

American Federation of State, County and Municipal Employees v. Washington, 578 F. Supp. 843 (W. D. Wash., 1983); 770 F. 2d 1401 (9th Cir., 1985), 59, 204

Argersinger v. Hamlin, 407 U.S. 25 (1972), 99

Baehr v. Lewin, 852 P. 2d 44 (Haw., 1993), 127

Bailey v. Drexel Furniture Co., 259 U.S. 20 (1922), 106

Baker v. Carr, 369 U.S. 186 (1962), 47, 211

Barenblatt v. U.S., 360 U.S. 109 (1959), 125

Barnett v. U.S., 376 U.S. 681 (1964), 67

Bates v. Arizona Bar Association, 433 U.S. 114 (1977), 26, 98, 103, 177, 215

Batson v. Kentucky, 476 U.S. 79 (1986), 32, 99–100

Beal v. Doe, 432 U.S. 438 (1977), 224

Bellotti v. Baird, 443 U.S. 622 (1979), 225

Bethel School District v. Fraser, 478 U.S. 675 (1986), 40

Bigelow v. Virginia, 421 U.S. 809 (1975), 224

Bob Jones University v. U.S., 461 U.S. 574 (1983), 150

Bowen v. Kendrick, 487 U.S. 589 (1988), 227

Bowers v. Hardwick, 478 U.S. 186 (1986), 40

Bowsher v. Synar, 478 U.S. 714 (1986), 193

Branzburg v. Hayes, 408 U.S. 665 (1972), 107

Brewer v. Lewis, 997 F. 2d 550 (9th Cir., 1993), 58n10

Brown v. Board of Education of Topeka, 347 U.S. 483 (1954); 349 U.S. 294 (1955), 2, 20, 34, 37, 42, 44, 47, 51, 55, 72, 78–79, 85, 102, 121, 125, 129, 166, 169, 205–207, 213

Buckley v. Valeo, 424 U.S. 1 (1976), 195

Calderon v. Thompson, 120 F. 3d 1045 (9th Cir., 1997); 118 S.Ct. 1489 (998), 58n10

California Liquor Dealers v. Midcal Aluminum, 445 U.S. 97 (1980), 100

Chaplinsky v. New Hampshire, 315 U.S. 568 (1942), 169

Chicone v. Chicone, 479 N.W. 2d 891 (S. Dak., 1992), 60n45

Chisholm v. Georgia, 2 Dall. 419 (1793), 149n7

Index

Citations of Authors